POSTMODERN FEMINISM IN THE FICTION OF AUDREY THOMAS

CONTENTS

LIST OF ABBREVIATIONS

BF	-	Blown Figures
GI	-	Graven Images
IL	-	Intertidal Life
LAT	-	Latakia
MB	-	Mrs. Blood
RM	-	Real Mothers
SMMTM	-	Songs My Mother Taught Me
TGB	-	Ten Green Bottles
TPT	-	The Path of Totality
WBY	-	Wild Blue Yonder

PREFACE

My research experience has been one of the most wonderful experiences of my life as it has helped me to grow as an individual. The present study has enlightened me as well as broadened my vision and I could identify myself with the women characters of Audrey Thomas's novels, feel their anguish and pain, and have got a lot of strength from them. The present study has also helped me to grow as a woman and rediscover myself.

Feminism fights against everything that discriminates between masculine and feminine and aims at placing women at their rightful position. Feminism is a movement for growth, through equal rights and opportunities. Its aim is to relieve women from the tyranny of ignorance, isolation, and vulnerability and involve them in larger problems of society as a whole.

Canada has produced a predominant number of women writers. Canadian women writers articulate in their fiction the silence and marginality of women which caused a sort of cultural alienation of women. The focus in their works is to reveal the experiences of woman from within, of the woman alone, of the woman with a man or another woman, and the projection of man through woman's eyes, and also the projection of the woman as mother/daughter/wife.

Audrey Thomas's novels deal with women's experiences in a male dominated culture. Her novels present women caught in oppressive stereotypes from which some women struggle to create a female space for themselves. This may be done through autonomy of thought, through self-definition and self-reconstruction of one's own history, that is, her story; through creative composition, oral or written, through bonding among women and through a refusal to take up the victim position or the role of subjugation.

The present study arches over Thomas's fiction from *Mrs. Blood* written in 1970 to that of *Graven Images* written in 1993 to map the evaluation of her postmodern feminist stance.

The women in her works have turned away from the catchword consolations of patriarchy, security, marriage, property, etc., and arrived at self-articulation, gender based vision of an alternative organizing of life through self-assertiveness and mother-daughter bonding.

In Chapter-I various trends and streaks of feminism, postmodernism, and postmodern feminism are studied. This chapter also surveys French feminism and contemporary Canadian feminist writers. An overview of writing in the feminine and postmodern techniques employed by Audrey Thomas in her novels to foreground her feminism is also discussed in this chapter. All this helps to comprehend Thomas's postmodern feminist perspective in her writings.

Chapter - II introduces the personal and literary life of Audrey Thomas. In order to critically analyze and study the works of Audrey Thomas it is imperative that her life and works should be studied together. She has written nine novels and seven collections of short stories. There is a wider range of female protagonists of varying dimensions in her novels and short stories. She gives remarkable portraits of women as lovers, artists and creators. Her novels are about women: in childhood, adolescence, maturity and old age, and also in relationships as daughters, sisters, lovers, and mothers.

Chapter- III is devoted to the study of the trilogy- *Songs My Mother Taught Me, Mrs. Blood* and *Blown Figures.* In the trilogy the centre of consciousness is Isobel and the trilogy is a search for her authentic self and identity. Since the study of the trilogy is thematic the chronological order of the novels is not followed. This chapter is divided into three sections. Section I concentrates on *Songs My Mother Taught Me,* Section II concentrates on *Mrs. Blood* and Section III concentrates on *Blown Figures.*

Songs My Mother Taught Me is a classic tale of adolescent growth up to the loss of physical and mental virginity. It introduces us to Isobel, the recurring persona in Audrey Thomas's later fiction. In *Songs My Mother Taught Me,* Isobel is embarrassed by her mother's intervention in her social life, and is also attentive to the family's financial instabilities. However, she rejects family bonding and moves ahead to be an independent, self-sufficient and distinct individual.

Mrs. Blood is not a tragedy of the miscarriage alone. The tragic moment occurs after the miscarriage, with Isobel, high on medication, calling out for Richard and then asking Jason's forgiveness. The protagonist's disgust with her own body results in crisis of identity- Mrs. Blood and Mrs. Thing.

Blown figures is an attempt to resolve the trauma of what occurred in *Mrs. Blood*. Here the focus is on Isobel's disintegrated self in search of the lost child. She returns to West Africa all alone and undergoes conventional and extraordinary experiences. The novel is punctuated by clippings from African newspapers and paradoxical definitions from the Oxford English Dictionary. In these novels, seen through a woman's eye, the narrator/ Isobel makes a narrative structure of the evolution of her own body.

Chapter-IV deals with the persistent self-psychoanalysis, the consequent realization of being oppressed which leads the heroines of Audrey Thomas to freedom of imagination and expression. The female protagonists confront society not only as women but also as female artists. Audrey Thomas has used intertextuality, puns, jokes, word playing, fragmentation, self-reflexivity and other postmodern feminist techniques to highlight woman's marginalization and subservient position. This chapter is divided into three sections. Section I focuses on *Latakia,* Section II focuses on *Intertidal Life* and Section III focuses on *Graven Images.*

In *Latakia,* Rachel's interest is in writing. Her creative potential throws a hint of a developing artist. Rachel rejects male dominance through the medium of art.

In *Intertidal Life,* the female narrator struggles against social conditioning and family injustices towards intellectual life which ultimately leads her to a successful career as a writer. Alice, who once felt rudderless without a man, learns to cope with the responsibilities and builds her career as a writer, and grows into a cool heroine towards economic, social as well as psychological independence.

In *Graven Images,* the mature and intelligent Charlotte works to retie the bond between her mother Frances and herself. Abandoned by her husband Michael, Charlotte retransforms her defeat into a successful career as a writer / journalist. For Charlotte, the feminine quest includes the search for freedom of imagination and expression through the medium of art.

Chapter-V in the form of conclusion seeks to recapitulate the observations and arguments made in the preceding chapters. Audrey Thomas's novels are women centered. Her central female characters range in age from girlhood to old age, cover the spectrum of single, married, separated, widowed and divorced women. They embrace a multiplicity of lifestyles, including that of single parenthood, pregnant mother, etc. Her heroines are creative women caught between the frequently incompatible functions of lover, mother and writer.

The debt to published scholarship has been duly acknowledged in the form of endnotes and the select Bibliography.

God has been kind enough to shower His blessings and bestow strength in me to complete my research. This book is developed from my Ph.D work. I would first like to thank the many people who aided and sustained me on this part of my journey. I express my deep gratitude to Dr. Gunjan Chaturvedi for her kindness and wisdom which made all the difference. I would specially like to thank Prof. Shyam Asnani for sending me numerous books and photocopied material on Audrey Thomas. Thanks are also due to Prof. B S. Dahiya, Prof. Gurupdesh Singh and Prof. Tejinder Kaur for their encouragement and astute comments on my work. I am deeply grateful to my friends and colleagues, especially Dr. Ranjana Maharotra, Dr. Anju Thappa, Dr Gurjeet Kaur, Prof. Vijay Dev Singh and others for their good cheer and kind support.

I express my gratitude to Dr. Joanna Daxell for her spontaneous response to email the important research material on Audrey Thomas. I am also grateful to Dr. Krishna Sarbadhikary for providing me the text *Graven Images*.

In particular, I would like to thank my colleague, my closest friend and critic Prof. Jasbir Singh without whose cooperation and guidance it would not have been possible for me to undertake this academic odyssey. I am deeply beholden to him for his attention when I despaired. I am thankful to him for his spiritual support, he kept me going each and every time I resolved to call it quits.

I always miss my parents. They taught me to believe in myself. Today whatever I am is due to them. It is their divine blessings which have always encouraged me in moments of gloom and desolation.

My son, Vivasvan (Vasu) deserves special thanks. Although away from me, he has always been a very sensitive and affectionate child. He is my source of strength. My visits to his school, his love for me, his telling me "I miss you" gave me the confidence, courage and compassion that this research work demanded of me. Vasu, my dear, how blessed I'm to have a son like you!

I owe special thanks to my sister Mrs. Neelam Nargotra for her continued support. She was available whenever I needed her help. She badgered me to work faster and finish my work soon. While talking of my gratitude there is one name I can never forget to mention and that is the name of Dee. Whatever I do, she remains a constant source of inspiration to me.

I also thank my publishers for without their efforts my research work might not have seen the light of the day.

Anupama Vohra

Chapter 1

INTRODUCTION

> **"Feminism has done many good things for women writers, but surely the most important has been the permission to say the unsaid, to encourage women to claim their full humanity, which means acknowledging the shadows as well as the lights."**

Man-woman relationship has, on the whole, evolved through centuries on a set pattern; man to rule and woman to obey; man the master and woman the slave; man the god and woman the devout. This centuries old mutely followed relationship is now challenged. Traditionally, man has been regarded as a protector, a master, and a guardian of woman. Simone de Beauvoir explains how even the mythology of female power in ancient civilization is misleading:

> That Golden Age of Woman is only a myth. To say that woman was the *Other* is to say that there did not exist between the sexes a reciprocal relation: Earth, Mother, Goddess–she was no fellow creature in man's eyes; it was *beyond* the human realm that her power was affirmed, and she was therefore *outside* of that realm. Society has always been male; political power has always been in the hands of men.[1]

Feminism as a concept as well as a movement has emerged as a reaction against the atrocities of patriarchy. As the image of women throughout history, and in all civilizations has been damaged and distorted under the overpowering male domination, Sara Grimke comments:

> Man has subjugated woman to his will, used her as a means to promote his selfish gratification, to minister to his sensual pleasure, to be instrumental in promoting his comfort, but never has he desired to elevate her to that rank she was created to fill. He has done all he could do to debase and enslave her mind; and now he looks triumphantly on the ruin he has wrought, and says, the being he has thus deeply injured is his inferior....[2]

Simone de Beauvoir states that men have always given a secondary place to woman and have always considered her just as a sexual being. "He is the Subject, he is the Absolute—she is the Other."[3] She further shows how woman is forced to behave in a so-called feminine way by constant cultural conditioning:

> ...man defines woman not in herself but as relative to him; she is not regarded as an autonomous being....Man can think of himself without woman. She cannot think of herself without man.[4]

Woman's personality is disfigured and she is confined to "the footnotes of history."[5] Kate Millet says: "The history of patriarchy presents a variety of cruelties and barbarities"[6] perpetrated on women.

Woman's idea of herself as inferior to man and dependent on him springs from her realization that the world "belongs to men.... Man–the–sovereign will provide woman-the–liege with material protection and will undertake the moral justification of her exisitence."[7] Feminism fights against everything that discriminates between masculine and feminine and it aims at placing women at their rightful position. Feminism is a movement for growth, through equal rights and opportunities. Its aim is to relieve woman from the tyranny of ignorance, isolation and vulnerability and involve them in larger problems of society as a whole.

According to Janet Radcliffe Richards, feminism has a strong fundamental case. It is intended to mean only that there are excellent reasons for thinking that: "women suffer from systematic social injustice because of their sex."[8] The proposition is to be regarded as constituting the essence of feminism. Here it must be understood that feminism does not aim at eliminating injustice in one or two groups of women but it stands against injustice done to women all around the world. It brings awareness among women as to how society has been unjust to them.

Lisa Tuttle observes that the term feminism taken from the Latin *femina* originally meant "having the qualities of females."[9] In the 1890s, feminism started being employed to denote the theory of sexual equality and the movement for the rights of women. It gradually replaced the word "Womanism,"[10] which had been in use till then. Alice Rossi attempted to trace the first usage of the word in print and reached the conclusion that it was first printed "in a book review published in *The Athenaeum*, 27 April 1895." [11]

Teresa Billington Greig has written that feminism is a movement which seeks:

> The reorganisation of the world upon a basis of sex-equality in all human relations; a movement which would reject every differentiation between individuals upon the ground of sex, would abolish all sex privileges and sex burdens, and would strive to set up the recognition of the common humanity of woman and man as the foundation of law and custom.[12]

Rosalind Delmar in her essay "What is Feminism?" deals with the meaning of feminism from different perspectives. "Feminism," she says, "is usually defined as an active desire to change women's position in society." Linked to this is the view that feminism is par excellence "a social movement for change in the position of women."[13] Casting a glance on the women's liberation movement and its aims, she writes that the introduction of an autonomous female subject, woman speaking in her own right, with her own voice, an attempt to transform woman from an object of knowledge into a subject capable of appropriating knowledge and to effect a passage "from the state of subjection to subjecthood"[14] – all these have been parts of the project of feminism in general.

There are different definitions and explanations of feminism in circulation because various thinkers have developed various insights to the term. Some have confined it merely to a political label or position. Others have called it an ideology or philosophy, which eliminates difference between femininity and masculinity, and many others have associated it with a demand for women's rights, and a revolt against social injustice. Adopting a very open attitude some have regarded that anything related with women can be called feminism, but none of them has been able to define the term perfectly. In fact, it is a dynamic, constantly changing ideology with many aspects including the personal, political and philosophical. "Feminism is a call to action. It can never be simply a belief system."[15] In simple terms, feminism means a doctrine which advocates for the equality of women with men in different walks of life, that is, political, social, legal, familial, cultural, academic, etc. At the same time it calls for the rights and freedom of women, including sexual, professional, personal, educational, cultural and religious. In general, it has a number of implications which have been summed up by Agate Nesaule Krouse in the following words:

> In its general, non literary applications, feminism has a number of different meanings and connotations. Thus man haters, lesbians, believers in free love, nymphomaniacs, and career women have occasionally been loosely described as feminists because they reject, consciously or unconsciously,

> the traditional definition of woman as one who finds her highest happiness in loving and being faithful to one man, living through his achievement, having children or making a home. All of the following have been more precisely described as feminists: the great nineteenth–century advocates of women's rights; suffragists; contemporary women interested or active in the women's movement; members of one of the liberal, socialist or radical feminist groups; authors of theoretical books or essays which expose sexism or injustice to women or which explore ways women can achieve justice and full humanity. A characteristic common to the members of this groups is that they advocate or support greater freedom or equal rights for women in politics, education, employment or personal life.[16]

Feminist movement started early in the twenties as a socio-political protest, in the form of demonstrations in the streets against the oppression of women. It soon became a matter of literary debate and discussion in academic circles. Feminism is not only a reaction to the patriarchal culture, which suppresses women in society but also a reaction to literature, which is the product of this culture.

The portrayal of women characters by male authors is biased against women and gives only men's view of life and experiences. This sexist bias becomes obvious in their misogynist attitude and misrepresentation of women in their works. Very often, the fictional woman in the male writings is shown as a shrew or an angel. She is seen as mother earth. She is not seen as a human being with all the agony, pain, exploitation and suffering.

Betty Friedan, the author of *The Feminine Mystique,* expressed the view that, like the East and the West, the twin worlds of the Masculine and the Feminine would never meet. She challenges woman's role inside her home, that she should find fulfilment only in domesticity and motherhood. She maintains that:

> .... for a woman as for man, the need for self-fulfilment, autonomy, self-realisation, independence, individuality, self-

> actualisation is as important as sexual need, with as serious consequences, when it is thwarted.[17]

Shoshana Felman states:

> Man has reduced the woman to the status of a silent and subordinate object...the woman is viewed by the man as *his* opposite, that is to say, as *his* other, the negative of the positive, and not, in her own right, different, other, Otherness itself.[18]

Julia Kristeva upholds the separatism between men and women. According to her:

> If women have a role to play...it is only in assuming a *negative* function: reject everything finite, definite, structured, loaded with meaning, in the existing state of society. Such an attitude places women on the side of the explosion of social codes: with revolutionary movements.[19]

In the words of Shirin Kudchedkar, feminism "aims at making woman the subject of her own story and not the object of male desire and male satisfaction or a whipping block for male frustration."[20]

Toril Moi's *Sexual/Textual Politics* more or less corroborates this idea of binary opposition between the masculine and the feminine. Toril Moi defines feminism in relation to terms such as feminism, femaleness and femininity. She states, "In a general way, I see feminism as a political position, femaleness as a matter of biology and femininity as a set of culturally defined characteristics." [21] At another place she says, "the words 'feminist' or 'feminism' are political labels indicting support for the aims of the new woman's movement which emerged in the late 1960s."[22] Feminist literary criticism aims at exposing the misrepresentation and marginalization of woman in literature to make woman's experiences as important as man's and as legitimate and valid subject of literature as man's experiences have been.

Elaine Showalter in her classic work, *A Literature of Their Own: British Women Writers from Bronte to Lessing*, divides the growth of feminism in three stages:

> The first feminine stage (historically from the appearance of the male pseudonym in the 1840's to the death of George Eliot in 1880) involves invitation of the prevailing modes of the dominant tradition and internationalization of its standards of arts and its view of social roles. The Feminist phase (winning of vote 1880-1920) is one of protest against these standards and values while the Female phase (1920 to the present, with a new stage of self-awareness about 1960) is a phase of self -discovery, a search for identity.[23]

Men ignored women writers in the eighteenth century by restricting their creative writing only to certain permissible areas of life. They were forbidden to focus in their works on all domains of human experience. As a result, the creative talent of women writers was suppressed and it was not possible for them to deliver a full-throated expression. Jane Austen makes a remarkable comment on the privilege of men:

> Men have had every advantage...in telling their own story. Education has been theirs in so much higher a degree, the pen has been in their hands.[24]

The social environment and the conditions of life have changed tremendously since the days of Jane Austen.

Feminist movement with its multidimensional character and concerns deeply influenced many an intellectual, especially the writers. It has been a major influence on many female fiction writers. A whole range of women writers of various political hues began looking at the realities as women and thus contributed new perceptions and perspectives.

Ellen Moers sees women's literature as an international movement:

> Apart from, but hardly subordinate to the mainstream: an undercurrent, rapid and powerful. This 'movement' began in the late eighteenth century, was multinational, and produced some of the greatest literary works of two centuries, as well as most of the lucrative pot-boilers.[25]

Women writers of fiction in the contemporary world enjoy a greater measure of freedom. Patricia Meyer Spacks finds that:

> For readily discernible historical reasons women have characteristically concerned themselves with matters more or less peripheral to male concerns, or at least slightly skewed from them. The differences between traditional female preoccupations and roles and male ones make a difference in female writing.[26]

Overthrowing the age-old dominance of the male view, in the world of letters, women writers of fiction have projected a feminist view of life and its problems in the context of recent fiction in English. There has been a renewed enthusiasm for the idea that "a special female self-awareness emerges through literature in every period."[27]

Postmodernism, which Arnold Toynbee introduced into critical discourse as a historical category sometime during the fifties was soon taken over by other disciplines. Andreas Huyssen claims that "the amorphous and politically volatile nature of postmodernism makes the phenomenon itself remarkably elusive," and the definition of its, "boundaries exceedingly difficult if not per se impossible."[28] Jean-Francois Lyotard defines postmodernism as a state of "incredulity with respect to metanarratives."[29] Ihab Hassan concurs on postmodernism: "We deconstruct, displace, demystify the logocentric, ethnocentric, phallocentric order of things."[30] Postmodernism unsettles and deconstructs traditional notions about language, about identity, about writing itself and so on.

Linda Hutcheon says, it is "a current cultural phenomenon that exists, has attracted much public debate, and so deserves *critical* attention."[31] Postmodernism exults in open-ended structures. For postmodernism, it is the process rather than the product that is important. Lyotard says:

> A postmodern artist or writer is in the position of a philosopher: the text he writes, the work he produces are not in principle governed by pre-established rules, and they cannot be judged according to a determining judgement by applying familiar categories to the text or to the work. Those rules and categories are what the work of art is looking for.[32]

Frank Davey says, "In the post-modern world of counter pointing influences, centres and traditions, the claim that a single tradition can be central or orthodox has become meaningless."[33] Postmodernism seeks therefore not a voice but many voices, not unity in disunity but disunity as unity.

Postmodernism seems to correspond to a culture's instinct for a new way to think and write about the prevailing situation, and produce a hybrid text. The text "reproduces in itself the basic cultural principle which only post-modernism has acknowledged as a working heuristic, that the meaning of the events depends entirely on the commentary gathering to them."[34] Postmodernism allows a large scope, offers a broad area to experiment, to create. Walker Benjamin in his essay "The Autnor as Producer" writes:

> There were not always novels in the past, and there will not always have to be; not always tragedies, not always great epics; not always were the forms of commentary, translation, indeed, even so-called plagiarism, playthings in the margins of literature; they had a place not only in the philosophical but also in the literary writings of Arabia and China. Rhetoric has not always been a minor form, but set its stamp in antiquity on large provinces of literature. All this to accustom you to the thought that we are in the midst of a mighty recasting of literary forms, a melting down in which many of the opposites in which we have been used to think may lose their force." [35]

Benjamin seems to have visualized postmodernist mode as early as 1943. A writer who thirsts for new forms and games can as well be called a postmodernist. The contemporary world with its diversions and diversifications seems to be a veritable treasure house to an artist to explore new form, content and technique.

Robert Wilson says that postmodernism in its application to literature contains:

> "Self-consciousness or reflexivity, a putting of the conventions of writing into the foreground of the text, a disregard for conventional forms of writing, perhaps an even greater disregard for conventional expectations of readers, a delight in puzzles, riddles, aporia of all types, a continuous breaking down of barriers, decanonization, and hence a wilful, self-conscious mixing of literary levels, kinds of discourse and genres. In a word, postmodernism seems to be highly intelligent (at least about literature), rather disrespectful, even nose –thumbing, innovative and (above all) playful."[36]

Since the mid 1980s, increasing numbers of feminists have been exploring the implications of postmodernism for feminism. Feminism has a positive approach to the possibilities of woman's release from patriarchal and social entrapments. It:

> Inherits a legacy that is thoroughly modernist, a legacy rooted in the emancipatory impulse of liberal humanism and Marxism....Modernist values are very much a part of contemporary feminist positions. The contradiction between these values and the postmodern themes of much contemporary feminism thwarts attempts neatly to categorize feminism as modernist or postmodernist."[37]

Jane Flax argues that feminist theories, "like other forms of postmodernism, should encourage us to tolerate and interpret ambivalence, ambiguity and multiplicity as well as to expose the roots of our needs for imposing order and structure no matter how arbitrary and oppressive these needs may be."[38]

In her anthology *Feminism/ Postmodernism,* editor Linda Nicholson claims there are "many points of overlap between a postmodern stance and positions long held by feminists," thus making the two "natural allies."[39] She points out that feminism has produced its own critique of scientific rationality, objectivity, and the autonomous self as masculinist constructions. Furthermore, critiques of white, western feminists' tendency to generalize from a limited perspective have been made by women of colour and women from developing countries. These criticisms, added to those of lesbian, disabled, and working class women, have produced a rethinking of key concepts in feminism that has led to more historically and culturally specific work. For example, gender is understood as a socially constructed, politically charged category. This is intertwined with other socially constructed categories such as race, class and sexual orientation. According to Nancy Fraser and Linda Nicholson, if feminism pursues this trend towards a more historical, non-universalising, non-essentialist theory, one that addresses differences among women, then feminism will become "more consistently postmodern."[40]

Feminism is said to have links with postmodernism. Linda Hutcheon points out:

> While feminisms and postmodernism have both worked to help us understand the dominant modes of representation at work in our society, feminisms have focussed on the specifically female subject of representation and have begun to suggest ways of challenging and changing those dominants in both mass culture and high art. They have taught us that to accept unquestioningly any fixed representations-in fiction, film, advertising or whatever-is to condone social systems of power which validate and authorize some images of women (or blacks, Asians gays, etc.) and not others. Cultural production is carried on within a social context and an ideology- a lived value system-and it is to this that feminist work has made us pay attention. Feminisms have, in this way, had a very profound effect on postmodernism.[41]

Hutcheon maintains that feminism has affected postmodernism in demonstrating how cultural production is carried on within a social context and an ideology. There is a two-way involvement of postmodernism with feminism. Feminisms have successfully urged postmodernism to:

> "reconsider-in terms of gender-its anti-metanarrative challenges to that humanist 'universal' called 'Man' and have supported and reinforced its 'de-doxifying' of the separation between the private and the public, the personal and the political...postmodern parodic and ironic representational strategies have offered feminist artists an effective way of working within and yet challenging dominant patriarchal metanarrative discourses."[42]

Postmodernism takes on a complementary and sustaining force in feminism. It rejects the dogmatism of enlightenment thought and formulates a new definition of truth. Nietzsche's words echo the connection between feminism and postmodernism:

> Supposing that Truth is a woman – what then? Is there not a ground for suspecting that all philosophers in so far as they have been dogmatists, have failed to understand women-that the terrible seriousness and clumsy importunity with which they have usually paid their addresses to truth, have been unskilled and unseemly methods for winning a woman?[43]

Feminism also questions the concept of rationality and the unitary definition of truth.

French feminist thought and the psychoanalytic discourse was promoted by the powerful group known as "Psychanalyse et politique" (psych et po). From the beginning, psych et po disdained feminism as "a bourgeois avant-garde that maintains, in inverted form, the dominant values." Instead, they argued, "If capitalism is based on the sexual division of work, the women's struggle is based on sexual difference. The only discourse on sexuality that exists is the psychoanalytic discourse. Therefore the women's struggle must of necessity deal with the dialectical relationship between historical materialism and psychoanalysis."[44]

French women's interest in psychoanalysis echoed the general trend of Parisian intellectual life after 1968. Sherry Turkle explains in *Psychoanalytic Politics* that a psychoanalytic culture emerged in France after the collapse of the revolutionary left. Disillusioned with the utopian promise of radical politics, "people... now turned to psychoanalytic ideas to explain what had happened" and "entered analysis to understand what it had meant to them."[45] In 1972-73, the subject of Lacan's Seminar XX was "Femininity" and, it "spoke to women in a way that few psychoanalytic texts have ever done."[46]

Lacanian psychoanalysis has played an important role in bringing about the transition from the concrete and political orientation of the French feminist movement to the more abstract theorizing of "the feminine." The three most influential French women theorists on cross-cultural feminist thought are Helene Cixous, Luce Irigaray and Julia Kristeva. They see post-saussurean linguistics, psychoanalysis, philosophy, semiotics and deconstruction as the most powerful means to understanding the production of sexual difference in language, reading and writing.

According to Ann Rosalind Jones, "Their common ground is an analysis of Western culture as fundamentally oppressive, as phallogocentric.... Symbolic discourse (language, in various contexts) is another means through which man objectifies the world, reduces it to his terms, speaks in place of everything and everyone else – including women."[47] In French feminist thought "Woman," or "the feminine," is "the privileged site from which western phallocentric thinking can be deconstructed. The feminine... is seen as a negation of the phallic, and thus the privileged carrier of utopian visions."[48] However, for deconstructionists "women," rather than "Woman," are not important. Alice Jardine notes that for Derrida and his disciples "the question of how women might accede to subjecthood, write texts or acquire their own signatures, are *phallogocentric* questions."[49]

Helene Cixous in *The Laugh of the Medusa* argues that, "Nearly the entire history of writing is confounded with the history of reason....It has been one with the phallocentric tradition."[50] Consequently, "writing is precisely *the very possibility of change,* the space that can serve as a springboard for subversive thought, the precursory movement of a transformation of social and cultural structures."[51]

According to Cixous, women must develop feminine writing to change the male defined world:

> "Woman must write her self: must write about women and bring women to writing, from which they have been driven away as violently as from their bodies.... Woman must put herself into the text...."[52]

She desires woman to gear up for her "inevitable struggle against conventional man" to bring "women to their senses and to their meaning in history."[53] She states: "I write woman: woman must write woman.... Write! Writing is for you, you are for you; your body is yours, take it.[54] She claims that women writers always retain a bit of the mother in them: "There is always within her at least a little of that good mother's milk. She writes in white ink."[55] Helene Cixous urges women writers to embrace "difference"[56] and to use it. In other words, women must write her self by putting into words her otherness.

Helene Cixous reinforces the idea of libidinal physical drives of woman for the definition of woman's sexuality. Regarding the unique libidinal economy of woman which is mystically superior to the limited phallic libidinal economy, she says:

> Though masculine sexuality gravitates around the penis, engendering that centralized body (in political anatomy)

> under the dictatorship of its parts, woman does not bring about the same regionalization which serves the couple head/genitals and which is inscribed only within boundaries. Her libido is cosmic, just as her unconscious is worldwide.[57]

Cixous finds an intimate connection between the woman's sexuality and the language which she often uses in the works of art. She links woman's diffuse sexuality to woman's diffuse language to state:

> Her writing can only keep going, without ever inscribing or discerning contours....She lets the other language speak – the language of 1,000 tongues which knows neither enclosure not death....Her language does not contain, it carries; it does not hold back, it makes possible.[58]

Cixous invokes other bodily drives in a continuum with woman's self-expression:

> Oral drive, anal drive, vocal drive - all these drives are our strengths, and among them is the gestation drive – just like the desire to write: a desire to live self from within, a desire for the swollen belly, for language, for blood.[59]

Cixous emphasizes that writing has sustained the opposition between male and female. "Woman" has been defined in language, as a signifier defined in opposition to "man." Cixous advocates the deconstruction of this opposition:

> If woman has always functioned "within" the discourse of man, a signifier that has always referred back to the opposite signifier which annihilates its specific energy and diminishes or stifles its very different sounds, it is time for her to dislocate this "within," to explode it, turn it around, and seize it; to make it hers, containing it, taking it in her own mouth, biting that tongue with her very own teeth to invent for herself a language to get inside of.[60]

Luce Irigaray agrees with Cixous that feminine sexuality and the female body are sources of feminine writing. Her strategy for liberation is that women should join together and speak boldly in the active voice avoiding false security.

Irigaray argues that the subject of knowledge and reason is always defined in the western tradition as masculine. A woman represents all that exists outside the subject and its truth. She is material, improper, indeterminate, incapable of conscious mastery, without self-mastery, without self-identity, indifferent, formless, and multiple. Nevertheless, as matter, she is the mirror, the specular scene upon which reason operates, providing reason with material for its concepts while yet remaining outside rational reality. Male reason is predicted on the subordination of the feminine, understood as the principle of connection in and to matter, which Irigaray associates with the mother's reproductive body. Men, she argues, have always appropriated women's reproductive powers for their own self-idealizing ends. Women's powers of reproduction have been exchanged between men to assure male alliances. There is a strong link between the philosophical elevation of the male mind over the female body, and the social institution of patriarchy: "For woman is traditionally a use-value for man, an exchange value among men; in other words, a commodity."[61]

Luce Irigaray finds femaleness in the specificity of the woman that distinguishes her from man. The sexual parts of the woman which are everywhere, sprawlingly present all over the body of the woman, are central to this specificity of woman. Irigaray posits female pleasure as auto-erotic:

> Woman "touches herself" all the time, and moreover no one can forbid her to do so, for her genitals are formed of two lips in continuous contact. Thus, with herself, she is already two-but not divisible into one(s)-that caress each other.[62]

Irigaray argues further that female sexuality explains woman's problematic relationship to masculine logic and reason:

> *Woman has sex organs more or less everywhere*...the geography of her pleasure is far more diversified, more multiple in its

differences, more complex, more subtle, than is commonly imagined-in an imaginary rather too narrowly focused on sameness. "She" is indefinitely other in herself. This is doubtless why she is said to be whimsical, incomprehensible, agitated, capricious...not to mention her language, in which "she" sets off in all directions leaving "him" unable to discern the coherence of any meaning. Hers are contradictory words, somewhat mad from the standpoint of reason, inaudible for whoever listens to them with ready made grids, with a fully elaborated code in hand. For in what she says, too, at least when she dares, woman is constantly touching herself.[63]

Irigaray perceives female language patterns as developing out of this pleasurable auto-erotic self-touching of a woman's sexual organs. A woman constantly touches herself in conversation:

> One would have to listen with another ear... *an "other meaning" always in the process of weaving itself, of embracing itself with words, but also of getting rid of words in order not to become fixed, congealed in them.*[64]

In contrast to masculine construct of language, which is rational, linear and privileged by the patriarchal culture, a woman's language is filled with ebb and flow, multiple beginnings, and multiple paths.

In France, *ecriture feminine* was represented by the work of Helene Cixous and Luce Irigaray among others. Since there is no adjectival distinction between "female" and "feminine" in French, *ecriture feminine* could mean both a "female" writing that is related to woman's sexuality and body, and a "feminine" avant-grade stylistics available to both sexes, and employing such techniques as gaps, breaks, questions, metaphors, "double or multiple voices, broken syntax, repetitive or cumulative rather than linear structure, and open endings."[65] Irigaray described a "woman's language or *parler femme* in which to inscribe female desire."[66] Cixous urged women to write as résistance to phallogocentric power:

> It is impossible to *define* a feminine practice of writing [*ecriture feminine*], and this is an impossibility that will remain, for this practice can never be theorized, enclosed, coded – which doesn't mean that it doesn't exist. But it will always surpass the discourse that regulates the phallocentric system; it does and will take place in areas other than those subordinated to philosophico-theoretical domination. It will be conceived of only by subjects who are breakers of automatisms, by peripheral figures that no authority can ever subjugate.[67]

Repression is gender blind and represses males as much as it does females. Males, too, can escape "philosophico-theoretical domination." Cixous chooses to call the subversive writing that she has in mind feminine or female because the forces of repression are so clearly male.

Julia Kristeva, author of the work *Desire in Language* (1980), links questions of desire to large issues of linguistic, political and historical change in her essay "Women's Time."[68] Using both psychoanalytic and socialist frames of reference, Kristeva casts doubt on the whole notion that women's desire is fundamentally different from men's, and pursues what ramifications of that desire would be if it were different. To do this, she sets out a history of the women's movement and links it to women's desire. Initially women wanted political, economic and reproductive equality, but "second generation" feminists have wanted to explore their own difference and the specificity of women's experiences and language.

Kristeva accentuates on the concept of "bodily drives"[69] for defining female sexuality. In her opinion, these "bodily drives" lead to a self-fulfilling sublimation through what she calls "semiotic discourse,"[70] which she describes, inheres in the "the gestural, rhythmic, preferential language"[71] of the texts. The writer gets a kind of textual "*jouissances*"[72] by constructing texts which violate the norms of the conventional language. Thematically, the semiotic discourse is a challenge to the symbolic order. Kristeva doubts whether women should aim to work out alternative discourses, or should persist in challenging the discourses that stand:

> A feminist practice can only be ...at odds with what already exists so that we may say "that's not it" and "that's still not it."[73]

To Kristeva, "woman" is "not so much a sex as an attitude."[74] Kristeva says, "By "woman" I mean that which cannot be represented, what is not said, what remains above and beyond nomenclatures and ideologies. There are certain "men" who are familiar with this phenomenon."[75]

Unlike Cixous and Irigaray, Kristeva resists identification of the "feminism" and the "masculine" with biological women and biological men respectively. She goes beyond sexual division to a pluralistic society that is not constructed by gender. Thus Cixous, Irigaray and Kristeva have distinctively postmodern feminist perspectives but they share a commonality of non-binary and non-oppositional thoughts. All of them believe that women can overcome binary opposition, phallocentrism, and logocentrism by breaking silence, by speaking and by writing.

Toril Moi notes that French theorists have contributed to feminist discourse by working on "problems of textual, linguistic, semiotic or psychoanalytic theory," and by writing texts "in which poetry and theory intermingle in a challenge to established demarcations of genre."[76]

The French theorists of feminism give primacy to the nationality of the woman as a subject on her own right. Far from becoming an object of desire for others, she enjoys the privilege of regulating herself in a way entirely independent of the patriarchal hegemony.

Levi-Strauss brings out the real worth of the woman when he invests her with "value". According to Levi-Strauss:

> Woman could never become just a sign and nothing more, since even in a man's world she is still a person, and since

> in so far as she is defined as a sign, she must be recognized as a generator of signs. In the matrimonial dialogue of men, woman is never purely what is spoken about; for if women in general represent a certain category of signs, destined to a certain kind of communication, each woman preserves a particular value arising from her talent, before and after marriage, for taking her part in a duet. In contrast to words, which have wholly become signs: woman has remained at once a sign and a value.[77]

Gynocriticism is used to describe the feminist study of women's writing, including readings of women's texts and analysis of the intertextual relations both between women writers, that is, a female literary tradition and between women and men. Elaine Showalter comments:

> In its earliest years, feminist criticism concentrated on exposing the misogyny of literary practice: the stereotyped images of women in literature as angels or monsters, the literary abuse or textual harassment of women in classic and popular male literature and the exclusion of women from literary history.[78]

She divides the feminist criticism into two categories. The woman as reader "feminist critique," and the woman as writer "gynocritics." The woman as reader concerns itself with:

> Woman as the consumer of male-produced literature, and with the way in which the hypothesis of a female reader changes our apprehension of a given text, awakening us to the significance of its textual codes....Its subjects include images and stereotypes of women in literature, the omissions of and misconceptions about women in criticism, and the fissures in male constructed literary history.[79]

When feminist criticism focuses on "the woman as writer," it concerns itself with:

> Woman as the producer of textual meaning, with the history, genres and structures of literatures by women. Its subjects include the psychodynamics of female creativity; linguistics and the problem of female language; the trajectory

of the individual or collective literary career; literary history; and, of course, studies of particular writers and works.[80]

Thus feminist criticism could be regarded as functioning in two distinct modes: "feminist critique" and "gynocritics." The former is concerned with women as the consumer of male produced literature and the way in which the hypothesis of the female reader changes the apprehension of a given text and the latter is concerned with women as the producers of the textual meaning, with the history, themes, genres and structures of literature by women.

Gynocritics seek to formulate a female framework for the analysis of women's literature, to develop new models based on the study of male experience rather than to adopt male models and theories. Gynocritics take into account the feminist research done in the field of anthropology, history, psychology and sociology to formulate their critical principles. Working as "gynocritics" women have tried reading male-created texts, producing a literary category as the women centered criticism.

Sandra Gilbert and Susan Gubar in *The Madwoman in the Attic* set out a new distinctively female literary tradition and developed a theory of "female literary response to male literary assertion and coercion."[81] They focused their attention on female literary creativity, struggling to find its way out of the strictures that contain it. The study charted:

> The difficult paths by which 19th century women overcame their anxiety of authorship, repudiated debilitating patriarchal prescriptions and recovered or remembered the lost foremothers who could help them find their distinctive female power.[82]

Gilbert and Gubar argued that patriarchal ideology in the 19th century thought of the writer as one who in the image of the "Divine Creator" fathers his work and they demonstrated that the pen was invariably imaged as phallic. Women could not, therefore, both write and remain feminine without transgressing the norms set up by patriarchal authority. Thus, the women writers were faced with the double burden. They had to confront these myths of creativity but they also had to work past the ideal of the "eternal feminine" that was set up as inspiration and complement to the male. Elaine Showalter writes:

> "Since 1979 insights have been tested, supplemented, extended, so that we have a coherent, if still incomplete, narrative of female literary history, which describes the evolutionary stages of women's writing during the last 250 years from imitation through protest to self-definition and defines and traces the connections, throughout history and across national boundaries of the recurring images, themes and plots that emerge from women's social, psychological and aesthetic experience in male dominated cultures.[83]

Gynocriticism has generated a vast literature on individual women writers, persuasive studies of the female literary tradition from the Middle Ages to the present in virtually every national literature, and important books on what is called "gender and genre,"[84] that is, the significance of gender in shaping generic conventions in their various and variegated forms. The theoretical programme of gynocritics in 1980s has been marked by increasing attention to "the analysis of female talent grappling with a male tradition,"[85] both in literature and criticism, a project that defined both the female literary text and the feminist critical text as the sum of its "acts of revision, appropriation, and subversion,"[86] and its differences of "genre, structure, voice and plot."[87] Gynocriticism assumes that all writing is marked by gender:

> Writers necessarily articulate gendered experience, just as they necessarily articulate the spirit of nationality, an age, a language."[88]

Feminist critics recognize that the meaning of gender needs to be interpreted within a variety of historical, national, racial and sexual contexts. However, they maintain that women writers are not free to renounce or transcend their gender entirely. As Sandra Gilbert asks,

> If a writer is a woman who has been raised as a woman-and I daresay only a very few biologically anomalous human females have not been raised as women-how can her sexual identity be split off from her literary energy? Even a denial of her femininity...would surely be significant to an understanding of the dynamics of her aesthetic creativity.[89]

A second assumption of gynocriticism is that women's writing is always "bitextual,"[90] in dialogue with feminine and masculine literary traditions. Showalter expresses the view: "there can be no writing or criticism outside the dominant culture."[91] Thus women's writing and feminist criticism were of necessity "a double voiced discourse,"[92] embodying both the muted and the dominant, speaking inside of both feminism and criticism. In reading women's texts, gynocriticism has freely experimented with a wide variety of interpretative tools. But it does not prescribe a particular mode of textual analysis, and has made extensive use of postmodernist insights, especially those having to do with the signification of the feminine.

There are several dimensions along which a critique of gynocriticism might be developed. But there are four major strands in its conceptual weave that are important to understand for the study or reading of women's literature in Canada. First is the idea of loss, which underwrites so much of the recovery of women's writing. Second, the notion of release or escape, which tropes itself into a feminist poetics in works such as *The Madwoman in the Attic*. Third is the problem that arises as a concept of experience, which in feminine practice has a critical, deconstructive charge, uncritically with an empiricist privileging of experience as the authentic source of truth and meaning. The fourth is the hidden politics of what some strands of feminism have set up as women's real experiences.

Feminism is a global and revolutionary ideology. Rosemarie Tong comments:

> ...change and growth are necessary to life and...what makes feminist thought liberating is its vitality, its refusal to stop changing, to stop growing.[93]

Feminist movement with its multidimensional character and concerns has been a major influence on Canadian women writers.

Canadian literature follows the usual colonial pattern. There have been two home cultures, French and British. The fact that the French and the British (English and Scottish) cultures exist side by side brings up the question of whether there is actually such a thing as a single indigenous Canadian culture even now.

The fiction written by Canadian women nurtures feminist awareness. The experiences of these writers cross national boundaries and are shared by women writers all over the world. There are close parallels between the historical situation of women and of Canada as a nation:

> Women's experience of the power politics of gender and their problematic relation to patriarchal traditions of authority have affinities with Canada's attitude to the cultural imperialism of the United States as well as its ambivalence towards its European inheritance.[94]

Canada's colonial inheritance of English and French language and culture is further complicated by the multiple origins of the Canadian population as a result of multi-ethnic patterns of immigration and settlement.

For years together women's writing in Canada was devalued. It was not judged objectively but treated as though it were women. Margaret Laurence described women's condition when in 1978 she said:

> These developing feelings [re Third World cultures] related very importantly to my growing awareness of the dilemma and powerlessness of women, the tendency of women to

> accept male definitions of ourselves, to be self-deprecating and uncertain, and to rage inwardly. The quest for physical and spiritual freedom...run [s] through my fiction.[95]

A linguistically divided culture of great ethnic diversity and the vast stretches of wilderness with varied regional concerns have resulted in the Canadian national identity being plural and decentralized. Within this fragmented national reality the female reality is further pushed to the margins. Virginia Woolf had expressed the frustrated sense of unbelonging suffered by the woman in *The Three Guineas*: "As a woman I have no country."[96] Atwood reiterated the grimness of this realization in the Canadian context in *The Journals of Susanna Moodie:*

> We are all immigrants to this place even if we were born here. The country is too big for anyone to inhabit completely and in the parts unknown to us we move in fear, exiles and invaders. This country is something that must be chosen - it is so easy to leave - and if we choose it we are still choosing a violent duality.[97]

The Canadian feminist fiction deconstructs the "traditional cultural dependencies"[98] in its quest for a physical and metaphysical freedom. Its thrust is the displacing of the authority of other traditions in order to acquire an autonomy in terms of a subjective tradition that originally was rejected to the marginal. This radical act of decentering leading to a willful occupation of the traditionally peripheral is the Canadian distinctiveness of women's writing.

In the Canadian context, feminist decolonization tends to be complex because of the presence of multiple European and native inheritances each one of which is supported on strong frames of patriarchy. Here there is an interesting distinction that separates male and the female writing in Canada. Both the male and the female writer have an ambivalent relationship with the lost and acquired traditions, caught by the urge to abandon and accept traditions in partial terms. But the feminist writing is characterized by the singularity and clarity of its resistance to the gender rooted aspect of any tradition that possessed it once or is now possessing it.

Patriarchal way of defining woman always subordinates her in the opposition. Women as such are associated both with madness and silence, whereas men are identified with prerogatives of discourse and of reason. Alienated from power structures, social recognition and crippled in expression with a language of which meaning is predicted by the male, the woman writer invents a language that:

> relates us, "takes us back" to where we are, as it relates us to the world in a living body of verbal relations, articulation: seeing the connections (and the thighbone and the hipbone etc.), putting the living body of language together means putting the world together, the world we live in: an act of composition, an act of birthing us, uttered and outered there in it."[99]

The revivification of the feminist movement since the 1960s has created the conditions for a change in women's consciousness. Women have struggled to find their own voices through which to challenge traditions which have marginalized and excluded them from power. Most of the novels written between the 1950s and 1990s in Canada have women writers as protagonists engaged in a struggle with language and inherited literary conventions to find more adequate ways of telling about women's experiences, fighting their way out of silence, projecting authentic images of how women feel and what they do. These stories are all told from the woman's angle. They register a feminized awareness of dislocation within the very literary traditions in which they are writing.

Canadian feminists challenge the power relationships in which males dominate. In the words of Barbara Godard:

> We are redrawing the circle from the circumference where we are circulating other knowledges. Often we seem to be speaking in paradoxes, negating even while we are

> advancing new values, in the very same word and breath. Such paradox is subversive, for it deconstructs the very notion of centre in which patriarchal monotheism is founded, by introducing multiplicity in thought and expression and by being resolutely eclectic and interdisciplinary in nature.[100]

Women have revolted against the map drawn by men showing that their difference is peripheral. Women are redrawing the map. Canadian feminist writers are not concerned with what people want to hear but with what their tongue wants to tell. These writers have taken up the task of re-reading which implies seeing again and seeing fresh. It changes the focus from what others see to what they as women see themselves. The aim here is to allow women freedom of movement through cultural, conceptual and imaginary spaces.

The feminist movement has struggled to create conditions for a change in woman's consciousness to challenge traditions which have marginalized and excluded them from power. Canadian women novelists pay attention to the problem of marginalization, exploitation and deconstruction of traditional authority structures in their writings.

The deconstructionist urge to displace traditional authority structures is a basic feature of women's writing in Canada. Fiction writing for these writers is a way of creating the illusion of order out of the random contingencies of experience, as a way of restructuring the past, as a way of self-assertion out of social or economic constraints. These writers create "a mosaic of alternative female worlds that have been hidden within the 'living body' of social history."[101]

Women's writing celebrates the power of the female imagination. However, this celebration is often accompanied by a deep unease about the activity and the purpose of writing. Writing is a deliberate displacement, a "fabrication"[102] as Morag calls it.

The aim of Canadian women's fiction is to make women "critically conscious of their own roles in conventional social structures."[103] Contemporary Canadian women writers have written feminist challenges into women's texts. Therefore, Canadian women's writing is characterized by the urge to "throw the storyline [of traditional power structures] open to question" and to implement "disarrangements which demand new judgements and solutions."[104] The stories narrated by these writers are concerned with exploration and survival, crossing boundaries, challenging cultural and psychological limits and glimpsing new prospects. Women writing in Canada is committed to bring about remarkable changes in the lives of Canadian women and society thereby "improving women's life-chances, and have the sense that women can contribute to the building of a major peaceful caring world."[105] In fact, women writers have aimed at restructuring social and economic relations in the light of gender equality in Canadian society. They stress in their writing the need for revision and a resistance to open confrontation with the power politics of gender.

The publication of women's magazines like *Branching Out, Broadside, Fireweed, Quebecoises deboutes, Les Tetes de pioche, Upstream* and *La Vie en rose* has helped to develop women's writing in the last few decades. Here the productions of women's writing are taken seriously among female audience.

Canadian women writers of fiction from Ethel Wilson down to Margaret Laurence, Alice Munro, Margaret Atwood, and a host of other women writers have registered a great measure of success as feminist writers and are acclaimed as major contemporary women novelists. The women's movement has provided many of these novelists with the courage and motivation to break out of traditional patriarchal forms to depict how women have been abused, exploited, and oppressed.

These women writers are concerned with a woman's struggle to rediscover her self and find self-fulfillment. Their stories deal with the woman's encounter with the world. Canadian women writing in the post -1960s played an important role in setting in motion many radical ideas in terms of women's individuality and autonomy, power and politics through their "own language through body-determined experiences, and their own strategies of rebellion through tropes of madness, silence, illness and guile."[106]

Margaret Atwood's novels present Canadian women's ambivalent relation to the literary and cultural traditions they have inherited through a variety of genres. Her works voice current ideas about alienation, women liberation, indigenous mythologies, ecology and commercialism. Alice Munro's stories reveal the contradictions of banality and secrecy within the daily lives of feminine protagonists. The works of Mavis Gallant question the enclosures caused by marriage and family, and provide assertions of independent identity. Marian Engel in her novels takes up the issues of marriage, pregnancy, childbirth and miscarriage. Morag Gunn in her fiction suggests the multiple functions of fiction writing for women.

Canadian women's writing constructs a private kingdom of subjective powers. It is a gendered, existentialist fight against invisibility and inaudibility, challenging authority, stereotypes, icons and sexist values. All this is a desperate act to find self-definition, that is, "a room of one's own" by the wilful occupation of the marginal space.

The present study is an endeavour to explore Audrey Thomas's theme of feminism as a major motif shaping her writing. Audrey Thomas employs "writing in the feminine" and postmodern strategies like metaphor, fragmentation, pun, wordplay, paranoia, intertextuality etc., to explore the dense allusive texture and subtle ironies in her novels to foreground her feminism. The restrained use of postmodern techniques to illuminate personal themes like pregnancy, abortion, childbirth, articulation of feminist consciousness, etc., puts Audrey Thomas in the realm of postmodern feminist writers in contemporary Canadian literature.

The following brief survey will concentrate on "writing in the feminine" and the postmodern techniques employed by Audrey Thomas to deconstruct, subvert, and decenter in her efforts to explore and express her feminist concerns.

Audrey Thomas's novels are governed by feminist consciousness which runs as an undercurrent and serves as the unifying principle. She emphasises the role of language as a strategic tool for identity formation and exploration for her protagonists. She uses female language to articulate female body. Language for her is a major feminist target for deconstructing and decentring. The site from which this is to be done is the female body, as there is a strong connection between language, sexuality and the body.

Maternity and creativity have appeared to be mutually exclusive to women writers. The historical separation evoked by the childbirth metaphor is so entangled with the language of creation and procreation that the metaphor's very words establish their own linguistic liberation. Words about the production of babies, and books abound with puns, common etymologies, and echoing sounds that simultaneously yoke and separate creativity and procreativity.

The wordplay reveals the structures of patriarchy that have divided "*labor* into men's *production* and women's reproduction."[107] Creation is an act of the mind that brings something new into existence. Procreation is the act of the body that reproduces the species. A man conceives an idea in his brain, while a woman conceives a baby in her womb. The pregnant body is female. The pregnant mind is the mental province of genius. Confinement of men suggests imprisonment and delivery from confinement suggests the restoration of men's autonomy, not its death. Confinement of women alludes to the final stages of pregnancy before delivery into the bonds of maternity, the very joy of which has suppressed their individuality in patriarchy. "Everything concerning woman is a puzzle, and everything concerning woman has one solution: it is named pregnancy."[108] The childbirth metaphor represents a symbolic reunion of mind and body, creation and procreation in Audrey Thomas's fiction.

Carolyn Heilbrun, in her book *Writing a Woman's Life,* writes, "Women must turn to one another for stories, they must share the stories of their lives and their hopes and their unacceptable fantasies."[109] She suggests four ways to write a woman's life:

> The woman herself may tell it in what she chooses to call an autobiography, she may tell it in what she chooses to call fiction; a biographer, woman or man, may write the woman's life in what is called a biography; or the woman may write her own life in advance of living it, unconsciously, and without recognizing or naming the process."[110]

Autobiography is ubiquitous in Audrey Thomas's fiction. Autobiography reveals gaps, and not only gaps in time and space or between the individual and the social, but also a widening divergence between the manner and matter of its discourse.

Patrica Meyer Spacks writes, "Autobiography assures the author of his [her] existence beyond all possibilities of philosophical denial. Through it he [she] comes to terms with his [her] past or exorcises it."[111] Women's autobiography writing is very often an attempt to mark a point of departure from their old selves, the selves which were handed down to them by the patriarchal culture, into a new world of self-sufficiency with an ample space for the self. Audrey Thomas's novels advocate sentiments of "maternal feeling, sisterly affection, *esprit de corps*"[112] for their readers. Her writing provides, "woman's view of life, woman's experience."[113]

Jonathan Baumbach observes, "you read a story nowadays and it's not a story at all, not in the traditional sense."[114] The postmodern writers distrust the wholeness and completion associated with traditional stories and have preferred to deal with other ways of structuring narrative. One way adopted by these writers is to break up the text into short fragments or sections, separated by space, title, numbers or symbols: "In those spaces there is nothing to write, the fiction writer can, at any time, introduce material (quotations pictures, diagrams, charts, designs, pieces of other discourse, etc.) totally unrelated to the story."[115] Another alternative adopted by these writers is the multiple ending, which resists closure by offering numerous possible outcomes for a plot.

Intertextuality calls attention to the importance of prior texts, insisting that the autonomy of texts is misleading notion and that a work has the meaning it does only because certain things have previously been written. Julia Kristeva suggests that: "every text is constructed like a mosaic of quotations, every text is absorption and transformation of another text."[116] Intertextual echoing has several narrative functions. One of which is to contest "the Romantic notion of uniqueness or originality and single meaning."[117] It is a "major means of articulating how textual meaning and sexual identity are fixed through and by literary representations of women."[118] In Audrey Thomas's works, intertextuality illustrates the impossibility of separating the social and the sexual from the literary when dealing with the writing and lives of women.

The protagonists of postmodern fiction often suffer from what Tony Tanner calls a "dread that someone else is patterning your life, that there are all sorts of invisible plots afoot to rob you of your autonomy of thought and action, that conditioning is ubiquitous."[119] This paranoia or threat of total engulfment by somebody else's system is felt by many of the characters of Audrey Thomas's novels.

Audrey Thomas the representative women novelist of the 20th century Canada shares to large extent the mainstream currents of feminism. Being a mother and a writer herself she knows about performing the double role of creativity, women as creator of children, and artist as creator of novels.

She incorporates many of the strengths of the past with a new range of language and experience in her novels. In her writings, she attempts to bring out the best of the self in the woman. "Sooner or later what is new and original in my self-image of woman ...meets up with the eyes of another woman. My eyes come across another woman: I recognise at last the essentille. I identify/myself."[120]

ENDNOTES

1. Simone de Beauvoir, *The Second Sex*, trans. and ed. H.M. Parshley 1949; rpt. (London: Vintage, 1997), p.102.
2. Sarah M. Grimke, *Letters on the Equality of the Sexes and the Condition of Women*, 1838; rpt. (New York: Source Book Press, 1970), p.10.
3. Simone de Beauvoir (1997), *op. cit.*, p.16.
4. *Ibid.*
5. Katarina Tomasevski, *Women and Human Rights* (London and New Jersey: Zed Books Ltd., 1993), p.xii.
6. Kate Millet, *Sexual Politics* (USA: Equinox Books, 1971), p.46.
7. Simone de Beauvoir (1997), *op. cit.*, p.21.
8. Janet Radcliffe Richards, *The Sceptical Feminist: A Philosophical Enquiry* (London: Routledge and Kegan Paul 1980), quoted in *Feminism: Theory, Criticism, Analysis* by Sushila Singh, (Delhi: Pencraft International, 2004), p.22.
9. Lisa Tuttle, *Encyclopedia of Feminism* (New York: Facts on File Publications, 1986), pp.107-108.
10. Sushila Singh, *Feminism: Theory, Criticism Analysis* (Delhi: Pencraft International, 2004), p.22.
11. Alice Rossi, "Women of Action: Frances Wright," *The Feminism Papers from Adams to de Beauvoir* (New York: Columbia University Press, 1973), quoted by Sushila Singh (2004), *op. cit.*, p.22.

12. Teresa Billington Greig, *Feminist Dictionary*, 1911, p.158, quoted by Sushila Singh (2004), *op. cit.*, p.24.
13. Rosalind Delmar, "What is Feminism?" in *What is Feminism*? eds. Juliet Mitchell and Ann Oakley, (Oxford: Blackwell, 1986), p.13.
14. *Ibid.*, p.23.
15. Sushila Singh (2004), *op. cit.*, p.23.
16. Agate Nesaule Krouse, "Feminism Prose Criticism," *Feminist Criticism: Essays on Theory, Poetry and Prose*, eds. Cheryl L.Brown and Karen Olson, (N.J. and London: The Scarecrow Press, 1978), pp.281-282.
17. Betty Friedan, *The Feminine Mystique*, 1963; rpt. (Harmondsworth: Penguin, 1971), p.282.
18. Shoshana Felman, "Women and Madness: the critical phallacy," *FEMINISMS: an anthology of literary theory and criticism*, eds. Robyn R. Warhol and Diane Price Herndl, (New Brunswick: Rutgers University Press, 1996), p.8.
19. Quoted by Ann Rosalind Jones, "Writing the Body: toward an understanding of l'écriture feminine," *FEMINISMS* (1996), *op. cit.*, p.359.
20. Shirin Kudchedkar, "Feminist Literary Criticism: The Ground Work," *Journal of Literary Criticism*, Vol. 8, No. 1 (June, 1996), p.34.
21. Toril Moi, "Men Against Patriarchy," *Gender and Theory*, ed. Linda Kauffman, (Basil Blackwell: Oxford, 1990), p.182.
22. Toril Moi, "Feminist Literary Criticism," *Modern Literary Theory: A Comparative Introduction*, eds. Ann Jefferson and David Rubey, (London: B.T. Batsford Ltd., 1968), p.204.
23. Elaine Showalter, *A Literature of Their Own: British Women Novelists from Bronte to Lessing* (Princeton: Princeton University Press, 1977), p.13.
24. Jane Austen, *Persuasion* 1818; rpt. (London: Oxford Uni-versity Press, 1964), p.84.
25. Ellen Moers, "Women's Literature: Profession and Tradition," *Columbia Forum*, 1 (Fall, 1972), p.27.
26. Patricia Meyer Spacks, *The Female Imagination* (New York: Avon, 1975), p.7.
27. *Ibid.*, p.3.

28. Andreas Huyssen, *After the Great Divide: Modernism, Mass Culture, Postmodernism* (Bloomington: Indiana University Press, 1986), p.58.
29. Jean-Francois Lyotard, *The Postmodern Condition: A Report on Knowledge*, trans. Geoff Bennington and Brian Massumi, (Minneapolis: University of Minnesota Press, 1984), p.26.
30. Ihab Hassan, "Making Sense: The Trails of Postmodernism," *New Literary History*, Vol. 18, No. 2 (1987), p.445.
31. Linda Hutcheon, *A Poetics of Postmodernism: History, Theory, Fiction* (New York and London: Routledge, 1988), p.ix.
32. Jean Francois Lyotard (1984), *op. cit.*, p.81.
33. Frank Davey, *From There to Here: A Guide to English-Canadian Literature Since 1960* (Erin, Ontario: Porcepic, 1974), p.19.
34. Padma Srinivasan, "Atwood's 'Lady Oracle': A Post-modernist Text," *Essays on Canadian Literature*, ed. K. Balachandran, (Bareilly: Prakash Book Depot, 2001), p.72.
35. Quoted by Padma Srinivasan, *Essays on Canadian Literature* (2001), *op. cit.*, pp.72-73.
36. Robert Wilson, "National Frontiers and International Movements: Postmodernism in Canadian Literature," *Ambivalence: Studies in Canadian Literature*, eds. Om P. Juneja and Chandra Mohan, (New Delhi: Allied Publishers, 1990), p.51.
37. Susan J. Kekman, *Gender and Knowledge: Elements of Postmodern Feminism* (Cambridge: Polity Press, 1990), p.2.
38. Quoted by Sue Thornham, "Postmodernism and Feminism," *The Routledge Companion to Postmodernism*, ed. Stuart Sim, (London and New York: Routledge Taylor and Francis Group, 2005), p.27.
39. Linda J. Nicholson, ed. *Feminism/Postmodernism* (New York and London: Routledge, 1990), p.5.
40. Nancy Fraser and Linda J. Nicholson, "Social Criticism without Philosophy: An Encounter between Feminism and Post-modernism," *Feminism/Postmodernism* (1990), *op. cit.*, p.34.
41. Linda Hutcheon, "Incredulity Toward Metanarrative: Negotiating Postmodernism and Feminisms," *Postmodernism and Feminism: Canadian Contexts*, ed. Shirin Kudchedkar, (Delhi: Pencraft International, 1995), p.78.
42. *Ibid.*, p.79.

43. Friedrich Nietzsche, *Beyond Good and Evil,* Trans. Helen Zimmern, *Complete Works,* Vol.12, ed. Oscar Levy, (New York: Russell and Russell, 1964), p.1.
44. Elaine Marks and Isabelle de Courtivron, eds. *New French Feminisms: An Anthology* (Amherst: University of Massachusetts Press, 1980), pp.117-118.
45. Sherry Turkle, *Psychoanalytic Politics: Jacques Lacan and Freud's French Revolution* (London: Burnett Book, 1979), p.9.
46. Stuart Schneiderman, *Jacques Lacan: The Death of an Intellectual Hero* (Cambridge: Cambridge University Press, 1983), p.30.
47. Ann Rosalind Jones, "Writing the Body: toward an understanding of l'ecriture feminine," *FEMINISMS* (1996), *op. cit.*, pp.357-358.
48. Gisela Ecker, ed. *Feminist Aesthetics* (London: The Women's Press, 1985), p.18.
49. Alice Jardine, "Pre-Texts for the Transatlantic Feminist," *Yale French Studies,* 62 (1981), p.225.
50. Helene Cixous, "The Laugh of the Medusa," *FEMINISMS* (1996), *op. cit.*, p.337.
51. *Ibid.*
52. *Ibid.*, p.334.
53. *Ibid.*
54. *Ibid.*, p.335.
55. *Ibid.*, p.339.
56. *Ibid.*, p.337.
57. *Ibid.*, p.345.
58. *Ibid.*
59. *Ibid.*, p.346.
60. *Ibid.*, p.343.
61. Luce Irigaray, "The Sex Which Is Not One," *FEMINISMS* (1996), *op. cit.*, p.355.
62. *Ibid.*, pp.350-351.
63. *Ibid.*, p.353.
64. *Ibid.*, pp.353-354.

65. Ann Rosalind Jones, "Inscribing Femininity: French theories of the feminine," *Making a Difference*, eds. Gayle Green and Coppelia Kahn, (London: Methuen, 1985), p.88.
66. Elaine Showalter, "Feminism and Literature," *Literary Theory Today*, eds. Peter Collier and Helga Geyer-Ryan, (New York: Cornell University Press, 1990), p.188.
67. Helene Cixous, "The laugh of the Medusa," *FEMINISMS* (1996), *op. cit.*, p.340.
68. Julia Kristeva, "Woman's Time," *FEMINISMS* (1996),*op. cit.*, pp.443-462.
69. Ann Rosalind Jones, "Writing the Body: toward an understanding of l'ecriture feminine," *FEMINISMS* (1996) *op. cit.*, p.358.
70. *Ibid.*
71. *Ibid.*
72. *Ibid.*
73. *Ibid.*, p.359.
74. *Ibid.*
75. *Ibid.*
76. Toril Moi, *Sexual /Textual Politics* (London: Methuen, 1985), p.97.
77. Levi-Strauss, *The Elementary Structure of Kinship*, trans. James Harle Bell *et al.*, (Boston, Mass: Beacon Press, 1969), p.128.
78. Elaine Showalter, ed. *The New Feminist Criticism: Essays on Women, Literature and Theory* (New York: Pantheon Books, 1985), p.5.
79. Elaine Showalter, "Towards a Feminist Poetics," *The New Feminist Criticism* (1985), *op. cit.*, p.128.
80. *Ibid.*
81. Sandra Gilbert and Susan Gubar, *The Madwoman in the Attic: The Woman Writer and the Nineteenth –Century Literary Imagination* (New Haven: Yale University Press, 1979), p.XII.
82. *Ibid.*, p.59.
83. Elaine Showalter, ed. *The New Feminist Criticism* (1985), *op. cit.*, p.6.
84. Elaine Showalter, "Feminism and Literature," *Literary Theory Today* (1990), *op. cit.*, p.190.
85. Elizabeth Abel, "Introduction," *Writing and Sexual Difference* (Chicago: University of Chicago Press, 1982), p.2.

86. *Ibid.*
87. *Ibid.*
88. Alicia Ostriker, *Stealing the Language* (Boston: Beacon Press, 1986), p.9.
89. Sandra Gilbert, "Feminist Criticism in the University: An Interview," *Criticism in the University*, ed. Gerald Graff, (Evanston: Northwestern University Press, 1986), p.117.
90. Naomi Schor, "Dreaming Dissymetry: Barthes, Foucault, and Sexual Differences," *Men in Feminism*, eds. Alice Jardine and Paul Smith, (London: Methuen, 1987), p.110.
91. Elaine Showalter, "Feminist Criticism in the Wilderness," *The New Feminist Criticism* (1985), *op. cit.*, p.263.
92. *Ibid.*
93. Rosemarie Tong, *Feminist Thought: A Comprehensive Introduction* (Boulder: Westview Press, 1989), p.237.
94. Coral Ann Howells, *Private and Fictional Words: Canadian Women Novelists of the 1970s and 1980s* (New York: Methuen, 1987), p.2.
95. Margaret Laurence, "Ivory tower or grassroots? The novelist as socio-political being," *Canadian Novelist and the Novel*, eds. Douglas Daymond and Leslie Monkman, (Ottawa: Borealis Press, 1981), p.258.
96. Virginia Woolf, *Three Guineas* (London: Hogarth Press, 1947), p.197.
97. Margaret Atwood, *The Journals of Susanna Moodie* (Toronto: Oxford University Press, 1970), p.62.
98. Robert Kroetsch, "Death is a Happy Ending," (1978); rpt. *Canadian Novelists and the Novel* (1981), *op. cit.*, p.248.
99. Daphne Marlatt, "musing with mothertongue," *In the Feminine: Women and Words/ les femmes et les mots Conference Proceedings 1983*, eds. Ann Dybikowski et. al.,(Edmonton: Longspoon Press, 1985), p.174.
100. Barbara Godard, "Redrawing the Circle: Power, Poetics, Language," *Feminism Now: theory and practice*, ed. Marilouise Kroker *et al.*, (Montreal: New World Perspectives, 1985), p.166.
101. Coral Ann Howells (1987), *op. cit.*, p.29.
102. *Ibid.*, p.30.

103. *Ibid.*, p.4.
104. Toril Moi, *Sexual /Textual Politics* (1985), *op. cit.*, p.43.
105. Sandra Burt, "The Second Wave of Canadian Women's Movement," *Canadian Politics: An Introduction to the Discipline*, eds. Alain G. Gagnon and James P. Bickerton (Ontario: Broadview Press, 1990), pp.548-549.
106. Malashri Lal, "Canadian Gynocritics: Contexts of Meaning in Margaret Atwood's Surfacing," *Perspectives on Women: Canada and India*, ed. Aparna Basu, (New Delhi: Allied Publishers, 1995), p.180.
107. Susan Stanford Friedman, "Creativity And The Childbirth Metaphor gender difference in literary discourse," *FEMINISMS* (1996), *op. cit.*, p.373.
108. Friedrich Nietzsche, *Thus Spake Zarathustra* (1883), trans. and ed., Rosemary Agonito, *History of Ideas on Women: A Source Book* (New York: Putnam, 1977), p.268.
109. Carolyn G. Heilbrun, *Writing a Woman's Life* (New York: W.W. Norton, 1988), p.44.
110. *Ibid.*,11.
111. Patricia Meyer Spacks, *Imagining a Self* (Cambridge: Harvard University Press, 1976), p.15.
112. Letter of October 6, 1851, *Letters of E. Jewsbury to Jane Welsh Carlyle* ed. Alex Ireland, London, 1892, p.426; quoted in Elaine Showalter, "The Female Tradition," *FEMINISMS* (1996), *op. cit.*, p.275.
113. Elaine Showalter, "The Female Tradition," *FEMINISMS* (1996), *op. cit.*, p.285.
114. Quoted by Barry Lewis, "Postmodernism and Fiction," *The Routledge Companion to Postmodernism* (2005), *op. cit.*, p.116.
115. Raymond Federman, ed. *Surfiction: Fiction Now and Tomorrow* (Chicago: Swallow, 1975), p.2.
116. Quoted by Barbara Godard, ""Heirs of the Living Body:" Alice Munro and the Question of a Female Aesthetic" *Canadian Literature: Perspectives*, ed. Jameela Begum (Madras: Macmillan India Ltd., 1994), p.73.
117 Linda Hutcheon, '"Shape shifters': Canadian women novelists and the challenge to tradition," *Amazing Space: Writing Canadian Women Writing*, ed. Shirley Neuman and Smaro Kamboureli, (Alberta: Longspoon Press, 1986), p.226.

118. Linda Hutcheon, *The Canadian Postmodern* (1988), *op. cit.*, p.111.
119. Tony Tanner, *City of Words: American Fiction, 1950-1970* (London: Jonathan Cape, 1971), p.33.
120. Nicole Brossard, *La Lettre qerienne* (Montreal: Remue-menage, 1985), p.116; quoted by Mary Jean Green, "Changing Subjects: Multi-Voiced Narrative and Feminine Textuality," *Postmodernism and Feminism* (1995), *op. cit.*, p.130.

Chapter 2

AUDREY THOMAS: HER LIFE AND WORKS

"... I am an instrument in the shape of a woman trying to translate pulsations into images for the relief of the body and the reconstruction of the mind."

Audrey Grace Callahan Thomas was born in Binghamton, New York, on 17 November 1935 to Frances Corbett and Donald Earle Callahan. Her father was a teacher and one of her aunts was a professor of mathematics. Her maternal grandfather was an engineer and inventor with IBM in Endicott. His big summer house in Adirondack Mountains of northern New York was a peaceful abode for Thomas during vacations. She was very close to her maternal grandfather who provided the thread of gold in her otherwise drab brown life. Her grandfather's punning and philology aroused Thomas's interest in words and provided her lessons in "reality and illusion"[1] in her literary career.

Her home life was not smooth. Her parents often quarrelled and she felt lonely and misfit. In later years, although they expected her to write "stories that ended happily."[2] She started school at the age of four with weak eyesight. She grew up during the war years preoccupied with death. At the age of fifteen, she won a scholarship to a girls' private school in New Hampshire. This was followed by another scholarship to Mary A. Burnham School in Northampton, Massachusetts. She took admission in Smith College on a tuition scholarship in 1953 and received her B.A. degree in 1957. While in college, she travelled to Spain, Italy, Belgium, Switzerland and Scandinavia during holidays. She went to Britain after graduation and taught in the Birmingham slums at Bishop Rider's Church of England Infant and Junior School.

Audrey married Ian Thomas, a sculptor and art critic at the Birmingham College of Art, in 1958. In 1959, after the birth of their first daughter, they moved to Vancouver, British Columbia. She enrolled in M.A. programme in English at the University of British Columbia. Her thesis "Henry James in the Palace of Art: A Survey and Evaluation of James' Aesthetic Criteria as Shown in His Criticism of Nineteenth Century Painting" was completed in 1963. She began doctoral work with the support of a Canada Council award. Her thesis "An Archetypal Reading of Beowulf" was not accepted. It was considered more like a novel than a dissertation. After this, Thomas opted out of academia. She taught English at the University of British Columbia from 1959 to 1963. She met numerous writers involved in the emerging Tish poetry movement, but always felt separate from them as a prose writer.

Audrey Thomas accompanied her husband to Africa. Her husband taught at the University of Science and Technology in Kumasi, Ghana, from 1964 to 1966. Her first published short story "If One Green Bottle..."appeared in *The Atlantic Monthly* (1965) while she was in Africa. After her return to Canada in 1969, she took up writing full-time and bought a house on Galiano Island, in the Gulf of Georgia, British Columbia, where she has lived since. Two more daughters were born to her during this period. She again visited Africa – French West Africa, Senegal, Mali and Ghana for three months of research in 1971. She separated from her husband in 1972 and got divorce in 1979. She took up teaching assignments to support her family.

Audrey Thomas has several honorary degrees, including an honorary SFU doctorate, conferred on her in 1994. She has written nine novels and seven collections of short stories. Thomas served on the panel of judges for the 2002 IMPAC Dublin Literary Arts Award, the most lucrative literary prize in English. Her books have been translated into several languages and she has twenty radio plays to her credit. A special issue of *Room of One's Own* (1985) highlighted her works and life. She lived in Greece, France, England and Scotland, but has chiefly resided at the north end of Galiano Island since 1969. During the 1970s, Thomas served on the Arts Advisory Board of The Canada Council and on its Reading Tours Committee. She is also a member of the Writers Union of Canada, on whose national executive she has served, and of P.E.N. All this helped her in getting Canadian citizenship in 1979.

Thomas as a child had a romantic dream of being "A Writer," desiring "to be *known* and all those things"[3] to compensate for being shy. She was an ardent reader introduced by her maternal grandfather to the magic of words, and a listener of her "Shanty Irish"[4] father's story telling. She wrote some poetry when she was about twelve, adding fiction at about nineteen: "I wrote several stories...when I was living in England."[5] None of her tyro work has been published and Thomas considers them "really terrible stories."[6] It was the stimulation at the University of British Columbia that turned her "on to words again."[7]

Thomas's first collection of stories *Ten Green Bottles* was published in 1967. In the stories, the characters grope for meaning, which would give them reassurance of their existence in a seemingly absurd world. According to Anita Raskia, it is the work of an author who "has clearly arrived"[8] to give an effective creation of a "mood of anxiety among the ordinary."[9]

Audrey Thomas's first novel *Mrs. Blood* (1970) is the story of Isobel's complicated pregnancy resulting in a miscarriage. Although first to be published, *Mrs. Blood* is second in a triptych about Isobel Cleary. *Songs My Mother Taught Me* (1973), and *Blown Figures* (1974) complete the series. The two novellas *Munchmeyer and Prospero on the Island* (1971) explore the "interpenetration of illusion and reality."[10] O.H.T. Rudzick states: "Prospero's magic does not get much above the mundane...."[11] However, Mary McAlpine expresses the view that Thomas is the "possessor of a strange talent... an oddly erratic style," which is "irritatingly brilliant."[12]

In *Munchmeyer and Prospero on the Island*, Part I "Munchmeyer" shows Will Munchmeyer as a graduate student who escapes the realities of wife and children by pretending to work on a novel in his basement refuge. Left alone, he transforms into the third –person centre of a fantasy in which he is chased through an empty department store by a mysterious cult of homosexuals. His trip begins and ends on a Stanley Park beach with a dream creation, his Miracle Girl, who is ultimately indifferent to him. He ends up reduced to being only a figure in his landlady's erotic invention, a man who cannot even create himself. "Munchmeyer" is a sad and complex metaphor for the vacuous realities met in contemporary experience, formed through a completely convincing male persona.

In Part II "Prospero on the Island," the central character is Miranda Archer, who has come to an island off the British Columbia coast with her youngest child and a Canada Council grant to write a novel about a character called Munchmeyer. She becomes close to another artist/painter Alex McKenzie who is the Prospero of the title. Miranda's diary entries, with reference to her novel, form the second part. If the male half of Thomas's double vision suggests suffocation and fragmentation, the female half offers an integrated sensibility in the making, and an invigorating air of expressed emotion. This work examines the relationship between the mind of the creator and the product of her creativity. The novel also suggests some of the similarities and differences in the circumstances under which the male and the female writers pursue their vocation.

Judith H. McDowell praises Thomas's "admirably realized people,"[13] in *Munchmeyer and Prospero on the Island*. Kildare Dobbs comments on the "completely convincing rendering of the mind of her male protagonist, even in his attitude to sex."[14] Thomas provides a veritable catalogue of narrative modes, ranging from jokes and anecdotes, through dreams, hallucinations, fantasies, to letters, journals, and novels. This is a very satiric and playful novel. Thomas admits: "I loved writing it. I had more fun writing that book than any book I've ever written."[15] To McDowell, Thomas's style and language show that "...hers is a superior, perhaps major talent."[16]

The stories in Thomas's second collection *Ladies and Escorts* (1977) are coextensive with her earlier periods of writing. The publication of this book along with a reissue of *Ten Green Bottles* made reviewers to comment that they are "companion volumes."[17] The stories can be classified into two categories. The African and Mexican stories focus on violent conflicts of culture, whereas other stories take up issues raised in *Munchmeyer and Prospero on the Island*, exposing the fake pastoralism of the hippy retreat to the islands and exploring the relationships between the quality of an artist's life and of his or her creations. Marion McCormick comments, "years have given greater confidence and skill"[18] to Audrey Thomas.

Latakia (1979) depicts the portraits of two artist protagonists, one male, and the other female. Jane Rule who nominated *Latakia* for the Governor General's Award contends that Thomas "perfects her method of maintaining multiple time streams for a marvellous economy of narrative."[19]

The title for Thomas's collection of stories *Real Mothers* (1981) comes from a line in *Latakia*: "I didn't measure up to their ideal. Real mothers weren't supposed to have obsessions like writing or separate identities."[20] In these stories, women characters relate to the issue of being a true mother, one who is loyal, self- sacrificing and carries out the tasks necessary to assure her children's well-being. However, these women are often unhappy, caught up in complex and conflicting emotions. They search for authenticity to displace the traditional notions and reconstruct new ideals. The stories narrate the actual experiences of "Real Mothers." These experiences are not the essence of motherhood but the actuality of it. Helen Hoyle is appreciative of Thomas's "metafiction[al] aims."[21]

Two in the Bush and Other Stories (1982) contains a selection of stories from *Ten Green Bottles* and *Ladies and Escorts*. These two books have close connection with respect to linguistic slippage of meaning between men and women. Some stories deal with the creative endeavours of both partners in a relationship; other stories show women's revolt against myths or conventions circumscribing their lives and language. The publication of *Two in the Bush and Other Stories* prompted Eleanor Wachtel to comment that Thomas now appears "relaxed," though her informality is "carefully crafted." This is a result of the more performative mode of the stories, anecdote having replaced "elliptical, personal imagery"[22] for narrative transitions.

In 1984, with the publication of *Intertidal Life* "an ambitious, complex work,"[23] a major shift occurred in the critical evaluation of Thomas's writing. This novel was short–listed for the 1984 Governor General's Award in Fiction. *Goodbye Harold, Good Luck* (1986), a collection of short stories, is introduced by an essay in which Thomas explains her method of composition through "correspondences."[24] Reviewers have preferred her short stories as Joel Yanofsky writes:

> Comparing this accomplished book with her last novel, *Intertidal Life,* an uneven, difficult work, it's easy to see why. Like Alice Munro and Mavis Gallant, Thomas is at her best working within the boundaries of the short story; she is at her most effective creating a fiction that is subtle and fragile, that is made up of hard choices and vivid moments.[25]

Wild Blue Yonder published in 1990 is another collection of stories written by Audrey Thomas. The stories in this collection are compact and self-contained narratives. Although the central characters in these stories are white, her minor characters represent a variety of cultures and races.

In *Graven Images* (1993), Thomas gives the story the mother and the daughter tell together. This is done in the process of writing a collaborative family history with Charlotte, incorporating her own autobiography and her mother's biography.

In *Coming Down from Wa* (1995), the protagonist, a white male on a quest to Africa, is represented by a third-person voice that records, orders, and observes the perspective of William Kwame McKenzie. William's parents served as Canadian volunteer workers in West Africa. His quest takes him from Abidjan on the Ivory Coast through Accra, Kumasi to Wa, to probe into the unhappy secret of his parents' past. The secret that William, with the help of his mother, finally discovers is his father's involvement with a young black student, Grace, which ends in tragedy. Thomas sets a challenge as she puts herself in a young man's body/mind and attempts to "make him... convincing."[26]

Audrey Thomas's novel *Isobel Gunn* (1999) is a fascinating exploration of history, culture, and the psychology of choice and loss. The novel is based on a few Hudson's Bay documents from the nineteenth century fur trade, which refer to a Scottish apprentice who turned out to be a young woman instead of a young man. Thomas reworks this persistent cultural story of the cross-dressing woman into a deeply moving account of one woman's, and one man's, encounters with the limitations of their world, both in the Orkney Islands where they are born and at the Hudson's Bay fort, in the early nineteenth century, where they first meet.

In *The Path of Totality: New and Selected Stories* (2001), Audrey Thomas describes female protagonists in Africa, Mexico and Greece as the means of exploring their identities. The stories are tales of female experience of life, power and fascination for words. Settings in non-English speaking countries frequently allow her to exploit her fondness for wordplay. Thomas ends this collection on what she describes in the preface as "a note of quiet contentment"[27] with a love story. The writer is in a mellow mood at a late stage in her career. The most outstanding quality of Thomas to cherish is her ascorbic wit, the sometimes savage indignation, and the bitterness that remains on the palate like a dish of good vinegar.

Apart from these, Thomas has written plays for CBC Stage, broadcast on CBC *Anthology* another half-dozen uncollected pieces, including a children's story. She has published more than a dozen book reviews in periodicals such as *Canadian Literature* and *Books in Canada.* She has also contributed essays to academic journals on subjects such as art criticism or women writers. Talon books of Vancouver and Penguin Canada of Toronto have mainly published her books in Canada.

Audrey Thomas is the recipient of several awards and honours. Some of her stories like "If One Green Bottle..." won Atlantic First Award from the *Atlantic Monthly* in 1965.

"Harry and Violet" won second prize in the National Magazine Awards fiction category, 1979. "Natural History" won second prize in the CBC Literary Contest fiction division, 1979-80. "Real Mothers" won second prize in *Chatelaine's* Fourth Annual Fiction Competition, 1981, and "Untouchables: A Memoir" won second prize in the CBC Literary Contest memoir division, 1981. She has also won the British Columbia Book Prize for fiction three times: for her novel *Intertidal Life,* for the short story collection *Wild Blue Yonder* and for the novel *Coming Down From Wa.* Thomas received the Marian Engel Award in 1987 and the Canada-Australia Literary Prize in 1990. She was nominated for the Governor General's Literary Award and Commonwealth Literature Prize in 1996.

In 2003, Audrey Thomas received the ninth Terasen Lifetime Achievement Award for an outstanding literary career in British Columbia. The audio book version of *Isobel Gunn,* read by Vancouver actor Duncan Fraser, was nominated for an Audio Award in 2003. She was honoured with the $20,000 Writers Trust of Canada's Matt Cohen Award in honour of a distinguished body of work.

Thomas has taught creative writing at the University of Victoria and at the University of British Columbia. She has been writer-in-residence at Concordia University and at Simon Fraser University. In 2004, she delivered the Margaret Laurence Lecture at the Writers Union of Canada AGM in Victoria. Thomas has a large variety of experience to share with readers because of having travelled widely. Landscapes to which she has travelled are spread through her works. Thomas is a writer whose world is surrounded by family, flora and fauna.

Audrey Thomas has selected Africa as a setting for several of her short stories and novels. This displays her fascination for the country where she has lived for several years and returned twice, the last visit having been in the1990s, which resulted in the writing of *Coming Down From Wa.* According to Edward Said, Africa is one of the "deepest and most recurring images of the Other"[28] that helped to define the West "as its contrasting image, idea, personality, experience."[29]

In Africa, the dream and the nightmare are substance and lie close to the surface. However, the surface itself is a cacophony of bright distracting images. The imposition of modernity on traditional modes of behaviour, the adoption of these western styles into indigenous rituals, the continuance of the rituals, and the resultant incongruous juxtapositions, all produce confusion. The Africa that meets the eye is complex, contradictory and a great camouflage for the real Africa.

Africa has appealed to Western and European writers because it is so unlike European. It is where the European culture meets with the primitive, where dream and reality are confronted and the European intellect is replaced by the African superstition and magic.

In Africa, the red hibiscus is a symbol of blood, the vulture of death, etc. They constitute what is tangible, sensuous and real in Africa. The expatriates seek the source of the unconscious, unknown and unknowable in Africa. Audrey herself admits:

> Africa is a metaphor for the unconscious. I think for a white person, you can never know Africa as an African.... Everything in Africa that I encountered was bigger, brighter. There's the sun to deal with; the colours are very intense. There's the terrific heat; there's a whole culture and background of superstition and ritual and myth which is so close to the surface – we keep ours for funerals and weddings but there's is everyday.[30]

In the late 1960s, travelling to Africa the "Shadow Continent"[31] became a new twist in the Canadian myth of the noble savage. This brings the works of Thomas within the orbit of the archetypal, which has been a marked feature of Canadian fiction in the 1960s and 1970s. Barbara Godard has commented on Thomas's "innate archetypalism."[32] Thomas did an archetypal study of Beowulf for her incomplete Ph.D thesis. The presence in her stories of innumerable archetypes is explained as "unconscious because I certainly never consciously put in any...I don't consciously use symbolism."[33] Her works attract academically oriented readers. However, she resents "being made into an intellectual writer. Because I'm not."[34]

The major influences on Thomas's writing are those of James Joyce, Joseph Conrad and Henry James. Audrey Thomas has adopted several themes, including the traveller, the interface of civilizations complicated by the blind innocence of characters, and the personality in flux, in her works. Thomas is intrigued by the moment when one thing turns into another. For her protagonists, travelling becomes a metaphor for the process of transformation, for self-discovery, just as Africa is often a metaphor in her works for the paradoxical intermingling of "dream" and "reality."[35] In this context, her works find comparisons with Conrad's *Heart of Darkness,* though she admits the real "Darkness is Canada."[36]

In her earlier writing days, Thomas saw herself as a failed poet. Her relationship with the Tish poets group comprising George Bowering, Frank Davey, Fred Wah and Daphne Marlatt was distant. She told Bowering it was difficult to "enter what you people were doing...because it was all poetry."[37] Now she thinks her prose is close to poetry "meant to be read aloud."[38] Thomas also shares with the Tish group an inheritance from phenomenology: "a *real* articulation of your experience of the real."[39]

Thomas's many stories are set in foreign countries, especially Greece and Africa, where she lived for a short time. In these stories, the characters, most of them on vacation in Greece, experience a sense of estrangement, dislocation and displacement. Being in an unfamiliar environment compels them to face their own sense of unfulfilment, to find a meaning to their lives, to dare challenge their fear of life and death in stories like "Miss Foote," "Local Customs," "Crossing the Rubicon," "Two in the Bush," etc. Death and cemeteries are also present in a number of stories like "Miss Foote," "The More Little Mummy in the World," "The Streets of Laredo," "Joseph and His Brother," etc.

The sea provides both a theme and a setting for some stories like "Local Customs," "The Man with Clam Eyes," and "The Wild Blue Yonder." In Audrey Thomas's short fiction, same characters appear in several stories, although the stories come from different collections like "The Albatross"(TGB), "Breaking the Ice"(TPT), "Ascension" (WBY), and "Local Customs"(RM), etc., thus providing the collection with some kind of coherence, a sort of loosely connected network of themes, characters and images.

Audrey Thomas's novels deal mostly with the complexities of family relationships, filial love between mother and son (*Isobel Gunn*), mother and daughter (*Graven Images* and *Songs My Mother Taught Me*), father and daughter (*Songs My Mother Taught Me*), and pain is always involved in these relationships. In her novels, "there is *no single* story of family life or marriage."[40] There are as many stories as there are individuals involved. Each character brings his or her story with him or her. The emphasis is not on the description of characters but on the act of telling stories. The characters leave the dominant impression rather than the landscape.

The many allusions in her works range from the Metaphysical poets, through the Romantics, to the great Modernists. Thomas has used writing to bring order to her varied existence, giving her a context through words.

Thomas's awareness of remote literary traditions has been a source of technical innovation in her writing. Studies of Old Norse and Old English gave her an interest in philology and a sense of the instability of the word as sign. Her break with the "linear stuff like medieval"[41] form of the organic novel was stimulated by interest in the cumulative forms of folk narrative and the circular forms of "Renaissance"[42] fiction. This broadening of perspectives is also evident in the works of another contemporary writer Hugh Hood, who, like Thomas, prefers "writing a *roman-fleuve* with recurring characters and motifs."[43]

If Audrey Thomas's roots were in the United States, her branches are in Canada. She has been there since 1959 and her first book, while published in the United States, was written in Canada and in West Africa. As a person, she is both very domestic and a wanderer. A reflection of this can be seen in the heroines of her novels. Her fiction finds its closest parallels with the works of writers such as Rudy Wiebe, who is interested in voice, or poet-novelists Leonard Cohen, Michael Ondaatje and Margaret Laurence, whose narratives also avoid traditional expository links and development occurring instead through a flux of images.

Thomas is concerned with the body, its foreignness and self-reflexivity, and with the process of writing. Thomas's writing is self-reflexive and autobiographical like that of Alice Munro and Rudy Wiebe. These writers question the representation of reality through words and this mode of fiction is popular in Canada. Munro makes a distinction between "autobiographical" works defined as being "life in its incidents," and "personal" works which "draw on experience"[44] to point out the impossibility of erecting definitive boundaries between truth and fiction. Writers like Munro, Laurence, Blaise and Ondaatje play with this paradox yet build credible characters, whereas Thomas's sense of writing as lying leads her at times to dissolve even this comfortable mimetic illusion.

Audrey Thomas is also a highly skilled writer of short stories, a genre that has been very vital in Canada in the last three decades. Critics compare her writing with the best short story writers of the country like Hugh Hood, Mavis Gallant and Alice Munro. Thomas, like these writers, builds her stories layer upon layer, generating paradoxes, ironies and creating a density of texture which "demands much more of her readers than most writers"[45] works do. Both her short stories and novels are experimental. They contain many intricate stories within stories, reflecting self-referentiality in her writing, which is a trait of postmodernism. Her first short story "If One Green Bottle..." serves as the embryonic source for much fiction that has followed. The experiment in this story continues to find its way into her subsequent stories and novels like *Mrs. Blood, Latakia, Two in the Bush, Intertidal Life, Graven Images* and *Coming Down from Wa.* All these novels focus on either a lost child, a lost lover or occasionally on both.

Thomas has written both short and long fictional forms with equal ease. She characterizes the shorter form as extremely demanding because the slightest error is magnified in them. Working so accurately has clearly been an important apprenticeship in her craft of writing. Continued practice has honed her use of highly allusive word and telegraphic detail so that the traits of density and compression are to be found in Thomas's longer fiction as well.

Thomas's works provide more scope for unearthing new dimensions of feminine imagination. Significantly, Audrey Thomas does not give up the conventional role of the responsibilities of a daughter and mother. Her life has been that of shifting from disturbed home life through education to marriage, to motherhood, divorce, economic crisis and then to stability as a writer. Her fiction has been and continues to be the evolution of feminism moving beyond conventions. For Thomas, personal experience and maternal experience are quite clearly connected and important to her art.

The recurrent motif of Thomas is the portrayal of female protagonist who needs warmth, company and human attachment despite having an established sensibility and a feeling of self-assuredness. She has been articulating her experience as a woman in a decade when women writers have been receiving much attention as a group. This places her works in not only Canadian context but also in an international context.

For Audrey Thomas, interest in language, change in meaning is related to personal association and experience. Her stress is always on the spontaneous, the unconscious, in sensing connections and not in any political motivation. She expresses the view that in order to confront patriarchy, one must "talk about forbidden subjects. That's the way in the end to defeat particular use of language."[46] Her fiction is a manifestation of postmodern feminist consciousness. Her interest in etymological roots of words, experiment and innovations with form, and narrative voice are found in all her novels.

Audrey Thomas portrays women's challenge to the patriarchal society. Her women aspire to rise above day to day business. They feel the painful dilemma of regarding themselves as the essential and the social pressure to accept them as a passive object. The apparent though masochistic willingness to belong, to conform, as well as the equally compelling urge for freedom and creativity felt by women is Thomas's major concern.

Thomas, like Margaret Laurence, makes ample use of biblical allusions and plots in her fiction; and like Margaret Atwood, she writes from knowledge of female rituals and rites. Margaret Atwood's novel *Surfacing* and Audrey Thomas's *Mrs. Blood* invite comparisons. Both these novels present explorations of the irrational, nightmare side breaking out of the order of male civilization.

Critics interpret changes in Thomas's writing as signs of increasing maturity and improvement. In "Thomas and her Rag-Bag," Butling places *Real Mothers* within the movement by women writers to redefine "the images of women"[47] in fiction. Thomas successfully deconstructs old images to make way for new images. Idealistic images are replaced by more realistic ones, where "Confusion, embarrassment, and mixed feelings"[48] become identified with mother love and with the construction of new ideals. Anne Archer in her essay "Real Mummies" writes:

> It is the purely personal aspect of much of Audrey Thomas' writing, coupled with her propensity to tell and retell a single story- to present us with a theme minus variation- that is both fascinating and problematic.[49]

The growth of women's self-awareness has considerably advanced in Canada during the 1970s. Thomas's novels, too, fit into the milieu of feminist writing. In her home on Galiano Island, Thomas is part of an artistic community, which has been said to "rival that of ancient Lesbos."[50] She acknowledges her writing has been:

> shaped by some of the great women of the past: Harriet Beecher Stowe, whom I read in an illustrated edition when I was very very very young (and who had an enormous influence on the women of her own and the succeeding generation), Louisa May Alcott, Willa Cather, Sigrid, Emily Dickinson, Edna St.Vincent Millay, Virginia Woolf, Doris Lessing and so on.[51]

Audrey Thomas, in her obsession with death, invites comparison with Sylvia Path who was at Smith College with her and whose obsession with death is expressed in poetic form. She writes from a woman's point of view. Her books focus on female characters and the stories are told from their individual point of view. Each of her protagonists is in search of her own voice/identity, troubled by the ambiguous relations between language and silence, speech and thought, words and power. Thomas's novels explore the constricting definitions of women and dramatize the ways a woman's voice becomes the means to her self-realization.

Audrey Thomas advances women's knowledge of themselves "to demonstrate the terrible gap between men and women"[52] and to "give women a sense of their bodies."[53] Her position is like that of Munro, Laurence, Atwood, Marian Engel, Constance Beresford-Howe, and Carol Shields. She documents the strictures on women's lives and attempts to articulate this experience in women's own words without positing alternate worlds. Thomas is different from the other writers of the period with regard to her experimentation and her interest in sexuality. Thomas finds sexuality in Munro's work mostly adolescent: "She's never really written an adult story,"[54] whereas Doris Lessing has written frankly about sexual relations "the sexual stuff between men and women."[55]

Thomas with her first short story "If One Green Bottle..." has inaugurated "gynecological"[56] fiction. Her concern for the body has drawn Thomas into the orbit of women's writing in French, especially the works of Helen Cixous, who advocates the translation of the body to create a new women's discourse. Her concern also with the language and the acts of writing and reading finds a correspondence in the works of Nicole Brossard.

Thomas has great admiration for the works of Quebec women writers, especially Marie-Claire Blais's *Mad Shadows*. She admits: "I feel a kinship with Marie Claire Blais.... A book like *Mad Shadows* – I wish I'd written that."[57] "Mademoiselle Blood," the title of Audrey Thomas's review of Anne Hebert's *Heloise*, underlines her affinities with "the theme of mastery"[58] and with the dark world where sex and death intertwine. These writers share a fascination with *Alice's Adventures in Wonderland*.

Femininity is of major interest to Audrey Thomas who questions and revolts against the acquired mode of behaviour of perceiving, thinking and acting in a manner the larger society demands of women to realize the roles assigned to them. Susan Brownmiller has described Femininity as:

> ...brilliant, subtle, aesthetic that was bafflingly inconsistent at the same time that is minutely, demandingly concrete, a rigid code of appearance and behaviour defined by do's and don'ts. [59]

Audrey Thomas explores the female quest for independence, identity and ultimate authority. Her keen sense of observation effaces her from the position of an ordinary didactic critic and puts her in the position of literary artist, who writes about woman's silence, madness, marginality, negativity and difference; and woman's body, woman's feelings and woman's desires.

Thomas's heroines do not always want to disentangle themselves of their femininity. It is their psychological requirement to love and be loved. Just as Susan Brownmiller says:

> The territory of the heart is admittedly a province that is open to all but women alone are expected to make an obsessional career of its exploration, to find whatever adventure, power, fulfilment or tragedy that life has to offer within its bounds. [60]

Susan Rudy Dorscht is of the view that Thomas's fiction insists that language is all: "Everything is word, everything is only word...."[61] Is life, like Africa, "something which you 'do' and then write up for the folks back home?"[62] Are the connections between being and nothingness, between life and death, just "a question of semantics?"[63] Is it "easier to conjure up a fairy tale...than to put one's finger on the pulse of truth?"[64]

The relationship between the word as sign and what it signifies is always an arbitrary one, but in the extreme situations in which Thomas's characters find themselves, that is, in foreign countries, in insane asylums, in sexual ghettoes, the gap between their experience and the language used around them is a vast one. This problem in communication is simultaneously cause and consequences of their alienation. Thomas explores and explodes limits and boundaries in a perpetual search for meaning.

Regarding Thomas's characterization, she "is skillful at peeling off the emotions."[65] Laurence Lafore says that Thomas's "speciality is not a region but a gender" and she is brilliant at portraying "neurotic women."[66] Frank Davey sees her style as fundamental to write: "an extreme kind of psychological realism."[67] The action involved in searching the essential self is an important component in the fiction of Audrey Thomas. She says, "The process of writing...may have brought me closer to myself, which may not have been where I thought I was."[68] For Thomas, the self is neither constant nor stable. It is a shifting identity and writing is one way to try to understand and clarify the position occupied by that identity. Her female narrators attempt to dislodge the male defined female identity and engage in a re-search of the self. This search is a continuing process, as her fiction remains open–ended and accessible to further exploration.

While calling herself a feminist writer, she does not want to be part of any institutionalized movement. She tells Robyn Gillam, "You can't add feminism to your work...it's not like vanilla; you don't go, tsk, tsk, needs a bit more feminism, and you put some more feminism in."[69]

Some important feminist readings appeared in the 1980's with critics like Joan Coldwell, Lorna Irvine, Wendy Keitner, Pauline Butling, Coral Ann Howells and Susan Rudy Dorscht making significant contributions to new readings of Thomas's works. Most of them dwelt on the connections between her fiction and western classics whose plots she sought to deconstruct. However, Lorna Irvine, who assigned allegorical meaning and took an archetypal approach to *Mrs. Blood* and *Blown Figures*, persisted in looking for an essential truth. Butling's reading of *Latakia*, while emphasizing Thomas's self–reflexive writing and foregrounding of language, saw the real meaning of the novel's form and method as the paradox of a Cretan proclaiming "All Cretans are liars."[70] This confusion of truth/lies ensured that all meaning is plural.

A new and positive feature identified by critics in her writing is humour. Reviewers appreciate the combination of "humor with heart-breaking pathos and realism with the odd dose of whimsy."[71] Thomas considers herself a funny person, but admits: "humour has not frequently appeared"[72] in her writing. However, her humour is most evident in "The Princess and the Zucchini" a witty fairy tale for adults about a princess who encounters a talking zucchini, with "a feminist twist to the theme of the captive prince."[73]

Thomas creates what Frank Davey terms "alternate stories,"[74] that is, scripts written by one character for another, stories from mythology and literature repeated by characters, stories contained within symbolic objects, and stories written by characters to justify their lives within "the apparent story,"[75] and ironically work to "demolish"[76] it, producing "disjunctive narratives."[77]

A shift in critical paradigms in the field of Canadian literature towards deconstructionist, feminist perspectives, and theoretical approaches, begins with the premise that language mediates our encounter with reality. These tendencies converge in Thomas's works with its subversions of the paradigms of dominant discourses.

The British critic Coral Ann Howells highlights Thomas's "treatment of narrative as a feminist issue."[78] In her essays, Howells is concerned with Thomas's women's need to tell stories, which are closer to their social realities and, consequently, with the need to revise or unwrite existing "old romantic fantasy narratives,"[79] "based on woman's adoration of the powerful male and on an exaggerated evaluation of him."[80]

Audrey Thomas offers play on the duplicity, the multiplicity of language and its paradoxes, thus opening up the space of the books for an active reader to work at its meaning. The stories are not in the words, but in the spaces between and around them, in the play between text and context. Thomas's stories evolve through "rhythm, calculation and selection,"[81] "plane grafted onto plane, perspective piled onto perspective."[82]

The works of Audrey Thomas thus also signal very clearly the remarkable emphasis in recent Canadian fiction on the active participation and involvement of the reader. This concern with reader response is in itself a matter of historical importance since it involves the placing of the reader as a participant in history, in the struggle for meaning. In acting as the producers of meaning, and not just its passive recipients, the readers of the text become "the actual and actualizing links between history and fiction, as well as between the past and the present."[83]

The central concept of Thomas's fiction is that personal memory allows one to become one's own saviour. She understands that the artistic validity of psychological drama depends on the influences of the past that the tension proceeds from "within the person who is drawn back to the past in order to orient himself to future."[84] In tracing Audrey Thomas's development, it is important to attend to the order in which the stories were written. Audrey Thomas says, "All my novels are one novel, in a sense...Each one extends, in a different style, offering more information, from a different perspective, what is basically the same story."[85]

A vigorous experimenter with narrative method and language, Thomas shows a keen interest in the derivation of words, their ambiguities and multiple connotations. She attempts "to locate a real language, a means of communicating...women's experiences and feelings."[86] She plays with literary allusions and puns, stretches language to catch the experience of people, mostly women, hovering on the verge of disintegration. Thomas is a demanding writer: "in her scrupulous avoidance of easy answers."[87]

Another important feature in Audrey Thomas's fiction is the reality, which proceeds from the female body. Susan Gubar comments on the relation between body and creativity:

> many women experience their own bodies as the only available medium for their art with the result that the distance between the woman artist and her art is radically diminished.[88]

Thomas does write the body to a certain extent such that her own physical ageing parallels the growth of her protagonists.

The distinguishing themes and invasive motifs in Thomas's fiction are quest, artistic creation, sexual identity, male/female relationships and mother-daughter relationships. There is a proliferation of biblical and literary allusions, references to rituals and rites of post-ages, female chaos and irrationality in her fiction. She is a serious writer who "has been discovered repeatedly."[89] Her novels map the evolution of her feminist thought.

In her feminist perspective, Audrey Thomas is not limited by the regional or geographical boundaries. In the present time, difficult situations, conflicting emotional demands, or role expectations are slipping women apart. Audrey Thomas in her novels has taken up the area where the struggle of contemporary women to redefine conventions is at its sharpest because convention here coincides with our deepest emotional bonds. It is in the intersecting paradoxes of Thomas's narratives that these conflicting demands are reconciled. Her novels reinforce wholeness and integration in a world that threatens to come apart and her stories appeal to the heart, just as their self-reflexive nature offers consolation of form to the mind.

ENDNOTES

1. Don Stanley, "Stories Audrey Told Me," *Leisure, The Vancouver Sun*, (September 9, 1977), p.7A.
2. Alison Appelbe, "Female Loners...and the Broken Marriage Syndrome," *Leisure, The Vancouver Sun*, (August 31, 1973), p.34A.
3. Pierre Coupey *et al.*, "Interview/Audrey Thomas," *The Capilano Review*, No.7 (Spring, 1975), p.94.
4. John Hofsess, "A Teller of Surprising Tales," *The Canadian, The Toronto* Star, (May 6, 1978), p.16.
5. George Bowering, "Songs and Wisdom: An Interview with Audrey Thomas," *Open Letter*, 4th Series, No. 3 (Spring, 1979), p.7.
6. Eleanor Wachtel, "The Guts of Mrs. Blood," *Books in Canada*, (November, 1979), p.5.
7. Pierre Coupey *et al.*, (1975), *op. cit.*, p.95.
8. Anita Raskia, review of *Ten Green Bottles, News*, [Savannah,Ga.], (October 8, 1967).
9. Jane Kay, "The Neglected Child of Literature," review of *Ten Green Bottles*, by Audrey Thomas, and four other books, *The Patriot Ledger* [Quincy, Mass.], (September 29, 1967), p.30.
10. Kildare Dobbs, "A Novelist Explores the Circles of Hell," review of *Munchmeyer and Prospero on the Island, The Toronto Star*, (April 1, 1972), p.59.
11. O.H.T. Rudzick, review of *Munchmeyer and Prospero on the Island*, "Letters in Canada 1972: Fiction," *University of Toronto Quarterly*, 42 (Summer, 1973), p.348.
12. Mary McAlpine, "I Cannot Wear Your Mark Upon My Back," review of *Munchmeyer and Prospero on the Island, Saturday Night*, (July, 1972), p.44.
13. Judith H. McDowell, review of *Munchmeyer and Prospero on the Island*, by Audrey Thomas, and *Daughters of the Moon*, by Joan Haggerty, *World Literature Written in English*, No.12 (April, 1973), p.58.
14. Kildare Dobbs (1972), *op. cit.*, p.59.
15. George Bowering (1979), *op. cit.*, p.26.
16. Judith H. McDowell (1973), *op. cit.*, p.59.
17. Deborah Scharbach, "Audrey Thomas," review of *Ten Green Bottles* and *Ladies and Escorts, Brick: A Journal of Reviews*, No. 4 (Fall, 1978), p.49.

18. Marion McCormick, "Love, Marriage and Related Disasters," review of *Ladies and Escorts, Quill and Quire,* (July, 1977), p.5.
19. Jane Rule, review of *Latakia, The Globe and Mail,* (December 22, 1979), p.10.
20. Audrey Thomas, *Latakia* (1979; rpt. Vancouver: Talonbooks, 1989), p.51.
21. Helen Hoy, review of *Real Mothers,* "Letters in Canada 1981: Fiction," *University of Toronto Quarterly,* No. 51 (Summer, 1982), p.322.
22. Eleanor Wachtel, "Contemporary Triangles," review of *Real Mothers* and *Two in the Bush and Other Stories, Saturday Night,* (April,1982), p.52.
23. Urjo Kareda, "Sense and Sensibility," review of *Intertidal Life, Saturday Night,* (January, 1986), p.50.
24. Audrey Thomas, *Goodbye Harold, Good Luck* (Toronto: Viking, 1986), p.xvi.
25. Joel Yanofsky, "Thinking Small," review of *Goodbye Harold, Good Luck, Books in Canada,* (June-July, 1986), p.14.
26. Robyn Gillam, "Ideals and Lost Children: An Interview with Audrey Thomas," *Paragraph: The Canadian Fiction Review,* Vol.18, No. 1 (Summer, 1996), p.2.
27. Audrey Thomas, *The Path of Totality: New and Selected Stories* (Toronto: Penguin, 2001), p.ii.
28. Edward Said, *Orientalism* (London and Henley: Routledge and Kegan Paul, 1978), p.1.
29. *Ibid.*, p.2.
30. Elizabeth Komisar, "Audrey Thomas: A Review/ Interview," review of *Blown Figures, Open Letter,* 3rd Series, No. 3 (Fall, 1975), pp.63-64.
31. Patricia Monk, "Shadow Continent: The Image of Africa in Three Canadian Writers," *Ariel,* Vol.8, No.4 (October, 1977), p.3.
32. Barbara Godard, *Audrey Thomas and Her Works* (Toronto: E C W Press, year not given), p.6.
33. George Bowering (1979), *op. cit.*, p.12.
34. Eleanor Wachtel, "Putting up Fences in the Garden: Audrey Thomas talks to Eleanor Wachtel," *Tessera,* 5 (September, 1988), p.68.

35. George Bowering (1979), *op. cit.*, p.10.
36. Pierre Coupey *et al.*, (1975), *op. cit.*, p.88.
37. George Bowering (1979), *op. cit.*, p.8.
38. *Ibid.*
39. Pierre Coupey *et al.*, (1975), *op. cit.*, p.107.
40. Barbara Godard, *op. cit.*, p.67.
41. George Bowering (1979), *op. cit.*, p.13.
42. *Ibid.*
43. Barbara Godard, *op. cit.*, p.6.
44. Linda MacKinley Hay, "Recurring Themes in the Fiction of Audrey Thomas," M.A. Thesis (New Brunswick, 1975), p.xii.
45. Barbara Novak, "Lunar Distractions," review of *Real Mothers, Books in Canada,* (February, 1982), p.20.
46. Eleanor Wachtel (1988), *op. cit.*, p.67.
47. Pauline Butling, "Thomas and Her Rag-Bag," *Canadian Literature,* No.102 (Autumn, 1984), p.195.
48. *Ibid.*, p.198.
49. Anne Archer, "Real Mummies," *Studies in Canadian Literature,* No. 9 (1984), p.214.
50. Hubert de Santana, "Wonder Women," *Today Magazine, The Toronto Star,* (December 13, 1980), p.15.
51. Audrey Thomas, "My Craft and Sullen Art: The Writers Speak," *Atlantis,* Vol. 4, No.1 (Autumn, 1978), p.152.
52. Pierre Coupey et.al., (1975), *op. cit.*, p.98.
53. *Ibid.*, p.107.
54. George Bowering (1979), *op. cit.*, p.31.
55. *Ibid.*, p.14.
56. *Ibid.*, p.20.
57. *Ibid.*, pp.30-31.
58. Audrey Thomas, "Mademoiselle Blood," review of *Heloise,* by Anne Hebert, *Books in Canada,* (February, 1983), p.11.
59. Susan Brownmiller, *Femininity* (New York: Fawcett Columbine, 1984), p.14.

60. *Ibid.*, p.215.
61. Susan Rudy Dorscht, "On Blowing Figures...and Bleeding: Post-structuralist Feminism and the 'Writing' of Audrey Thomas," *Canadian Fiction Magazine,* No.57 (1986) [*Tessera,* No.37], *op. cit.*, p.68.
62. Audrey Thomas, "Omo," *Ten Green Bottles* (1977), *op. cit.*, p.56.
63. Audrey Thomas, "Still Life With Flowers," *Ten Green Bottles* (1977), *op. cit.*, p.22.
64. Audrey Thomas, "A Winter's Tale," *Ten Green Bottles* (1977), *op. cit.*, p.142.
65. Nikki Moir, "A Symphony of Birth That Is Unforgettable," review of *Ten Green Bottles, The Province* [Vancouver] (January 12, 1968), p.5.
66. Laurence Lafore, "Short Turns and Encores," review of *Ten Green Bottles*, Audrey Thomas, *The Courtyards of Jerusalem,* Chaim Brandwein, *Dear Me,* Edita Morris, and *The Best American Short Stories 1967*, eds. Martha Foley and David Burnett, *The New York Times Book Review,* (December 10, 1967), p.55.
67. Frank Davey, "Audrey Thomas," *From There to Here: A Guide to English –Canadian Literature since 1960* (Erin, Ont.: Porcepic, 1974), p.254.
68. Eleanor Wachtel, "An Interview with Audrey Thomas," *Room of One's Own*, Vol. I0, Nos. 3 and 4 (March, 1986), p.49.
69. Robyn Gillam (1996), *op. cit.*, p.5.
70. Audrey Thomas, *Latakia* (1989), *op. cit.*, p.29.
71. Barbara Gunn, "Writer with Dazzling Gift for Short Fiction," review of *Goodbye Harold, Good Luck, The Vancouver Sun,* (June 14, 1986), p.E15.
72. Eleanor Wachtel, "The Guts of Mrs. Blood," (1979), *op. cit.*, p.28.
73. Ronald Hatch, "Stories for Now," review of *Goodbye Harold, Good Luck, The Canadian Forum,* (August-September, 1986), p.34.
74. Frank Davey, "Alternate Stories: The Short Fiction of Audrey Thomas and Margaret Atwood," *Canadian Literature,* No.109 (Summer, 1986), p.5.
75. *Ibid.*
76. *Ibid.*, p.9.

77. *Ibid.*, p.5.
78. Coral Ann Howells, "No Sense of an Ending: Real Mothers," *Room of One's Own*, Vol.10, Nos.3-4 (March, 1986), p.111.
79. *Ibid.*
80. Coral Ann Howells, "Margaret Lawrence: The Diviners and Audrey Thomas: Latakia," *Canadian Woman Studies*, Vol.6, No. I (Fall, 1984), p.99.
81. Audrey Thomas, *Real Mothers*, (Vancouver: Talonbooks, 1981), p.35.
82. Barbara Godard, *op. cit.*, p.66.
83. Linda Hutcheon, *The Canadian Postmodern: A Study of Contemporary Fiction* (Toronto: Oxford University Press, 1988), p.65.
84. Arthur Miller, *Psychology and Arthur Miller*, interviewer Richard Evans, (New York: E.P. Dutton, 1969), p.56.
85. John Hofsess, (1978), *op. cit.*, p.17.
86. Donna Bennett, "Naming the way home," *Amazing Space: Writing Canadian Women Writing*, ed. Shirley Neuman and Smaro Kamboureli, (Alberta: Longspoon Press, 1988), p.235.
87. John Hofsess (1978), *op. cit.*, p.18.
88. Susan Gubar, "The Blank Page and the Issues of Female Creativity," *The New Feminist Criticism*, ed. Elaine Showalter, (New York: Pantheon Books, 1985), p.296.
89. Eleanor Wachtel, "The Guts of Mrs. Blood," (1979), *op. cit.*, p.3.

Chapter 3

ISOBEL'S TRILOGY

SECTION-I

SONGS MY MOTHER TAUGHT ME

"a sensitive and touching portrait of a girl growing up."

Literary tradition has portrayed woman as weak, passive, gentle and modest, "the proper woman in male texts has been the selfless, self-effacing, docile, acquiescent, mute and submissive one, an angel in the house who accepts without demur the gender defined role assigned to her by the patriarchal society."[1]

For female writers, the act of writing is self-conscious. Annis Pratt remarks:

> Women novelists...have dug the goddess out of the ruins and cleansed the debris from her face, casting aside the gynophobic masks that have obscured her beauty, her power, and her beneficence. In so doing, they have made the woman's novel a pathway to the authentic self, to the roots of our selves beneath consciousness of self, and to our innermost being."[2]

In her narratives, Audrey Thomas shatters female stereotypes and emphasizes women's competence and independence. Her protagonists single or separated posit themselves in a world of independence, which provides alternative definition of what it means to be a female. The emancipated woman faces crisis with confidence and courage. She faces the dilemma and struggle through adversity, self-knowledge and authenticity. Her heroines free themselves from the desire of what women must become and achieve the desirable feminist synthesis, exploring and exposing the heroic possibilities in them. They cease to "swing in the ancient orbits"[3] and embrace new orbits of definition and define themselves in relation to artistic values other than those of male superiority stressed by patriarchy.

In some of her earlier works, Audrey Thomas has repeated the same subjects. Her three novels, *Mrs. Blood* (1970), *Songs My Mother Taught Me* (1973), and *Blown Figures* (1974), written during the 1970s, record the saga of self-discovery of a single female character Isobel Cleary. An extensive part of the world is seen through her consciousness. Each novel picks up Isobel at a particular stage of her psychological life. Isobel's wartime childhood and postwar adolescence form the subject matter of *Songs My Mother Taught Me,* the second novel of this trilogy. *Songs My Mother Taught Me* is "an impressionistic period piece"[4] and serves as a narrative bridge between *Mrs. Blood* and *Blown Figures.*

Songs My Mother Taught Me is a family centred story set in and around Utica, New York, in the 1940s and 1950s. It is the story of Isobel: "Daughter of Warren Joseph Cleary, and Clara Blake, née Goodenough, Cleary" and "younger sister of Jane Elizabeth."[5] The novel traces Isobel's psychological and emotional development from the age of five to seventeen. Isobel as a child is shy and self-conscious. During her teenage years, she gropes for her valid identity as an intelligent and sexy adult female and potential poet.

Songs My Mother Taught Me projects Isobel growing up in New York state. The novel begins with five-year old

Isobel misreading a map of New York, as she tries to trace "Utica" (SMMTM, p.13) instead of "Ithaca" on way to "Journey's End" to spend the summer vacation with her grandfather ""Harry" or "Uncle Harry"" (SMMTM, p.17). Isobel and her elder sister Jane are deeply attached to him:

> And he would scoop us up, leaving the lantern on the bottom step, carry us squealing and kicking up to the top, where the three of us, Harry, Jane and Isobel, would stand looking down in arrogant superiority at the superfluous couple below (SMMTM, p.16).

As a child, Isobel faces disturbance at home. Her parents do not get along well: "if my parents weren't quarreling they were snoring heavily and then it was very hard to get to sleep" (SMMTM, p.20). In her family, comprising of four members, Isobel still finds herself lonely: "I had addressed all the postcards to myself. 'Dear Isobel. Having a swell time. Your friend.I'" (SMMTM, p.27).

All the characters in *Songs My Mother Taught Me* suffer from a kind of madness or disorder in their emotions. Isobel is afraid of her mother bursting in rages inspired by trivial incidents: "I trembled to think of my mother, in one of her sudden rages, picking up the heater and flinging it ..." (SMMTM, p.31). Her father, a teacher, is the member of Masonic League. He is a henpecked husband. He is unsuccessful as a breadwinner and in sex: "a homosexual or homosexually inclined" (SMMTM, p.63). He is considered to be a misfit and burden by his wife Clara who has "endless complaints about his inadequacies" (SMMTM, p.114). Her parents sleep in separate rooms. The father sleeps in the back bedroom, whereas the mother sleeps in her bedroom: "Ashamed of one another, hating one another, blaming one another" (SMMTM, p.111). Her father is an enigmatic person to Isobel. Her parents live in a world of their own:

> my father worked on his garden or went up to his room and marked or practiced for one of his Degrees. My mother

> lay across her bed and read her books and magazines (SMMTM, p.106).

Isobel finds the cordial, affectionate communication between husband and wife missing in her parents' life. Isobel's father is timid. He proves to be "weak both physically and morally" in front of his wife. Even on occasions when he tries to assert himself: "Mother would quickly chop him down" (SMMTM, p.54). Isobel feels sad to reflect that though her parents live under the same roof there was no:

> closeness between them except when they combined efforts to borrow money or ward off bill collectors. I grew up, for the first sixteen years of my life, knowing only this woman and this man (SMMTM, p.64).

Her father has a duck like voice and mother does not hesitate to call him "Donald Duck" (SMMTM, p.20). Isobel rejects the role model provided by her mother Clara. To Isobel, she is a dominating housewife, full of rages, suffering from feelings of guilt and sexual repression. Isobel remembers Clara's hatred: "Your precious father...contemptible-a pervert" (SMMTM, p.98). The dreadful fate of reproducing her mother's wasted life is symbolised for Isobel in her two eroded, corpse-like rag dolls, ""Me" and "Mimi,"" a mother and daughter symbiotically intertwined as their names suggest, "bleached featureless" and rendered almost indistinguishable from each other, which she initially interprets as her "totems" (SMMTM, p.19).

Isobel is also dissatisfied with the images of single womanhood presented by her two spinster aunts. Aunt Hettie is: "a large, fat woman who wore a laveliee" (SMMTM, pp.114-115). She is powerless and housebound: "cooked and cleaned or read the Bible...was a fanatical housekeeper and even kept...starched shirts and detachable collars rolled up in the icebox before she ironed them" (SMMTM, pp.121-122), whereas Aunt Olive is a university professor with a Ph.D. in English. Isobel's father is dependent on her for regular loans. As she is better educated and economically independent, she arouses instant fury and resentment in Clara, "I don't want your filthy money" (SMMTM, p.76). Seeing her mother, Isobel becomes conscious of the psychological self-effacement and economic powerlessness inherent in the domestic role of housewife and mother. However, to her dismay, she discovers in the life of her professional spinster aunt equal and opposite limitations. Isobel is filled with shame and disgust at Clara's heavy body disfigured by stretch marks and oozing menstrual blood. But she equally repels Aunt Olive's shapeless figure concealed in dark brown skirts, opaque stockings, and heavy shoes. Isobel cannot help asking herself: "did I really want to end up sack-shaped, on a Greyhound bus, honorary house mother to a group of sorority girls" (SMMTM, pp.75-76). And the answer is no.

Isobel is in a state of shock and despair when she compares the old female members of her family with the slim waist, well-groomed models of the women's magazines. She desires neither to be shackled by a bad marriage nor to live the half-life of an unmarried woman. She confesses: "What I really wanted to do was to remain forever fixed... like the little girl in the glass paperweight at home" (SMMTM, p.123). To Isobel, living with unsociable parents is a heavy burden:

> "In the eighteen-odd years I lived "at home" (if only on the holidays), they *never*, together or separately, had a real guest in for the evening" (SMMTM, p.106).

Her mother's constant criticism of Isobel as a misfit and failure depresses her. She longs to die. The night of her senior prom, she seriously considers committing suicide. She is embarrassed by the sham parade of angora sweaters, ballet slippers and salon perms purchased on her father's shaky credit. She detests her mother's manipulations to secure invitations and friendships for her. Isobel realises she will never become the "golden girl" (SMMTM, p.136) of her mother's aspirations.

For Isobel, her mother Clara signifies deprivation, nameless frustrations and fear. Thomas's use of the locked door symbolises the exclusion and splitting away from the mother as well as the fear of an engulfing presence. The narrator looks back and interrogates the absent self, asking: "Which was worse, Isobel? The sound of the key from the inside, locking her in, or sitting downstairs or waiting in your bedroom for the key to turn again?" When Clara would burst out "like the real Grace Poole, roaring, biting, eager to attack" (SMMTM, p.49).

Isobel duplicates Clara's behaviour later. She, miserable at her classmate's rejection of her invitation to her home, shuts her bedroom door and wishes to have "a key, like Mother's, to lock it once for all" (SMMTM, p.61). Audrey Thomas uses the images of doors and windows to connote both the entrapment and the power of suppressed quest for identity and self-authenticity. Isobel closes the door of her room so that she is shut off from the world gaze. Fleenor makes a similar observation:

> The writer's feelings are frequently illustrated by the image of enclosed space and image which conveys repression and frustration.... Spatial imagery, images of enclosed rooms or houses, suggests either the repressive society in which the heroine lives or the heroine herself and some times compulsively both.[6]

She attempts to decode the rules of her mother's world: "was it better to be married than to be an old maid??" wonders the sixteen year old Isobel. One was supposed to feel sorry for old maids like Aunt Hettie, "at least that's what I gathered. Old maids married Jesus. Grandfather had "warped" her (that was my mother's word)" (SMMTM, p.123).

One of the earliest memory traces Isobel has is of: "A shadow-mother on the bedroom wall," memories that are constantly "dissolving, re-creating themselves" (SMMTM, p.18). The "twisted braid of affects" that besets Isobel in her relation with her mother signifies "abjection."[7] According to Kristeva, abjection is a state related to the child's initial splitting from the mother, the breaking of the pre-oedipal links, and its resultant primal repression of a "want"[8] that continues to trouble the child. The resulting fear, insecurity, and sense of exclusion give rise to a "revolt"[9] within the abject subject. Feeling threatened from outside and inside, both by exclusion and rejection, the subject, as a means of self-protection, abject and excludes the other. "Fear cements the compound" of the world from which the child has been "driven out, forfeited" and the "solace" offered instead of the maternal object/other, is the father, "loving but unsteady, merely an apparition."[10] This fear shades off metonymically "like a mirage and permeates all words of the language with non-existence...."[11]

While abjecting the mother, splitting the self from the other, Isobel testifies to the power of the mother's word: "My mother said terrible things and then changed her mind and wanted you to forget them, but how could you? Look how well Isobel remembers" (SMMTM, pp.37-38).

Isobel yearns for freedom from physical as well as psychological inhibition. She is irritated by the sheltered, extremely protective attitude of the family towards her: "My mother bawled me out about the smoking ... and that "nobody respects a girl who plays fast and loose"" (SMMTM, p.168).

After an account of her mother's neurotic behaviour: "mother left us, got as far as Scranton, Pennsylvania, and returned," with its aftermath of emotional and often physical violence: "she smashed all the glass in all the frames of the countless family photographs" (SMMTM, p.99), Isobel confesses:

> In school we learned to conjugate the verb "to be." Be/Is/ Are/Was/Were/Am/Being/Been (SMMTM, pp.99-100).

Here she conjugates present, past and signifies the stasis of her life as just being in hell and not becoming one. Isobel moves from childhood to adulthood into ever widening circles of the complexity of the connections to make more and more complex decisions about belonging, about love and resistance, and decisions related to acceptance or rejection.

She admits "the burden of my family too heavy to try and share" (SMMTM, p.57) with anyone. Parental quarrels, unpaid bills, the lies and hypocrisy involved in the pathetic charade of the children being exploited to get loans, are some of the reasons for "misery spread like the damp along the walls" (SMMTM, p.111) of the Cleary home. This message is proclaimed by Isobel "GOD BLESS OUR HO -" (SMMTM, p.55). Her uncommunicative father and her deeply disturbed mother cause irreparable damage to Isobel's self and cripple her psyche. She remembers the Christmas when Clara: "tore the ornaments off the Christmas tree that night…crushed them under her heel, scattered the turkey carcass, wrenching it apart, outside in the backyard in the darkness…." Isobel and Jane in order to escape Clara's wrath "rushed upstairs, howling, … and utterly heart-broken," and their father: "outside in the dark, weeping, trying to find the bits of turkey with a flashlight, blubbering, "My God, my God, my God"" (SMMTM, pp.82-83). At one stage, her adolescent anger against her parents verges on thoughts of murdering "one or both of them before the summer was out" (SMMTM, p.138).

Harry Goodenough "an ascetic in his habits- little food, no tobacco, no alcohol" (SMMTM, p.92) has more physical dynamism than his son-in-law Warren who is "Weak. Lily-livered" (SMMTM,p.67). Harry's sense of humour, his virile, and affection for Isobel and Jane, makes him father archetype. The girls look forward to spend the summer vacation in his cottage. However, Clara finds his behaviour "perverted" (SMMTM, p.63).

The only solace for Isobel in her world of misery is her grandfather's house and all it stands for. The presiding deity of this world is her grandfather. Jane and Isobel: "The Pin-up Girls of H.B.Goodenough" (SMMTM, p.87) are dependent on him for gifts and presents. He gave them ten dollars each on their birthday and Christmas. For Isobel, Harry symbolizes power, success and other male identified virtues. However, when "Journey's End" is sold Isobel's sense of exclusion and betrayal surfaces in a dream. In the dream, old Harry with "death spots on the back of his hands," calls out to Isobel and is ignored. She drops "the match near Harry's cardboard feet" (SMMTM, p.184) to see him go up in flames.

For Isobel, sexuality is part of both maturity and belonging. She has adolescent fantasies of perfect man with whom she will share these pleasures. During teenage turmoil, she meets Christopher Meyer in the mountains and falls in love with him. He is "tall and brown" with his "teeth stuck out a bit... all my strength resting, trusting, on his arm." In his company, it turns out to be "such a beautiful, beautiful summer" (SMMTM, p.127). However, her first love does not last long. He goes away. He sends her a few letters and then it stops. She comes to know eight months later that he was killed in a car crash.

Isobel is lonely and sad after Christopher's death. She comes across Digger, the lifeguard at the country club: "Bandy-legged and with a gravelly voice. Short. Dark. Possibly Jewish" (SMMTM, p.172). This affair like the previous one with Christopher is short-lived. Digger realizes the vast age gap between them: "I'm twenty-two and you're sixteen." Moreover, he tells Isobel: "If I wasn't the lifeguard and the whole thing wasn't a great big adventure, you'd pass me by on the street" (SMMTM, p.181). They part with a heavy heart.

Two unexpected things happen to Isobel at seventeen. First, her grandfather sells his summer house. She has to spend the summer in the city for the first time in her life as a result of the unprecedented move. To her, "it was like a cruel and unnecessary amputation," leaving her "minus a vital limb, helpless, pain-wracked" (SMMTM, p.133). Second, she goes to work. After her sister Jane leaves for Maine to take up the job of a counsellor at a summer camp, Isobel is left all alone: "I was there, *all the time,* apparently friendless, ambitionless…" (SMMTM, p.136). She gets the job of a "female aide" in a mental hospital. In the beginning, she was reluctant:

> My first impulse was to turn and walk straight out of there. In many ways my upbringing had been as sheltered as that of a girl in a convent…I had always turned my head away from the blind pencil seller at the corner of Main and Chenango streets. I had never seen a dead person, let alone a mad one (SMMTM, p.139).

Isobel to escape from the madness at home decides to take up the assignment. The thought of economic independence and "Freedom had never seemed so sweet" (SMMTM, p.140) to her. In the hospital, she works in ward 88 with Mrs. Reynolds and Mrs. Kolodzy, the two senior nurses. The side rooms of ward 88 are reserved for full – blown cases of madness. An old woman suffering from cataleptic occupies the first room. This woman stands for hours together and has to be forcibly moved to bed by the nurses. The second room's occupant is an old Lady Hazel, suffering from typhoid. Her door is shut all day. None of her relatives visit her. Mrs. Reynolds tells Isobel: "She was transferred here, years ago, from another hospital" (SMMTM, p.160). Beatrice is another patient lying in one of the tiny rooms. She is retarded and schizophrenic. She looks:

> a great long creature with coarse skin and twisted limbs. She had coarse reddish hair on her arms, her legs, her face. Spoke from the back of her throat in thick gutterals, like a

caveman. With her broken teeth, her nostrils close together like a monkey's... (SMMTM, p.161).

The madness of ward 88 makes her remember the severity of Beatrice. This mad girl, "who could have been seventeen! Crippled in mind, in body," (SMMTM, p.162) is not only incapable of communication with Isobel, but also hostile to the friendly overtures Isobel makes. She eats the roses Isobel brings her from the family garden as a gesture of unselfish love. She even physically hurts Isobel: "turn on me and grab my hair, pulling harder and harder until I yelled and one of the nurses had to come" (SMMTM, p.161).

Isobel, at the age of seventeen, working in the mental hospital encounters dirt, madness and shit all around her. She admits: "I could pick up a ball of shit and toss it ...I know what reaming is...I have seen a woman drink from a bedpan" (SMMTM, p.148). This forces her to loose her mind's virginity yet physically she "was still a virgin" (SMMTM, p.167).

After serving for three weeks on ward 88, Isobel is shifted to "Operation Room." Here she starts working with Ruth and Lorna, the senior nurses. Isobel who has lived most of her:

> life in chaos and disorder and who had found on ward 88 a kind of undistorted mirror image of the madness of my family, found in the OR a beauty and self-control that was created out of pain and ugliness and decay (SMMTM, p.199).

One afternoon, while cleaning the basin, she cuts her finger open with a scalpel blade. The male nurse, John Kristoff, gives her a pill and applies dressing to the wound. He gathers the confidence to tell her:

> "I've been by your house about ten times, trying to get up the nerve to come and talk to you." "How did you know where I lived?" "I looked it up." "I never saw you." "I know. I made damn sure of that" (SMMTM, p.202).

She loses her virginity to the sexually attractive John Kristoff.

Isobel, away from the world of her mother, for a short duration accepted the domination of the male world. The most dominating male personality in her life was Harry whom she rejected after being betrayed. Then came Christopher in her life. He rejected her through his death. Next was Digger who also rejected her desire for sexual fulfilment. In the end, she lost her virginity to Kristoff, " and began to laugh again for the sheer delight of at last doing something that I had wanted to do for so long and which was, after all, *pace* mother, such a slippery, strange and utterly delightful experience" (SMMTM, p.203).

Isobel is sensitive and emotional. The unpleasant memories of childhood keep haunting her in youth. She is unable to forgive her grandmother for spoiling her kindergarten concert and party. She desired her grandmother and mother to be present at the Christmas party. Seeing them sitting in the audience gave her a lot of confidence: "I loved singing, and for the first time...I felt at peace" (SMMTM, p.45). Soon after a chair tipped over and some one called, "Somebody's granny is lyin' on the floor" (SMMTM, p.47). This incident shatters young Isobel. She is unable to control herself and wets all over the floor. The teacher is annoyed and sends her home. Isobel feels she would never forgive her grandmother for having a heart attack at her kindergarten Christmas party: "To fall backward out of her chair like some circus acrobat. It was too much..." (SMMTM, p.48).

In *Songs My Mother Taught Me*, Thomas brings three generations of female members of a family together. Grandmother Goodenough belongs to the first generation of traditional womanhood. Mother Clara, Aunt Hettie, and Aunt Olive belong to the second generation. Clara eyes with jealousy Aunt Hettie for her economic independence, but is unable to completely reject the traditional role of woman. Clara's husband is unsuccessful to carry out the economic burden of the family. He is also unsuccessful to satisfy her sexually. Clara is frustrated on account of marital difficulties. Even then, she continues to live in the family "because of the children" (SMMTM, p.54). Isobel and Jane belong to the third generation which finds the past represented by Clara, Aunt Hettie and Aunt Olive as well as the past represented by Grandmother Goodenough not in tune with the present time. The collapse of grandmother in Isobel's Christmas party symbolizes that the foundation of the past is weak. Grandmother is like wreckage, which easily collapses and crumbles when unable to adjust to the present time.

There exists emotional tension between Isobel and the other elderly women in the family. None is able to impress young Isobel so that she can look forward to choose them as her role model. The memory of the time spent with them brings about hatred and rejection for them in her mind. Her reflection of the past impinges on her present. She vividly recollects Aunt Hettie's biased attitude to prevent the sisters (Jane and Isobel) from visiting "Saturday nights" dance party. When Jane seeks grandfather Harry's permission to visit the "Square dances" party, Aunt Hettie bursts: "And not to a dance hall," ... "Cer-tain-ly-not-to-a-dance-hall" (SMMTM, p 120).

Like Mrs. Ramsay's family in *To The Lighthouse,* in *Songs My Mother Taught Me,* food is the foundation of the domestic and social interaction for the members of the Cleary family. The family is very fond of eating and spends a lot of money every year on food. The family enjoys eating: "roast beef or chicken ...roast potatoes, salad, bread and butter...a plate of celery and radishes, green onions, pickles, pimento–stuffed olives" (SMMTM, p.71). Both mother and father cook. Quarrels are expiated with offerings of food:

> "Clara! Clara!"..."Aren't you gonna come down and eat some of this nice stew?"...."I've got some nice lamb stew here for you" (SMMTM, p.72).

Food is quite appropriately shown as the artistic presentation of feminine imagination. Eating is a clan fetish, a celebration of self-indulgence, misplaced sensuality and a reminder of the simple lack of communion in the family.

Isobel's lack of self-assurance in early adult life can be seen as a direct outcome of her childhood experiences. Her deep rooted desire to be an adventurous, romantic hero finds expression in fantasies and day-dreams. In her school days, she wished that like her new classmate "Heather Martin," who "had been evacuated from Britain" and was "being looked after by one of the richest families in town," (SMMTM, p.95) someone claims her too:

> Missing Heiress found at last. Elects to return to War-Torn Homeland (SMMTM, p.96).

In the character of Isobel, Thomas has presented a woman who is both the mother figure and the wanderer, the questor involved in a journey, which carries with it a promise of revelation. *Songs My Mother Taught Me* throws light on Isobel's conscious search for self and her struggle to destroy maternal links for the purpose of creation in future. The ancient glittering eyes of the mad women on ward 88 shock, horrify, attract and finally liberate Isobel. The experiences on ward 88 give her the confidence and stability to confront problems larger and more painful than her own. Isobel undergoes a marginal change in perspective at the end of the novel. She gets an insight to better understand her past and a new self emerges.

In *Songs My Mother Taught Me,* Thomas substitutes for a conventional omniscient narrator an elusive narrative, which shifts perspective, truncates, juxtaposes, catalogues, and employs various other devices. Isobel is exposed not by her actions and accomplishments, but by the quality of her perceptions and by her facility with words themselves. Her home life seems "some of the old, faded, slightly out-of-focus snapshots in one of my mother's innumerable candy boxes." For Isobel, the "me" who took the bus to the hospital and back "had nothing to do with the "me" who had a life on 88" (SMMTM, p.150). Like Rachel Cameron, at the conclusion of Laurence's *Jest of God,* Isobel does manage in the end to dare rejection and ridicule in order to commit herself to human and sexual relationship.

The earlier self-centred, self-pitying girl learns to see herself from the perspective of the unfortunates in the asylum. Her attitude towards her parents becomes more tolerant. Before leaving home for Europe she voicelessly articulates her feelings for Clara: "I wanted to comfort her – realized not that I had never loved her but that she had never let me love her and that these were two entirely different things" (SMMTM, p.205).

Death surrounds Isobel in her childhood years and teenage:

> Death was all around us and in some ways, like most children, we were attracted to it. We buried dead birds in juice tins or cigar boxes....Stamped on ants or crushed them between our fingers, gently but hard enough to kill (SMMTM, p.35).

The two visits in a year to the family graveyard to tidy up the graves and trim the plants were an adventure to Isobel and Jane. They enjoyed looking around at stones with "lots of carving on them" (SMMTM, p.37). Isobel constructs her younger self as lonely, fearful, rejected and afraid of two things – death and the passage of time. This fear is conveyed through an extremely short chapter:

> 9:01
> 9:02
> 9:03
> '48,' 49,' 50 (SMMTM, p.111).

Isobel encounters life and death in its most unnatural form. The amputated limb is carried around in the ward and offered as a chicken or turkey drum- stick:

> "We don't see you at lunch any more."..."What've you got there?" "A leg." "You're kidding." "No, I'm not..." (SMMTM, p.197).

The title of the novel *Songs My Mother Taught Me* is ironic. It signifies the bonding of the female child with the mother from the feminist point of view. Susan Walker praises Thomas's "sharp-edged sense of irony" and "tinge of self-parody."[12] The novel is divided into two parts. Part- I is addressed as "Songs of Innocence" and Part II as "Songs of Experience." This shows a direct association with Blakean romanticism. The child forced to come to terms with the adult world of contradiction and repressed anxieties has Blakean romanticism. Isobel's favourite childhood story is *The Ugly Duckling*. Isobel, like the Ugly Duckling, is conscious of her thin body and feels her breasts "much too small. "Rat-Bites"" (SMMTM, p.169).

Her summer job in the hospital increases her self-division. The asylum world is a mirror of her mother's world. In her first attempt at a total break, she steps through the looking glass rather than out of it. The Alice in wonderland atmosphere is build up on the first day at work. Isobel follows "white-clad...figures" (SMMTM, p.143) who ignore her. Carrying "great bunches of keys jangling in their pockets," they "disappeared into the building," (SMMTM, p.144) leaving her: "blinking, like Alice down the rabbit hole" (SMMTM, p.145).

Songs My Mother Taught Me concludes with the excerpt from the Alice story, which synthesizes the Alice parallels and that sense of wonderland, which Thomas has woven into the trilogy through the child naive Isobel:

> "But I don't want to go among mad people," Alice remarked.
> "Oh, you can't help that," said the Cat, "we're all mad here.

> I'm mad. You're mad." "How do you know I am mad?" said Alice. "You must be," said the Cat, "or you wouldn't have come here" (SMMTM, p.207).

The Alice figure is the archetypal child in adult world forced with contradictions and serious choices expressed here in a false promise. Alice is an extension of a romantic possibility to step through a looking glass and live in the world of dreams, a wôrld always tense against the one that must be lived in its place. Isobel's relationship to Alice is one of emotional kinship.

An in-depth study of *Songs My Mother Taught Me* from postmodern feminist perspective refutes Alix Kates Shulman's observation that the book is "almost lacking in plot," and is "a collection of vignettes."[13] The novel has a coherent plot. It throws light on the early childhood and youth of Isobel. In Part I of *Songs My Mother Taught Me,* Isobel takes on all the impressions without considering whether they are good or bad. She is more troubled by the relationship with her mother:

> Why did she hate us so? Perhaps we were a constant affront to her, the awkward and visible proof to herself, as well as to Harry, the neighbors, society at large, that she had been intimate with this FAILURE, this lame excuse for a man (SMMTM, p.63).

Clara unable to accept Warren as her husband hates everything linked to him. In Part II, in her grown up years, Isobel remembers the songs her mother taught her. She is neither paralysed by the past's weight nor does she allow it to silence her. Remembering the songs, from her unpleasant experiences, she gains experience. The division of the novel into two parts separates Isobel's girlhood years from those of her emerging adulthood.

References to *Life Magazine, National Geographics, Atlantic Monthly* and True Confessions occur in the novel. By hovering over things, naming and cataloguing them, and building up a rich complex of minutely detailed observations, Thomas transfixes sensory experience in the more enduring patterns of language. Her ability to find the precise words, brand name, or quotation from a popular magazine enables her to evoke the world of a child on the east coast of the United States in 1940s. Thomas in an interview given to Robyn Gillam says, "Playing around with words is what I do....I love playing with words."[14] Her love for words is apparent in the novel:

> All Things Bright and Beu-uu-tee-full. All crea-tures Great A–and Small (SMMTM, p.35).

Isobel is fond of reading Nancy Drew. Her grandfather Harry among his prized possessions possessed the book *Gone With The Wind.* Isobel's reading out the poem written by her at school assembly:

> As solemn faces pass my/ tomb/ I lie within my world of/ gloom (SMMTM, p.101), reflects Thomas's love for writing: "I love words. I love the way they suddenly surprise you; I love the way *everyone,* high or low, uses them to paint pictures - that is to say metaphorically."[15]

Songs My Mother Taught Me is spread out with nonsensical jokes, rhymes and puns. Isobel admits: "Because of my love of words...I mistakenly associated Germany and germs" (SMMTM, p.95). Thomas has introduced ridicule to highlight the dissatisfaction of Isobel. Ridicule is always with a feeling of dissatisfaction:

> Missing Heiress found chooses to return to Homeland Dear Robert Walker I am 11 years old and very unhappy (SMMTM, p.163).

Isobel puts into black and white her restlessness through these foolish escapades.

"The boat circled slowly. Like a feather. Like our lives" (SMMTM, p.119). Sentence fragments such as these incomplete thoughts, lacking the action of verbs are endemic in the first half of the novel, repeating the theme of purposelessness of Isobel's adolescent years. Part II shows Thomas's increasing interest in paradox and nonsense. Isobel also pays increasing attention to language. Her word playing with names:

> "Knock, Knock." "Who's there?" "Isobel." "Isobel who?" "Is a bell necessary on a bicycle?"(SMMTM, p.142)

throws light on her moving beyond innocence to the darkness of individual mystery.

Isobel's decision to work in the mental hospital asserts her independence from her cloistered family. The lines between sanity and madness are blurred. She comments:

> "In many ways it was easier for me to cope with the avowed madness of ward 88 than the glossed-over violence of my home" (SMMTM, p.149).

In the end, when Isobel is initiated into sexual experience and released into joy, the agonizing tensions between fear and desire are resolved. She finds within herself the strength to change from a passive observer into a full participant in the vibrant and devastating cycles of life.

"Play, freewheeling play," as Jacques Ehrmann suggests, "is articulation, opening... of and through language," its "ludic function," holding out the goals of "true culture and civilization," freeing all from a false, systematized reading and an appropriation of a "singular truth."[16] It is the magic of Harry's talk: "You two brats. C'm here. Have you been growing while I wasn't looking" (SMMTM, p.22) that Thomas endures rather than Isobel's magical words:

> Be Careful Now
> And Don't Get Funny
> Remember Birds
> These Signs Cost Money
> Burma Shave (SMMTM, p.92).

Isobel is closer to being a writer when she makes her "way through the adventures of Big C and little c" (SMMTM, p.45) at the age of five than when she egoistically plans to immortalize herself in novel in her freshman year at college. Isobel thinks that names given to objects are not "real name" and is encouraged to find her own name. Isobel asks Harry: ""Is my real name not Isobel?" Only to be told: "It might be. Wait and see"" (SMMTM, p.88).

Isobel, frightened by her father's pusillanimity and her mother's rage, spins a protective web of words around her. She escapes into a poetic, pastel coloured, picture book world to savour the "cool, fragrant smell of the night" in which "frogs, startled into silence for a moment, began again to saw away at the dark" (SMMTM, p.16), and to notice "houses the color of blackboard chalks-pale and dusty in the hot afternoon" (SMMTM, p.14).

The landscape in *Songs My Mother Taught Me* reflects the emotional life of Isobel. Isobel recalls the early years of her disturbed home life. Thomas portrays the landscape: "a few houses, the cemetery, a rundown general store, a church....Everything was dust-colored and decaying," (SMMTM, p.40) as correlative of the repressed emotional stance of Isobel. Images of houses, doors and windows are also presented as reflections of the state of female repression in male dominated culture. Isobel after one of her fights with her mother runs to her room and draws the curtains aside to look "at the falling snow" (SMMTM, p.69). Her bedroom is the only place in "that terrible house" where she finds "a kind of sensuous peace" (SMMTM, p.61). At the end of the novel, Isobel makes herself mentally androgynous to resolve the tensions between the sexes in our "savagely fathered and unmothered world."[17]

Isobel has inherited Harry's preoccupation with signs, as her bending over the map suggests. Isobel as a child was fascinated by the "illustrious names" bestowed on the towns of upper state New York, names like "Rome. Syracuse. Ithaca. Troy," which are traces of epic adventures. Isobel learns to spell from them:

Utica was one of the first words I could spell, and "U" was, for a long, long while, a magic letter. "U" Dear Harry, How ar U? (SMMTM, p.13).

"U" leads to Harry and to Utica. It also leads onwards to Ulysses. Isobel is no less than the Greek adventurous hero Ulysses. Like Ulysses, she wants to go on fresh voyages and seek new experiences and more adventures. Isobel rejects the unreal innocence of the child's world, desiring the more real experiences of the world outside. For Isobel, loosing her virginity to the sexually attractive Kristoff becomes the rejection of her mother's knowledge and experience. Isobel's first independent decision to move away from home/mother none the less leads her into another world of madness. Her summer job in the mental asylum increases her self-division. In the closing pages of the novel, she bends over a map with the same city names written on it. It is the map of Europe she is studying, while dreaming of foreign odysseys.

Audrey Thomas has portrayed male characters with a sense of rejection and distrust. The filtering process of memory in Isobel's mind shows gradual exclusion of male characters. The male characters, grandfather Harry and father Warren, lovers-Christopher and Digger, who come into her life in childhood as well as in adulthood show lack of commitment and fulfilment. The sexual ambivalence that Isobel feels is a direct outcome of her experiences with them. None of them is able to win her confidence and become an ideal companion. They are considered as intruders who spoil the peace and serenity of her life. She loses her virginity to Kristoff: "So this is what it's all about" (SMMTM, p.203). This short experience initiates her search for self. Heroic in her own small way, she plans to "go away" (SMMTM, p.205). Isobel becomes aware of her own resilience, openness and her capacity to love and care for others.

Isobel is the female hero of this family centred story. She moves away from her amputated conditions, with what Carol Christ calls, an "experience of nothingness." According to Christ, women experience "emptiness in their own lives in self-hatred, in self-negation, and in being a victim; in relationships with men; and in the values that have shaped their lives." Women: "Experiencing nothingness, reject conventional solutions and question the meaning of their lives, thus opening themselves to the revelation of deeper sources of power and value."[18] Having acquired this kind of awareness, Isobel wrestles with the archetypes that confront her to reach a stage of individuation.

Isobel's relationship with her mother reveals intergenerational failure. Lorna Irvine observes that in English-Canadian fiction, women's quests are bound up with the mother. "The psychological journey," according to her, "reveals the ambivalence that characterizes the daughter's feelings about her mother. In her efforts to achieve autonomy, anger and affection vie with each other so that she suffers from a desired separation, often felt to be a desertion of the mother, while at the same time, she resents her child-like dependence."[19]

The English-Canadian novelists suggest that "the angry posturing and dreams of radical independence characteristic of much recent feminist writing form a necessary phase in the process that ideally culminates in reconciliation."[20] Isobel absorbs the positive influences of the past, rejects the negative ones and moves ahead with a life-affirming attitude. Her multiple and ambivalent relationship with her mother reveals the characteristics underlined by Lorna Irvine. This alienation from those of the other sex is marked in the failure of her relationship with her father Warren Goodenough. She looks forward to moments of peace and tranquillity even at the cost of losing her father:

> When my father had one of his asthma attacks I would lie in bed and listen to him coughing, coughing, coughing, gasping for breath and wheezing – would imagine him getting more and more red in the face until his heart would burst and he'd fall down dead in a pool of his own heart's

> blood. I fully expected it at any minute and secretly wished it so" (SMMTM, p.35).

In *Songs My Mother Taught Me,* Audrey Thomas has created a text, which demonstrates female desire that the parental world of security and safety is often an impediment to the discovery of self.

The epigram preceding chapter one in *Songs My Mother Taught Me* has grandfather Harry telling Isobel and Jane:

> "Listen," he said, "I'll teach you a little story." "The night was dark and stormy the rain came down in torrents. The King said unto Antonio, 'Antonio, tell us a tale.' Antonio began as follows..." (SMMTM, p.11).

This epigram focuses on Thomas's style of "circular representation and doubling back."[21] Here again a tale is told, but it is different this time. It is significant that the circular tale of the epigram is told to Isobel and her sister, Jane, by their grandfather Harry. The tale is another of his many practical jokes, of his many punning and paradoxical signs, like a sign affixed near his cottage:

> "Journey's end and, underneath, private property: trespassers will be prosecuted" (SMMTM, p.15).

It is old "Harry! Mythical at the top of the stairs," (SMMTM, p.85) who is the prankster in this novel. His theory of art as play ultimately shapes the aesthetic of mature Isobel: "Unclenched my hands one day and said, 'Nothing in life is worth clenching your hands about'" (SMMTM, p.92).

Elaine Marks points out that in feminist texts: "the women are up and the men are down."[22] In *Songs My Mother Taught Me* the standard literary model is eroded by Audrey Thomas, who has the élan and energy for demystifying and deconstructing. This is a tale told from a woman's point of view. The epigram at the end of *Songs My Mother Taught Me* shows Alice's reluctance to "go among mad people," and the Cat's retort: "Oh, you can't .... You're mad" (SMMTM, p.207). The novel subsists on a circular structure ending where it began. Thus, the inexperienced innocent girl of the opening pages evolves into a mature and enlightened individual at the end.

According to Rachel Du Plessis, until the twentieth century, ""story" for women has typically meant plots of seduction, courtship, the energies of quest deflected into sexual downfall, the choice of a marriage partner, the melodramas of beginning, middle, and end, the trajectories of sexual arousal and release."[23] But Isobel is a young woman of twentieth century who mentions lovers quite casually. Her quest is for self-knowledge and self-realization. Thomas is more interested in quest plots, as Rachel Du Plessis argues, are many twentieth century women writers.

Songs My Mother Taught Me is the beginning of Isobel's search for her essential, authentic womanhood as an independent and autonomous member in a patriarchal society. It is a lyrical novel couched in terms of optimism and hope. Isobel firmly slaps the door on social forces, parents, sister, aunts, grandfather, lovers etc., who would enclose her and limit her power and sets off on a quest for authenticity. She understands:

> Life was cruel, people hurt and betrayed one another, grew old died alone. And did not rise again (SMMTM, p.205).

She evinces characteristics usually considered masculine such as courage, aggression and ambition. When Isobel pours over the map, a new world, different and subversive from the world of her childhood, invites celebrations.

ENDNOTES

1. Shyam Asnani, "The Female Identity," *The Sunday Tribune*, (December 13, 1992).
2. Annis Pratt, *Archetypal Patterns in Women's Fiction* (Bloomington: Indiana University Press, 1981), p.178.

3. Nancy Poland, "Margaret Drabble: There must Be a Lot of People Like Me," *Midwest Quarterly*, XVI, 3 (April, 1975), p.265.
4. Jean Mallinson, "Song Sung Blue," review of *Songs My Mother Taught Me, Leisure, The Vancouver Sun,* (April 5, 1974), p.32A.
5. Audrey Thomas, *Songs My Mother Taught Me* (1973; rpt. Vancouver: Talanbooks, 1988), p.29. All subsequent references in parentheses belong to this edition of the text.
6. Juliann E. Fleenor, *The Female Gothic* (Montreal: Eden Press, 1983), p.12.
7. Julia Kristeva, *Powers of Horror: An Essay on Abjection,* trans. Leon S. Roudiez, (New York: Columbia University Press, 1982), p.1.
8. *Ibid.*, p.5.
9. *Ibid.*, p.1.
10. *Ibid.*, p.6.
11. *Ibid.*, p.5.
12. Susan Walker, review of *Songs My Mother Taught Me, Quill and Quire,* (January, 1974), p.12.
13. Alix Kates Shulman, "Surviving Childhood," review of *Songs My Mother Taught Me,* by Audrey Thomas, and *Now Molly Knows,* by Merrill Joan Gerber, (April, 1974), p.33.
14. Robyn Gillam, "Ideals and Lost Children: An Interview with Audrey Thomas," *Paragraph: The Canadian Fiction Review,* Vol.18, No.1 (Summer, 1996), pp.5-6.
15. Audrey Thomas, "Basmati Rice: An Essay About Words," *Canadian Literature,* 100 (Spring, 1984), p.313.
16. Jacques Ehrmann, "Homo Ludens Revisited," *Game, Play, Literature,* ed. Jacques Ehrmann, (Boston: Beacon Press, 1971), p.56.
17. Adrienne Rich, "An Old House in America," *Poems: Selected and New* (1975) reproduced in *Adrienne Rich's Poetry, The Poet on her Work: Reviews and Criticism,* eds. Barbara Charlesworth Gelpi and Albert Gelpi, (New York: W.W. Morton and Co., 1975), p.78.
18. Carol Christ, "Nothingness, Awakening, Insight, New Naming," *Diving Deep And Surfacing: Women Writers on Spiritual Quest* (Boston: Beacon Press, 1980), p.13.

19. Lorna Irvine, "A Psychological Journey: Mothers and Daughters in English – Canadian Fiction," *The Lost Tradition: Mothers and Daughters in Literature,* eds. Cathy N. Davidson and E.M. Broner, (New York: Frederick Ungar Publishing Company, 1980), p.243.
20. *Ibid.*, pp.243-244.
21. Krishna Sarbadhikary, *Dis-Membering /Re-Membering: Fictions of Audrey Thomas* (New Delhi: Book Plus, 1999), p.22.
22. Elaine Marks, "Women and Literature in France," *Signs*, 3, 4 (Summer, 1978), p.835.
23. Rachel Du Plessis, *Writing Beyond the Ending: Narrative Strategies of Twentieth- Century Women Writers* (Bloomington: Indiana University Press, 1985), p.151.

SECTION-II

MRS. BLOOD

"...it is all blood and breaking...
she has made herself again
out of flesh out of dictionaries."

The preceding section on *Songs My Mother Taught Me* introduces Isobel the recurring persona in the ongoing section on *Mrs. Blood* and the next section on *Blown Figures.* Although first to be published *Mrs. Blood* is chronologically second in triptych about Isobel. The epigram at the end of *Songs My Mother Taught Me* is repeated in the preface of the first part of *Mrs. Blood,* stressing Alice/nameless narrator/ Isobel's reluctance "to go among mad people," and the cat's retort, "Oh, you can't help that... we're all mad here. I'm mad. You're mad."[1] This gives a hint that the nameless narrator in *Mrs. Blood* is, in fact, Isobel only.

Helene Cixous claims: "woman's body, with its thousand and one thresholds of ardor... make the old single-grooved mother tongue reverberate with more than one language."[2] *Mrs. Blood* chronicles a difficult pregnancy and ultimate miscarriage in Ghana with frequent flashbacks to Britain and North America. The self-division and madness of Isobel's adolescent world is explored and extended in *Mrs. Blood,* together with the artifice of writing. In the novel, the focus constantly shifts between the recent past of Isobel's marital relationship with Jason and her early student past with its troubling memories of Richard, her ex-lover.

In *Mrs. Blood,* Isobel is married and lives in Africa with her husband Jason who is an art teacher. She has two school going children Nicholas and Mary, and is expecting a third child. In *Songs My Mother Taught Me,* the split between domestic and independent woman is portrayed as an external conflict among Clara, Aunt Hettie, Aunt Olive and Isobel. In *Mrs. Blood,* Thomas takes up this conflict as a rupture within the heroine herself. The character of Isobel is divided: "Some days my name is Mrs. Blood; some days it's Mrs. Thing" (MB, p.11). Anthony Boxill points this division as Isobel's "schizophrenic state of mind."[3]

Woman's ability to confirm to the expectations of parents and others as well as an ability to form distinct and separate self results in schizophrenia. Even before Isobel's visit to Africa, she has problems with her self-identity. She recalls when Jason left for work in the morning, she would find it impossible to occupy herself: "It was as though, when he left the house, he took the real me with him and I was just a stand-in, waiting in another person's part" (MB, p.146). However, Thomas declares, "she's not a schizophrenic."[4]

Isobel presents a complex, confusing, fragmented record of her third pregnancy, which is threatened by uncontrollable bleeding. Richard, her ex-lover in England, who forced her to undergo an abortion earlier, is not physically present in *Mrs. Blood*. Mrs. Blood's memories create him. Richard using litotes to address her: "Madam, you are no philosopher," introduces the absence with which he is paradoxically identified throughout in *Mrs. Blood.* As Mrs. Blood says, "And now I have a horse called Nothing and when you ask me where he rides I'll answer, "Nowhere"" (MB, p.77). She has with Richard: "held hands in a movie called "The Man Who Never Was."" Richard, the lost lover, becomes confounded with the lost child: "Love, *L'oeuf.* Nothing. Nothing will come of nothing" (MB, p.217). He is the shadow of her personality, drawing her down into the world of heat, fertility, sexuality, violence, unreason and death.

Mrs. Blood has a postmodern life. It marks the woman's bodily presence in the text. *Mrs. Blood* is divided into three parts. Part I is the longest. It takes place in the hospital. Here Mrs. Blood speaks 50 times while Mrs. Thing speaks 42 times. In Part II, Isobel returns home still pregnant. At the end of this part, she begins to bleed again and is rushed back to the hospital. Mrs. Thing in this part speaks 29 times and Mrs. Blood speaks 39 times. Part III is very short. Mrs. Thing speaks only once, rest of the section is in the voice of Mrs. Blood. Mrs. Blood speaks nine times. The baby dies. *Mrs. Blood* is a female text and in the words of Mary Jacobus illustrates "the transgression of literary boundaries," the "moments when structures are shaken, when language refuses to lie down meekly," when "the marginal is brought into sudden focus" and "intelligibility itself refused." [5] Isobel loses her intelligence:

This is my body which was riven, my body which was roven:

> my flesh all scattered and tattered and torn, and Rosie is the riveter who nailed me there as a totem in front of the door (MB, p.59).

Part I of the novel begins with Mrs. Thing's silent ride to the hospital gripped in fear and waiting in vain for some words from the unspeaking African nurse who accompanies her. The initial silence is replaced by her unceasing series of observations, musings, memories, hallucinations, dreams, fantasies, literary parodies and liturgical revisions. Lying in her hospital bed, she remembers the cruelty of an earlier lover. She hears him talking to his friends, describing women as obscene, disgusting and expendable. She recollects an earlier scene when wandering through a Japanese garden where they have just made love, the man looks at the gold fish: ""Ugh," he said. "They look like blood-soaked bandages".... "What d'you know of blood–soaked bandages?" I asked and spoiled his poetry" (MB, pp.23-24). Surrounded by female nurses, Esther, Grace and Alexandria, her hospital room is presented as a female enclave. She lies on the hospital bed protecting "the child, my nutmeat, my centre, my dying darling" (MB, p.26).

Dr. Shankar and Dr. Biswas are the two Indian gynecologists serving in this African hospital. Isobel is under the supervision of Dr. Biswas. He asks her every morning in his soft voice "Is there any pain?"(MB, p.90) She finds closeness with him. He is young and intelligent. She admits: "Dr. Biswas and I, both being foreigners, both "educated," both parents (and I think both lonely), enjoy our daily ritual of talk" (MB, p.93).

Isobel's mental state is described in her dialogue with Dr. Biswas who visits her and comments on her negativity. He feels she has "become too introspective" (MB, p.121). The conversation makes Isobel cry:

> "But what is the matter?" "Nothing. I don't know." "I think," he gives me a traitor's smile, "it is time for you to go home." "Home?" (MB, p.122)

Mrs. Thing feels abandoned and betrayed by the doctor when he permits her to go home. Mrs. Thing does not show emotions but transfers her emotions onto other people when she finds the situation traumatic:

> Why am I crying? Dr. Biswas is obviously exasperated.... And if I lose the baby? Screaming in an upstairs room, windows wide open against the heat, the compound listening and Jason losing face forever (MB, pp.121-122).

Mrs. Thing is aware of her tendency to transfer her feelings onto people close to her and explains doing this:

> It is impossible for me to see other people as separate from myself. Jason is my husband; Mary, my daughter; Nicholas, my son. I can only imagine what they are thinking by imagining what I would think if I were in Jason's position – which is quite different from imagining what I would think if I were Jason! Thus when I was in the hospital, ashamed and defensive because of my physical weakness, I saw Jason as ashamed and embarrassed too (MB, p.191).

By transferring her emotions and dissociating from them, Mrs. Thing is able to alleviate the anxiety they provoke. She expresses why she must not let herself become emotional, "because once started I knew I would be carried screaming to a place far worse than this" (MB, p.36). It is Mrs. Blood who protects Mrs. Thing from becoming irrational from reacting in what Mrs. Thing would consider an inappropriate fashion. Part I ends with Mrs. Blood's fragmented clippings from the local newspaper:

> A precious mother is Jane. A voice we loved is stilled ....May the Lord preserve you till we meet. REST IN PEACE....PEACE. He was for peace; he fought for it; and he actually achieved it before he died.... They can pick the *quality* drink even when blindfolded. Reine/ Marie/ A compliment of Fine Taste! "Adam and Eve and Hitme were on a raft. Adam and Eve fell off. Who was left?" "Hitme." "Ha. Ha" (MB, pp.123-125).

Here the recollection of past events is no longer sufficient to keep out the overwhelming emotions that will keep Isobel from losing her sense of self. The newspaper clippings take Isobel's dissociation a step further by shutting out any personal responses to the world around her. Joanna Daxell comments:

> Part One...oscillates between Mrs. Thing's rather matter-of-fact narrative, dealing primarily with her everyday experience, and Mrs. Blood's hyper-reflexive narrative, infused with memories and fantasies.[6]

Part II is told from Isobel's home. Still she is pregnant. In this part, she attempts to reconstruct her mother's life, particularly the moment Isobel was born:

> "When I had you," Mama said, "they put a bit of gauze over my eyes. I think they did it always, then. Just to make sure everything was all right, you know, before they let the mother see her baby"(MB, p.138).

Problems related to woman's physical body dominate Isobel's thoughts. She remembers "Sears Roebuck catalogues," with their advertisements for "Sanitary napkins in bulk" (MB, p.158). An episode from the sixth grade when a student discovers "a dirty Kotex underneath her chair," (MB, p.163) keeps haunting her memory. Isobel also recollects her cousin's agony because she "got her period the morning of her wedding... but the doctor gave her something to stop it" (MB, p.158).

In *Mrs. Blood*, contradictions in the present deal mainly with Africa and its struggle to reconcile a tribal heritage with what Isobel mockingly refers to as the "new heaven and new earth" (MB, p.84) of modern western technology. Contradictions in the past deal mainly with the conflicting memories of Richard, her lover from her student years and the only man to whom she has ever committed herself passionately and wholly. She juggles the memory of the real Richard, gentle, caring man who tried to cushion the impact of their break up with soft words, with the memory of the unreal Richard, brutal, unsympathetic, impatient, unmoved by her appeals standing behind the compartment door: "ignoring the irate looks of people....And then he fixed his coat against the glass and said, "I've never made love between Oxford and Watford Junction." And I said,

"What if somebody comes?" And he laughed and said, "What if?"" (MB, p.147) Isobel feels "alone on a never-ending beach" (MB, p.180) after Richard deserts her. Richard is the most troublesome element to reconcile in her memory. Audrey Thomas admits: "Richard in *Mrs. Blood* has a major part to play in her memories. He does not have a major part to play in the book."[7]

In Africa, the country of taboos, she remembers silent Canadian taboos on menstruation and pregnant women. Part II also concentrates on the act of writing. Thomas makes an attempt to translate the female event of pregnancy into narrative. Mrs. Thing consciously draws attention to the opening of Part II when she announces to "begin at the new beginning" (MB, p.131). According to Edward Said such announced beginnings have certain psychological intentions for they involve reversal, a "change of direction" that "constitutes an authorization for what follows from it."[8] Isobel, by attempting to change direction, endeavours to substantiate her precarious pregnancy through narrative structure. She alters the story and changes its direction. She also consciously struggles to overcome her fear by cleverly manipulating language: "Controlling the panic by speaking in careful sentences" (MB, p.196).

In spite of Mrs. Thing's attempts to narrate the story, the voice of Mrs. Blood breaks in, out of place and at times is irrational and wild. George Bowering comments: "Mrs. Thing is covered with pain, and Mrs. Blood is covered with memories."[9] For Mrs. Blood, words and fragments of sentences assume terrifying meanings, dominated by her body. "Avez-vous du pain?" (MB, p.150); *"Ne rien ins erer"* (MB, p.216). Even the dictionary harbours evil meanings. The word *"grave"* metamorphoses into *"gravid*... Pregnant," then into *"grieve"* (MB, p.150).

Part III is the shortest of the three parts. Isobel is shifted back to the hospital. Dr. Biswas feels sorry for her: "So. It has not worked out as I had thought" (MB, p.203). Isobel is exhausted both physically and mentally at this moment. She makes endless effort "to hold the baby in and keep the pain away" (MB, p.213). However, she delivers off a stillborn baby and the narrative ends. In *Mrs. Blood*, Thomas experiments with what it means to write a female text. The stillborn baby and the psychological return of Isobel's earlier abortion are at journey's centre and evoke fears of narrative failure, but Isobel orders her experience and turns it into legend from which all stories and all story tellers originate. Isobel physically dominates space and time. She is able to produce and structure language that describes her desires, even her body.

The events in *Mrs. Blood* continually move backward and forward in time. The past happenings in the life of Isobel are told through flashbacks, dreams and the substance of memory. Here she repeats the life of her own housewife mother whose image she had struggled to resist as an adolescent. Isobel's marriage lacks to give her peace and serenity. She and Jason are: "Wedlocked to one another; and no keys" (MB, p.119) can set them free. Isobel honestly confesses:

> the burden of my lust for Richard which I carried with me for a long, long time and finally set down with relief on Jason as a hobo might set down a bundle which has suddenly became too burdensome to bear (MB, p.170).

Mrs. Thing's comment on her husband's visit to the hospital is indicative of how Isobel loses contact with the outer world. She is unable to maintain connections with Jason and others, with whom she ordinarily would have a close relationship:

> To him I am a creature from another planet and sometimes he talks too loudly at me....And yet his loud words come to me from far away as though I am already dead and buried....And he shows me the drawings they have made me, which I stare at with the polite disinterest one shows

Her husband fails to give her the emotional support she needs during pregnancy. Richard is the man of true romance in her dream world. Her fatal flaw is her inability to control her dreams in the face of reality around her. The dreams eventually possess her. In her state of honest confession, Isobel acknowledges that Jason is "never so violent" (MB, p.166) as he seems to be in moments of her anger. Isobel calls out to him, "I am not what I am" (MB, p.218). She is unknown to him. She is a woman bound into a passionless marriage: "...irrevocably joined to one another, in a back-to-back position. Not looking at one another, *unable* to, lying wide-eyed in the darkness and wondering how it happened" (MB, p.172).

The middle age Isobel is surrounded and engulfed by unsatisfactory, traditional domestic ties. Before going to the hospital in an alien country (Africa) she thrusts the responsibility of her children to the manservant: "Look after the children, Joseph" (MB, p 14). Joseph, like his Old Testament namesake, is a good, honest and patient man. When Isobel is in the hospital, he affectionately looks after the children. The children are also fond of him. In his company, they do not miss their mother. To Isobel: "he is always polite and deferential and concerned" (MB, p.176).

Isobel worries what other women might say about her, if her children are not properly dressed for school. She is concerned about the missing button on Nicholas's shirt and Mary's asymmetrically braided hair. She is conscious of the variegated aspects of her lack, which "the ladies will discuss it over coffee" (MB, p.137). The thought of her death in Africa makes Isobel fantasize the other women tending her grave, setting up committees, and having her become an object of ritualized devotion passed on from hand to hand until the people looking after her grave no longer even know anything about her: "If I die here Jason and the children go back home, who will bring flowers or water my grave with their tears?" (MB, p.31) This mind talk characterizes the inactivity of the patient and marks a degree of self-indulgence as unhealthy to the mind as her physical state is to the baby she carries.

The nurses in the ward, her servant and the doctors with their skin colour differences and their cultural differences parade in front of Mrs. Blood with a sense of strangeness obvious in their manner. Isobel feels embarrassed when Alexandria and Elizabeth praise her white skin and wash her "very carefully and tenderly as though I were a precious relic" (MB, p.46). The way these nurses talk to the local patients, share jokes, laugh, and get bossy with them, she finds missing in their talk to her. They maintain distance from her:

> they always treat me like a guest and it is this that embarrasses me and not the fact that they gaze upon my naked body (MB, pp.46-47).

They look upon her as superior. She remains an outsider, a white woman being looked after by black women.

When at home, Isobel is most of the time confined to bed. She is fearful for her unborn baby. Her present condition frees her from social obligations. She is not eager to reconnect with the community and would rather stay at home than join her husband and children when they go out. She has not been able to establish herself in her new surroundings: "The cheese stands alone" (MB, p.161). Isobel's self-alienation and feelings of rejection can be traced to several sources. She is alienated from the colonial society, particularly its ladies. They are "Vultures in terylene dresses" (MB, p.29). She feels disadvantaged by such "rugged, capable, cope-able" (MB, p.139) women and wants to look up a dictionary for "what a cope is" (MB, p.13). She is a part neither of the African community nor of the British colonial community. At the hospital, she is kept behind a curtain most of the time and therefore cannot interact with the "other women in the ward" who have "much good-natured banter..." (MB, p.110). She listens to what goes on around her at home from her second-floor bedroom: "she looks around her and things aren't being conducted in a way that she understands at all. She's immobile, she's a prisoner."[10]

She fears her emotional responses are considered irrational and inappropriate. When she hides her tears on seeing Dr. Biswas, he utters: "Big girls don't cry. Madame must not cry in the presence of the natives" (MB, p.91). Her obsession with her own feelings engenders the hyper-reflexive state that makes it nearly impossible for her to interact with other individuals around her. She confesses: "I am not, really, very self-reliant or very sociable" (MB, p.161).

Audrey Thomas makes an endeavour to study the psychology of the character. In an interview given to Elizabeth Komisar, she admits:

> In *Mrs. Blood* there was one protagonist but I split her into two so that there's the visceral woman, Mrs. Blood, and there's the objective distanced woman, Mrs. Thing, although they're the same woman. [11]

Mrs. Thing is the woman acted upon. She is passive, performing perfunctory roles that have blurred her identity and transformed her into an object to function. Mrs. Blood is the woman in touch with a universal source of female strength, yet wholly overwhelmed by her reproductive capacity. Mrs. Thing and Mrs. Blood joined together still do not make a whole. In either state, Isobel is reduced to a condition in which the missing and lacking features of her life have been projected more prominently. The split throws light on the fragmented nature of woman, divided not only from other women, but also from her own self by language, tradition, religion and law in order to be someone else.

The female body is both the page on which the story is inscribed and the author of its events and characters. The story is a geography of the pregnant female body. In *Mrs. Blood*, legends, the Bible, dramas, novels, nursery rhymes appear altered from a woman's perspective. The novel is an epic struggle of a female hero Isobel, on a female journey, that is, pregnancy. The novel a "spectacular de force"[12] records the long days of waiting before the birth of a dead baby. The split between sanity and insanity is present throughout *Mrs. Blood*:

> "Richard. I've got to talk to you." *Jason. Forgive me, I was not strong enough. The child is dead. They are washing my face now with soft cloths, and Elizabeth holds me, weeping* (MB, p.220).

Isobel imagines herself a hero wandering through wastelands where the path is narrow and where she is followed by "whatever it was that I had felt behind me, stalking me, for all those years" (MB, p.12). Her major task is to keep shedding blood and, like Noah, to preserve in the ark of her body the life she carries. Noah, the patriarch, built a ship in which he, his family and animals of every species survived the flood. Isobel in her attempt to make the child in her womb to survive is no less than the legendary hero Noah. Her goal is the same as it was for some of the knights of the Holy Grail, to bring life to the wasteland and to preserve the fish. The narrative of pregnancy becomes the romance of the Grail in which the mother and the baby are major actors.

The nameless narrator/Isobel is both quester and fisher, carrying in her body the secret of the Grail: "I keep my secrets hidden, like grenades, beneath the pillow" (MB, p.103) which could blow apart the present as well as the past. Holy Grail in medieval legend was a cup or chalice associated with unusual powers, especially the regeneration of life and it was much sought after by medieval knights. To protect and save the life growing in her womb is greatly desired and cherished objective for Isobel. She connects human life with the land and defines women's blood as the origin and preserver of the human race. She becomes the hero of her own life drama. She fluctuates, sometimes rewrites with her blood, the journey of the hero. Sometimes she is the blank white page on which the story is inscribed.

Part I of *Mrs. Blood* brings forth series of fragments that symbolize the deconstruction that has dominated the text. A sign advertising the forthcoming performance of two musical bands merges with the female body rhythms. The musical programme is entitled "The Mid-Month Blues." A photo printing establishment is named "THE DEO GRATIAS STUDIO" and an advertisement for the return of lost key "AWARD FOR FINDER" (MB, pp.123-124), metaphorically signifies Isobel's simultaneous desire to keep her secrets locked inside her which means to keep the baby safe and the narrative silent, and to open the same to let the narrative speak.

She imagines the African nurses passing her "bloody garments from hand to brown hand," (MB, p.83) as if participating in a ritual of blood. The drama of birth and death, and sacrifice is feminized and articulated entirely by the female voice. The female body becomes a metaphor for religious sensibility and a correlative for the rituals that accompany it. Mrs. Blood "a Christ figure... goes thru the whole crucifixion business to get wisdom."[13] Thomas reviews the Christian structures based on passive, virginal motherhood, on a female body that is no more than a receptacle for male existence. The condensation of birth and book for the woman writer becomes an extension of her own body. The connection is so important that Susan Gubar insists:

> The startling centrality of childbearing in the *Kunstlerromane* of women represents a response to the hegemonic texts and contexts of our culture that either appropriate the birth metaphor to legitimize the 'brain children' of men or, even more destructively, inscribe female creativity in the womb to insult women whose productions then smack of the mere *re*petition of *re*production, its involuntary physicality.[14]

In *Mrs. Blood,* Audrey Thomas uses language and imagery appropriate to women and thus "alters the psychoanalytic paradigm of language and culture acquisition."[15] The landscape reflects the narrator's moral state. Blood red hibiscus flowers metaphorically illustrate an invisible interior, a female space: "They have opened too early and too wide and all their energy has been sucked out by the sun" (MB, p.154). Isobel finds "a plucked hibiscus, like a fresh clot..." (MB, p.206). The hibiscus symbolizes Isobel's deflowering and the ripening and peeling of her endometrium. The secretions of the female body mark *Mrs. Blood.* Blood and milk form the words of the story. She remembers driving with her father and seeing an accident. A "milk truck on its side and another car smashed underneath it and blood and milk together running all across the road" (MB, p.20).

Isobel's dreams become grotesque. They are filled with images of dismemberment and decapitation, of infants torn apart, of voices shrieking in the night. The outer world confirms her inner terrors. She fears she will bear a deformed baby. Newspapers repeatedly describe malformed babies, for example, a two year old girl was born with "those redundant arms and legs which hung around her body like the symbolic limbs of Krishna" (MB, p.207). Her neighbours discuss a mongoloid child who will probably not live to be twenty. As her journey continues, the image of fish signals the Grail story and highlights the fish's importance to early Christians. "These images- like the images in T.S Eliot's *The Wasteland* suggest regeneration."[16] Isobel at times imagines herself as a fish: "for making love....Just smooth, from the waist up to the shoulder and over into the neck" (MB, p.181). She often imagines the baby as a fish, swimming in its mother's womb. She recalls Jason's anxiety to get away from the hospital where he visits her after the birth of their first child, Mary. She compares Jason to the "Japanese fishermen who will frantically cut their lines rather than touch the dreaded wolf fish" (MB, p.183). Towards the end of Part II, a crude drawing of fish appears on the page and an advertisement of:

> THE STATE FISHING CORPORATION SAYS
> Good fresh fish gives you
> Good eating
> Good health
> Good value (MB, p.191).

In *Mrs. Blood,* bizarre linguistic transformation occurs, for example, the word "Vulture" metamorphoses into the word "Vulnerable,"(MB, p.207) and "fireflies" turn into "evil eyes" (MB, p.206). Fragments of literary works, of the Bible, newspaper articles, of old songs continue to flash through her mind. Their appearance is dictated by her constant awareness of the loss of blood. Each fragment speaks of death: "Did ya ever think/ When a hearse goes by/... geraniums or flags." A man with "Eyes like rubies," (MB, p.210) reflects a landscape of the womb, the other side of the mirror. The recitative, "Listen, I think I am bleeding" (MB, p.211), blends into a wasteland where the floods are turned "into a wilderness, and drieth up the water springs" (MB, p.212). Logic breaks down and the flow of consecutive narrative stops. Isobel's consciousness mingles with past scenes of imagined or real events:

> Everyone was very kind...from Calgary right through to Toronto...to the New York Central.... Jason ordered wine for every lunch and dinner. We even danced (MB, p.211).

Ironic reversals infect the language and homonyms describe Isobel's latent anxiety. "It is very meat and write so to do" (MB, p.212); "I have no cope, I cannot cope" (MB, p.13). She suffers the pangs of hell. On the third night, it is over. Like a dried and wilted flower, Isobel survives in a desiccated land. Excerpts from "The Song of Solomon," from the Shakespearean tragedies, from folklore, from *The Duchess of Malfi,* from airplane manuals, from past events document the novel. Mrs. Blood's unborn child reminds her of her badness. Using the words of Shakespeare she tells her husband: "Jason, my love, I have done a deed without a name" (MB, p.218). The quote refers to a scene in *Macbeth* where the three witches, the most evil and powerful of *Macbeth's* characters, respond to Macbeth who is asking what they are concocting:

Macbeth: How now, you secret, black and midnight hags!

What is't you do?

All: A deed without a name.[17]

Comparing herself to Shakespeare's evil witches, Mrs. Blood counts herself among the evil and powerful women that historically have challenged patriarchal society and had to suffer for it through their society's contempt or even their own death.

As Mrs. Thing, Isobel is dissociated from her past and from any feeling of guilt. However, Mrs. Thing has an existential fear closely related to the abortion she had many years ago. This fear is closer to paranoia or anxiety than it is to any feeling of guilt:

> "I can't remember a time when I wasn't afraid; and now I felt the hour had come round at last - and time has proved me right" (MB, p.12).

Mrs. Blood, on the other hand, is very conscious of her guilt. The daily routine at the hospital is to Mrs. Blood an attempt, by the people surrounding her, to conceal her guilt. She is kept behind curtains where she is bathed and made to spit into what her nurse calls "the Nemesis basin". In Greek Mythology, Nemesis avenges any violation of sacred law. Seeing the bed sheets soaked in blood Isobel is reminded of the line uttered by Lady Macbeth in *Macbeth*: "All the perfumes of Arabia could not sweeten..." (MB, p.15). This line points out that there is no way her sin or guilt can be washed away. The reference to Lady Macbeth suggests that

Mrs. Blood believes Isobel will always carry her guilt, the "smell of blood" (MB, p.16) with her. The smell of blood has become an essential though repressed part of her. After all, she calls herself Mrs. Blood and says at one point in the novel in a very postmodern way: "I stink therefore I am" (MB, p.21).

Worried about her baby's safety she recollects: "Macduff was from his mother's womb untimely ripp'd and Caesar too" (MB, p.54). Sometimes gaps in communication between the protagonist and her husband force her to reflect on Mrs. Ramsay's character in *To The Lighthouse*: "One only tries to get to Z if one believes that Z is there. Mrs. Ramsay was wrong to admire her husband for such a ridiculous attempt" (MB, p.94). The epigraph at the beginning of Part II is taken from Oscar Wilde's *Teleny*. Mrs. Thing thinks with the passing time guilty emptiness is replacing her deep love for Jason. This makes her dwell on the different dictionary meanings of cleave:

> *Cleave*[1], to split. (E) Strong verb. *Cleave*[2], to stick. (E) Weak verb (MB, p.172).

In a subtle way, the phrases and images are juxtaposed and dissolved speedily in the last few pages of *Mrs. Blood*. The blood that signifies the unborn child is the visible sign of guilt. A rush of multiple voices culminates in the final sentence of the novel. The words of her former lover come back to haunt her: "Get rid of it" (MB, p.220). This is the sign of the unspeakable, but because it has become taboo Isobel does not feel guilt about the abortion. Her guilt is existential and something from which she cannot escape. It resembles the guilt many schizoid individuals or schizophrenics experience. R.D. Laing suggests that the guilt is not:

> so much in respect to specific thoughts or acts ...it is superseded by a much more inclusive sense of badness or worthlessness which attacks their very right to *be* in any

> respect...guilt is the urgent factor in preventing active participation in life, and in maintaining the 'self' in isolation, in pushing it into further withdrawal.[18]

Mrs. Blood describes the physical details of Isobel's character. Her body provides her own most tangible reality. Her past and present world appears fragmentarily, from oblique angles, vivid but not solid. Her husband, her steward and her neighbours exist only in her perception of them from her hospital bed and then from her home, while convalescing. Her ex-lover, the past shaped by her sexuality, the past and the present that made her passive and frightened, and the world of childhood, of summer work in an insane asylum, of in-laws and old friends, of domesticity all collide in the anxiety sustained by her traitorous body. George Bowering remarks: "Mrs. Thing is paying attention to what's happening right now, and Mrs. Blood is remembering stuff."[19]

Audrey Thomas creates a world defined by Isobel's own feelings. The novel is the journey of Isobel's pregnancy which culminates in miscarriage. It is also the journey of Isobel's self-discovery. Thomas ties everything into an amorphous whole with delicate skill. There is little plot in the novel. Episodes emerge as tableaux without movement.

The opening epigraph in *Mrs. Blood* is taken from Lewis Carroll's *Alice's Adventures in Wonderland*:

> "But I don't want to go among mad people," Alice remarked. "Oh, you can't help that," said the Cat: "we're all mad here. I'm mad. You're mad." "How do you know I'm mad?" said Alice. "You must be," said the Cat, "or you wouldn't have come here" (MB, p.9).

This epigram is an interesting choice taken from a children's book that has its greatest success with childish adults. Alice's two vehicles are the rabbit hole and the looking glass. The latter is the more intellectually striking device. There are many other allusions in the novel to Carroll's book to show a world where things "aren't always what they seem to be"(MB, p.11). The narrator is outside Carroll's story when she dresses her children for a costume party as "Alice and the White Rabbit" (MB, p.180) and inside when she herself is Alice, aware of the strangeness she must hold for these March Hare Africans. Finally, she is the food and drink which cause Alice to lose all sense of proportion:

> I put a sign on my breast, "Eat me," and on my lips a notice, "Drink me," but only the mosquitoes came (MB, p.26).

The passage continues with these associations to collide with allusions to the mass, and Isobel becomes Christ, the sacrificial victim. These actions of eating and drinking echo some of the other puns in the novel. While Mrs. Blood casts herself as Christ, elsewhere she plays the role of Mary. This conflating of herself with both mother and son make the story a revision of that earlier story of the creation of the world, told this time from the woman's perspective. This is a story of waiting for others, of the abdication of the self to the invasion of others. This is a story, which culminates in the loss of everything: "the universal calamity of pain and birth and blood" (MB, p.83).

Another reference to eating is the punning phrase of Richard *"Avez – vous du pain?"* (MB, p.147). Audrey Thomas acknowledges it as "one of the major puns"[20] in *Mrs. Blood*. It evokes Isobel's desire to remember what is causing so much pain and loss. The pain paradoxically contains both nourishing presence and painful annihilation. The protagonist of the novel surfaces from under the swamp of the male discourse by narrating her experiences in her own discourse which is distinctly feminine. The title of *Mrs. Blood* is related to women. Blood for women is both life giving and life taking. Birth, miscarriage, abortion, stillbirth, menstruation, etc., connected to women are associated with the flow of blood.

Isobel is both prophet and scribe. "I heard a voice from heaven, saying unto me, Write" (MB, p.151). Isobel rejects

Eve's role as subservient to Adam and insists on the right to interpret. She does not deny moral and spiritual necessities rather she redefines them. In her revision, life and death assume immediate physical presence and the symbolic significance "of the bloody and bawd of Christ...bloody Mary, who propelled Him, shrieking, into the musty straw and thought all over that which had just begun" (MB, p.193).

The story of Isobel in *Mrs. Blood* is a spiritual odyssey, a retelling of the Bible. She assumes responsibility for her own guilt. She imagines the mother addressing her newborn infant with Christ's words:

> This is my body which was given for thee. Feed on me in thy heart by faith and by thanksgiving (MB, p.183).

Thomas has glorified motherhood as a heroic and sacrificial act by using the childbirth metaphor. The narrator's broken body and the "wine" that "dries sticky on the sheets" (MB, p.21) suggest the body / text analogy. The conflation of "mind and body, word and womb"[21] seems to promote a poetic of the female body. When a woman writer makes use of this metaphor cultural and historic realities lead to a polarization of creativity and procreativity. Here the meaning of the writer's symbolic employment of the metaphor is easily understood to establish "a matrix of creativities based on woman's double-birthing potential." [22]

Thomas makes an endeavour to deconstruct the binaries of creation/procreation, while simultaneously confronting the ambiguities of possible fusion of "literally and literarily"[23] motherhood. The mind/body duality is more pertinent to Mrs. Thing since she claims both and tries to solve this duality. She tries to overcome her obsession with her "traitor body," as she looks forward to "hone the intellect" (MB, p.93) in her daily ritual talk with Dr. Biswas.

Unlike Milton's Eve whose duplicity made her the mother of lies in a patriarchal tradition, the heroine is a committed writer in this novel. She "alters the nature of the conflict between fiction and reality and refuses Adam his monopoly on the Word."[24] To Hemingway's male universe she responds as the woman writer: "But you want to be a writer. Stay. Why nervous in a clean, well-lighted place?" (MB, p.81)

The narrative also throws light on her language making facility. At one end of the scale, *Mrs. Blood* is denotative, documentary and mocking. Isobel verbalises a catalogue of horoscopes, advertisements, and trivia from the local newspapers. She reports the domestic chatter at the ladies' "Thursday coffee morning" (MB, p.74) parties. She reproduces someone else's diary of food consumed on a ship crossing. At the other end of the scale, *Mrs. Blood* is connotative, evocative, haunting, moving through curdling descriptions of mutilation, decapitation, decay and disease. The narrator manages to transmit emotional and physical pain as understandable phenomena, capable of communication, despite her fear that pain has isolated her, not only from the main stream of life but also from those whose well-being she deeply cares.

In *Songs My Mother Taught Me,* young Isobel saw herself as the murderer of her parents. In *Mrs. Blood,* she sees herself as the murderer of her child. "Do you play Duplicate?" (MB, p.204) is the refrain occurring throughout the last part of the novel. Isobel's feelings of guilt, sinfulness and fear of death recall misreading a film advertisement outside a petrol station: "REX 8.30 TONIGHT. PAY UP OR DIE" (MB, p.143). The abortion leaves a scar on her psyche "...the pain of aborting life unhinges the mind to a degree that it creates an alternate 'truth' to the event."[25] She considers Richard at whose behest she had the abortion as the murderer of her foetus. She finds a reflection of her tragedy in the African landscape, which too is mutilated:

> There are smells here which will always be part of Africa for me; and yet if someone asked later what Africa was like

and I said "Mansion Polish," or "Dettol," or "the smell of drying blood" (MB, p.43).

Barbara Godard speaks of *Mrs. Blood's* narrator "as nonsensical, in a world where all is in flux."[26] This view is reminiscent of the anti-psychiatric movement, which considers all mental illness as a construct of the medical establishment without biological basis. According to this belief, what is considered madness is a natural and sane response to living in an insane world. Although this may sometime be true, it does not help the individual to cope with reality or explain why some people react to this insane world in the way Isobel reacts.

The opening epigram of *Mrs. Blood* suggests that the novel is the story of a displaced and disoriented woman trapped in what she perceives to be a mad world. Shoshana Felman argues, "madness is the impasse confronting those whom cultural conditioning has deprived of the very means of protest or self-affirmation...a manifestation both of cultural impotence and political castration."[27] Chesler suggests that women's madness is "an intense experience of female biological, sexual and cultural castration."[28] Madness, whether its origin is a medical disorder or cultural disease, is thus one form of being in the world similar to that of the culturally or socially deviant. Joanna Daxell suggests that this "splitting is a result of an irreconcilability between on the one hand the social and cultural norms that have shaped the view of women and their bodies and on the other hand the delusion of an autonomous self."[29]

The world is not really mad in *Mrs. Blood*. It only appears mad in Isobel's mind because she cannot relate to the world around her, not only because of her situation, which prevents her from interacting on a physical level but also because of the cultural alienation she feels in her surroundings. In order to deal with this rift, which causes her anxiety, she has split into two selves, one linked to the body, Mrs. Blood, and one linked to her mind, Mrs. Thing. Isobel projects her disease with her own body on to the unfamiliar society in which she finds herself. She cannot feel at ease in society because she cannot feel at ease within herself. She cannot feel at ease with her own pregnant body. Her body reacts in ways she is unfamiliar with, causing her much fear and anxiety, as a result of the pregnancy and its complications. This situation makes her not only highly attuned to what is happening in her body but also highly attuned to anything unusual in her surroundings.

Immobile in her hospital bed, Isobel with regard to her domestic identity says, "I can cook. I'm educated...My husband is...admired" (MB, pp.160-61). But beneath this identity is hidden another identity, like "men in peat," (MB, p.33) that of a young aspiring poet. *Mrs. Blood* is the struggle to achieve a female symbolic language. The split dialogue in *Mrs. Blood* questions women's place in literary text. Moreover, Isobel's split character signifies an acting self and a writing self.

Mrs. Blood reveals that "under the surface alienation and the second-level blur" of words, there is "a living barrage of meaning."[30] This meaning opens the doors to a different world. This novel is the saga of Isobel's disjointed and disorganized thoughts as she struggles to give birth to what will be a stillborn baby.

Thomas's use of the travel metaphor draws attention to the duplicity of signification involved in language and the process of communication. Isobel being English is associated with culture, education and all refined qualities. Africa is a primitive land close to nature. It is the land of savages. She explores this alien land and encounters realities. The alien feeling of guilt haunts her. She finds the natives strangers because of cultural gaps. In a moment of honest self-appraisal, looking at the alien environment, with its strange sights, smells, colour, and a nature threatening and alive,

Isobel comments, "usually it does not bother me. It is all part of the other we came to seek" (MB, p.173). Though the authorial presence behind Isobel's consciousness is personal, the metaphorical quest for self/child is a focus for consolidation of identity in an alien environment.

The white and black colours are a metaphor for writing. Isobel's own whiteness contrasts with the blackness of those around her. White culture superiority for Isobel becomes her inferiority in the presence of the black women around her. In fact, the black and white colours describe the conflict experienced by Isobel in connecting words with her experience. The self-pity and spatial splitting experienced by Mrs. Thing in the alien environment leaves her marooned:

> ...with all the new sounds coming in from outside and the new kind of brightness and the whole new thing that was out there and I couldn't get at-like Alice and her garden (MB,p.12).

Mrs. Blood presents a "moral landscape, a romance controlled entirely by the female body."[31] Sexuality seems diseased to the pregnant Isobel. Her concern is to protect the unborn child. The female sexual organs appear like "the Venus flytrap... mouth open wide to catch the unsuspecting guest" (MB, p.107). Isobel imagines herself "wilting on a too thin and bloody stalk" (MB, p.29), and the surrounding world becomes a mirror of the women's inner narrative: "And that spring I noticed for the first time that the street-lamps looked like onions growing the wrong way up and wilting in the sun. Or chive plants gone to seed" (MB, p.28).Thus "body and plants metaphorically join."[32]

R.D. Laing points out in *The Divided Self*, "...the split in the experience of one's own being into unembodied and embodied parts is no more an index of latent psychosis than is total embodiment any guarantee of sainty."[33] Anybody can feel this way at some point or other. It is often the only defence mechanism available to a distressed individual.

Isobel's two parts correspond to the "embodied and unembodied self" which Laing describes as:

> The embodied person has a sense of being flesh and blood and bones, of being biologically alive and real: he knows himself as subject to the dangers that threaten his body, the danger of attack, mutilation, disease, decay and death.[34]

The unembodied self, as onlooker at all the body does, engages in nothing directly. Its functions come to be observation, control and criticism vis-à-vis what the body is experiencing and doing, and those operations which are usually spoken of as purely 'mental.' The unembodied self becomes hyper-conscious.[35]

This split reflects the conflict that many women experience and is largely the result of the cultural double bind imposed on women by patriarchal society. Joanna Daxell remarks, "schizophrenia serves as a metaphor for the considerable difficulties encountered by many women as they, like Isobel, try to mediate society's predetermined expectations of women with their, often unconscious, need for self-affirmation and actualization."[36] Isobel did not choose to become pregnant. In fact, she warns her husband: "If you get me pregnant I won't go with you" (MB, p.27).

Mrs.Blood is the story of a woman's culturally assumed silence and marginality. The stillborn baby and the psychological return of the earlier abortion are at the journey's centre. Laurie Ricous calls *Mrs. Blood* "the most female novel in Canadian literature."[37] The subject matter of this novel is birth and miscarriage and male indifference to woman's pain and desire: "Birth and copulation and death. That's all there is" (MB, p.212). Joan Coldwell suggests: "the miscarriage suffered in *Mrs. Blood* has haunted the narrator with guilt and loss until she has gone mad."[38]

Isobel in *Mrs. Blood* is the representative of all women. Her voice is like the voice of Christ: ""Take this," I said, "in remembrance of me..."" (MB, p.26). She believes:

no one will assay to touch me because of the shards which gleam greenly against the white altar and the wine shall run over and down and expire in a hiss when the sun sticks his finger in the window. Drops of red pain, rivers of pain and the earth outside rusty with blood. This is my body (MB, p.99).

In *Mrs. Blood,* Audrey Thomas writing about issues connected with the women's body like childbirth, abortion, menstruation and " a lot of nasty things...sometimes you don't have the baby or the baby's deformed"[39] makes women realize: "the two great archetypal things that happen to you in your life are birth and death; and you can't remember your own birth. The only way you can get back to anything close to it is when you yourself have a child."[40]

At the end of the novel, Mrs. Thing is left rootless and lost positioned "between two worlds, one dead, the other powerless to be born" (MB, p.189). *Mrs. Blood* questions and challenges women's place in traditional discourse and suggests a rejection of such discourse. It confronts: "...convention and ideology, questioning what the masculine tradition has defined as "right" and "acceptable," and work toward opening a space from which a woman can speak her desire- and in her discourse."[41] The novel is an exploration of a contemporary problem, the search for unity that has become divided.

ENDNOTES

1. Audrey Thomas, *Mrs. Blood* (1970, rpt. Vancouver: Talonbooks, 1988), p.9. All subsequent references in parentheses belong to this edition of the text.
2. Helene Cixous, "The Laugh of the Medusa," *FEMINISMS: An Anthology of Literary Theory and Criticism,* eds. Robyn R. Warhol and Diane Price Herndl (New Brunswick, N.J.: Rutgers, 1991), p.342.
3. Anthony Boxill, "Portraits of the Artists: Three Novels by Audrey Thomas," *The Fiddlehead,* 95 (Fall, 1972), p.114.

4. Elizabeth Komisar, "Audrey Thomas: A Review/Interview," review of *Blown Figures, Open Letter*, 3rd Series, No. 3 (Late Fall, 1975), p.59.
5. Mary Jacobus, ed., "*Women Writing and Writing About Women* (London: Croom Helm, 1979), p.16.
6. Joanna Daxell, "Body/Mind Split: The Social Logic of Schizophrenia and the Dissolution of Self in Mrs. Blood" *Intercultural Journeys/Parcours Interculturels* eds. Joanna Daxell and Natasha Dagenais, (Baldwin Mills: Topeda Hill, 2003), p.171.
7. George Bowering, "Songs and Wisdom: An Interview with Audrey Thomas," *Open Letter*, 4th Series, No. 3 (Spring, 1979), p.30.
8. Edward Said, *Beginnings: Intention and Method* (New York: Basic Books, 1975), p.34.
9. George Bowering (1979), *op. cit.*, p.22.
10. *Ibid.*, p.16.
11. Elizabeth Komisar (1975), *op. cit.*, p.59.
12. Martin Levin, "review of Mrs. Blood," *The New York Times Book Review*, (January 3, 1971), p.23.
13. George Bowering (1979), *op. cit.*, p.23.
14. Susan Gubar, "The Birth of the Artist as Heroine: (Re) production, the *Kunstlerroman* Tradition, and the Fiction of Katherine Mansfield," *The Representation of Women in Fiction*, eds. Carolyn Heilbrun and Margaret Higonnet, (Baltimore: The Johns Hopkins University Press, 1983), p.26.
15. Dianne Sadoff, *Monsters of Affection: Dickens, Eliot and Bronte on Fatherhood* (Baltimore: The Johns Hopkins University Press, 1976), p.167.
16. Lorna Irvine, *Sub/Version: Canadian Fictions by Women* (Toronto: ECW Press, 1986), p.32.
17. William Shakespeare, "*Macbeth," The Living Shakespeare: Twenty-Two Plays and The Sonnets*, ed. Oscar James Campbell, (New York: The Macmillan Company, 1958), p.963.
18. R.D.Laing, *The Divided Self: An Existential Study in Sanity and Madness* (New York: Penguin, 1965), p.169.
19. George Bowering (1979), *op. cit.*, p.10.

20. *Ibid.*, p.17.
21. Susan Stanford Friedman, "Creativity and the Childbirth Metaphor: gender difference in literary discourse," *FEMINISMS* (1991), *op. cit.*, p.373.
22. *Ibid.*, p.390.
23. *Ibid.*, p.389.
24. Lorna Irvine (1986), *op. cit.*, p.35.
25. Malashri Lal, "Canadian Gynocritics: Contexts of meaning in Margaret Atwood's Surfacing," *Perspectives on Women: Canada and India*, ed. Aparna Basu, (Delhi: Allied Publishers, 1995), p.186.
26. Barbara Godard, *Audrey Thomas and Her Works* (Toronto: ECW Press, year not given), p.26.
27. Shoshana Felman, "Women and Madness: the Critical phallacy," *FEMINISMS* (1991),*op. cit.*, p.7.
28. Phyllis Chesler, *Women and Madness* (New York: Avon, 1972), p.27.
29. Joanna Daxell (2003), *op. cit.*, p.183.
30. Dennis Lee, "Cadence, Country, Silence: Writing in Colonial Space," *boundary*, 2, 3, No. 1 (Fall, 1974), p.164.
31. Lorna Irvine (1986), *op. cit.*, p.28.
32. *Ibid.*
33. R.D.Laing (1965), *op. cit.*, pp.70-71.
34. *Ibid.*, p.69.
35. *Ibid.*, p.71.
36. Joanna Daxell (2003), *op. cit.*, p.175.
37. Laurie Ricous, "Phyllis Webb, Daphne Marlatt and simultitude," *Amazing Space: Writing Canadian Women Writing*, eds. Shirley Neuman and Smaro Kamboureli (Alberta: Longspoon Press, 1986), p.205.
38. Joan Coldwell, "Memory Organised: The Novels of Audrey Thomas," *Canadian Literature* 92 (Spring, 1982), p.48.
39. George Bowering (1979), *op. cit.*, p.15.
40. *Ibid.*, p.21.
41. Sally Robinson, "The Anti-Logos Weapon: Multiplicity in Women's Texts," *Contemporary Literature*, 29, 1 (Spring, 1988), p.122.

SECTION-III
BLOWN FIGURES

"I stand in the ring
in the dead city
and tie on the red shoes
....
They are not mine,
they are my mother's,
her mother's before,
handed down like a heirloom
but hidden like shameful letters."

Blown Figures, the concluding novel of Thomas's Isobel trilogy, set in Africa or "MAFROKA, the broken, the divided land"[1] demonstrates womanhood's fragmentation and loss. Thomas admits *Blown Figures* is "a novel about writing a novel or about creativity."[2] Madness has been an important theme in literature from Greek tragedy onwards, but in the nineteenth and twentieth centuries it has been associated with women. Many of the key texts of feminist literary studies have been centrally concerned with the figures of the mad woman, like Charlotte Bronte's *Jane Eyre,* Virginia Woolf's *Mrs. Dalloway,* Sylvia Path's *The Bell Jar,* Doris Lessing's *The Golden Notebook,* and Marge Piercy's *Woman on the Edge of Time* etc. The reason for women writers' interest in madness has been immediate and personal. Elaine Showalter in *The Female Malady* writes:

> Biographies and letters of gifted women who suffered mental breakdowns have suggested that madness is the price women artists have had to pay for the exercise of their creativity in a male-dominated culture.[3]

In *Blown Figures,* set a few years after her traumatic miscarriage, Isobel, "wife of Jason, and mother of Mary and Nicholas," (BF, p.22) is haunted by the memory of the dead foetus. She is terrorised by the fear of her crumbling sanity and grotesque dreams. Trapped by her fears, "I'm afraid...I'm afraid all the time. Of everything" (BF, p.20), she questions the reality of her existence and, correspondingly, her own sanity. She returns to Africa alone in *Blown Figures*. She leaves behind her husband and children in Vancouver. Her return is prompted by a visceral desire to regain the spark of life, which has been taken out of her and by the need to tone down a spiritual agony that has left her overwhelmed by guilt. She embarks on a journey of "exorcisms" (BF, p.218) convinced that unless she goes back to Africa and the "small ghost" of her first abortion and second miscarriage can be "propitiated and set free" (BF, p.194), there can be no happiness for her and Jason. Isobel loses the maternal sense of guilt and fear during her journey and enters wholly into her quest for self.

Blown Figures focuses on madness to explode character boundaries. The excerpts from journals, magazines and newspapers spread throughout the novel point toward the madness of the outer world. Phyllis Chesler in *Women and Madness* addresses the gender specificity of woman's madness. She writes women by bearing children enact "a blood sacrifice for the perpetuation of the species" and mark themselves as symbols of self-sacrifice because of their biology. Chesler argues that denied cultural supremacy, "some women are driven mad," and their madness is "an intense experience of female biological, sexual and cultural castration, and a doomed search for potency."[4] Although mental illness is debilitating, women have occasionally found that the experience of losing and having to remake their identity gave them a hard won independence from conventional ways of seeing the world and of using language.

Gilbert and Gubar in *The Mad Woman in the Attic* write about: "literary works that are in some sense palimpsestic, works whose surface designs conceal or obscure deeper, less accessible levels of meaning."[5] According to them, the less accessible meanings are contained in projections of woman writer's own despair that result in the creation of "melodramatic characters who act out the subversive impulses every woman inevitably feels when she contemplates the 'deep-rooted' evils of patriarchy."[6] In the fiction, written by women, the madwoman is the author's double. Forced to recognize her double, the female character often discovers in madness a cleansing that allows her to face the actual madness of her culture, to "recognize and reject not only the pathology of social and sexual arrangements but her own participation in these arrangements as well."[7] In *Mrs. Blood,* such doubling occurs between Mrs. Thing and Mrs. Blood, and it occurs between Isobel and Delilah in *Blown Figures*. When women confront their mirror selves, when they create characters that have the "power to reach toward the woman trapped on the other side of the mirror/text and help her to climb out,"[8] they move towards literary autonomy.

The novel begins on board the "H.M.S. *Pylades*" (BF, p.11). Isobel is standing beside a woman "who held a screaming baby in her arms" (BF, p.12). The story is fraught with anxiety. Even before the boat leaves shore, Isobel panics:

> GET OFF GET OFF booms the big bass drum. GET OFF GET OFF GET OFF. It wasn't too late. The gangplank still connected her with the shore (BF, pp.13-14).

When the boat embarks, her past threatens to rise up and engulf her. The boat's tug looks as if: "it were sitting in one of her father's old rubber overshoes" (BF, p.40).

The people and events on the boat give depth to Isobel's narrative. They like the material of dreams, represent the phenomena of her mind. The young Dutch boy with "a slight lisp and a very pink and white skin" (BF, p.63) reminds her of a baby. She sleeps with him. The ocean crossing is filled with sexual allusions and with descriptions of erotic play, a dramatic condensation of the act and results of copulation. The past events flash through her mind: "The apotheosis of dear Isobel's education, Clara's sacrifices, Warren's drawers full of unpaid bills..." (BF, pp.18-19).

Isobel is worried and concerned about her family:

> Where are Nicholas and Mary?
> What are they doing....Where is Jason? (BF, p.66)

She is unable to weed out her ex-lover Richard from her thoughts: "Richard is ubiquitous, like God. He is everywhere and nowhere" (BF, p.26). When the group briefly disembarks at Dakar, the heat, the beggars and the souvenir seller threaten to suffocate her. When she returns to the ship, she is enclosed with a couple travelling with a four-week-old baby. The ship becomes becalmed, the dinner at the home of two members of the British Council and the visit to the beach illustrate Isobel's hysterical state.

Isobel is on the brink of suffocation on the train because the "fan in the ceiling did not work and the sweat ran down her fingers" (BF, p.137). She leans out of the window to catch air. Baobab trees cast their ghostly reflections as the train speeds past. An African man prays in the next compartment. The train passes into Mali, where the trees give way to "striated rock and heat and light" (BF, p.140). At one of the stops, a uniformed soldier takes Isobel off the train. She has not paid enough money for the trip and her traveller's cheques are not accepted. Finally, an unknown English speaking man pays her fine and she is released. At midnight, she leaves the station, finds a taxi and goes to the Grand Hotel. There are no rooms. Rescued again by a man, Isobel is offered a room.

Time passes. She is sitting in a café called "*La Croix du Sud*" with her friend Delilah Rosenberg and a black man named Hyacinth, "a clerk in the Hotel Continental" (BF, p.151). Delilah regales Isobel with stories of her various abortions. She is "twenty-eight and had had four abortions; the babies were all by black men," (BF, p.153) and confesses she is again pregnant. The pregnant Delilah is the mirror which reflects the body Isobel wants to exorcise, along with her own demons. Her most important and revealing friendship is with the ruthlessly liberated Delilah Rosenberg. She becomes Isobel's travelling companion for a major part of the journey. Delilah is life loving and Isobel is "fascinated by her" (BF, p.152). Both enjoy the shared closeness of sisters, yet Isobel condemns the irresponsible and promiscuous woman. There is "no quick intimacy," but "a kind of tension between them..." (BF, p.159). The men, who have helped Isobel, hang around. One offers further help, while the other elicits sexual payment. Isobel and Delilah have to wait till morning for the banks to open and then for the taxi to take them across the border.

When the taxi arrives, it moves slowly and erratically. It is stopped by the police and then by the driver's girlfriend who "smoked and chewed gum and chatted..." (BF, pp.166-167). Isobel crowded by other passengers again imagines suffocation:

> being stifled by the body heat and body odors of three Moslems, two white American ladies, one African girl and possibly part – Arabic driver, not to mention three other pungent gentlemen in the back seat (BF, p.167)

Isobel's anxiety is compounded by the news of the death of a young motorcyclist, by the sound of drums, and by political references to conflict between French and English Canada. Isobel and Delilah follow "the French-Canadian priest in silence" to meet an old nun "dying of a cancer" (BF, p.238). Paranoia spreads. Isobel and Delilah "act out myth and legend"[9] as they wait for a ferry to take them across the river: "pacing back and forth on the jetty, were out of harmony with the rest of this strange, waiting crowd. Just so might the dead souls have waited for Charon and his ferryboat" (BF, p.462). In the classical myth, the ferryman called Charon conveyed the souls of the dead across Styx river. Here Isobel is waiting for the boat to carry her across the river to search for her lost child. It also implies purification of mind and body for Isobel. The landscape drained of colour:

> was somehow depressing, almost surreal. Tops of dead trees stuck out of the water like withered drowned arms, the flesh collapsed and wrinkled; the water, like the trees, was a strange grey color (BF, p.461).

Delilah affected by the sun and her pregnancy becomes ill. When the boat arrives they are not able to board it. Isobel desires to abandon Delilah to her fate yet she remains with the pregnant woman through the ferry journey and onto the bus that takes them into the jungle. Their journey is again halted when Delilah miscarries. Delilah authenticates Isobel's need to explore her self though other women rather than to separate herself from their experiences as she has done since childhood. Isobel confirms she shares with Delilah and all other women a link of blood: "The blood which links all women was linking them..." (BF, p.479). This event frees Isobel from her connection with Delilah. In nightmarish fury, Isobel leaves the hotel, and hails a taxi that takes her to the border of the old town. It is a symbolic ride. She recognizes that "Death is all around her" (BF, p.494). After walking some distance, she is picked up by a lorry marked by the painted words: "TWO SHADOWS" (BF, p.509). The ghostly lorry carries her into the depths of the forest. Amidst the ritual enactment of guilt and retribution, Isobel:

> danced to the God's drums with the smashed egg still plastered on her head.... "I have journeyed here," she said, "to get my destiny changed" (BF, p.524),

and the narrative ends.

Aboard the *Pylades* at Southampton, recorded older tunes heard by Isobel are described as "musical ghosts," a lead-in to her exaggerated concern with her miscarried child. The "screaming baby" (BF, p.12) is the first in a series of foetuses, infants and children that impress upon her consciousness.

It is later epitomised in the ceremony of disposing of a dead offspring carried as a "head load" (BF, p.202), literally and psychologically. The line from the song:

> OOOOOOOO OH-KLAHOM-A / WHERE THE SUN SHINES BRIGHT-LY ON THE HAY (BF, p.12),

signifies her ongoing neurosis about the harsh and revealing quality of unclouded light. Another song, "GETTING TO KNOW YOU" ironically points her isolation. The bass drum booms "GET OFF GET OFF" (BF, p.13) to Isobel's unnaturally heightened sensitivities, while the boat's supposed "breakdown" (BF, p.12) and delayed departure are prefigurements of her own psychological dislocations throughout the novel.

Isobel remembers books left by her grandfather Harry: "a ten volume Photographic History of the Civil War, a Life of General Grant, The Quiver Readings, Don Quixote and Paradise Lost" (BF, p.16). These books suggest to Isobel her own social and spiritual trials and ambitions. She has earlier confessed to the psychiatrist her fears of: "Nearly everything. Transportation especially. And things that shut you in" (BF, p.20), so that in a real sense her quest acts as therapy for her paranoia. Louis K. Mac Kendrick comments:

> Many of the transports she will encounter are named in accord with her estimate of her situation: the circuitous claustrophobic taxi *Pitie de Moi,* the lorries "Two Shadows," "People Weep to See Me," and "Life Changes."[10]

Isobel's memory of letters from her mother which "always said TO BE DESTROYED in the upper left hand corner" (BF, p.21) indicates her major concern with the dissolution of her personality, a persistent motif reinforced by Jason's accurate observation: ""Isobel doesn't live"... "she exits." He meant to say "exists."" Even a stamp machine card in her purse urging "STICK TO YOUR JOB" (BF, p.22) is the first of many messages she receives from popular sources and which are seen as unexpectedly specific. Ironically, in her final dream ritual of purification, Isobel learns that her destiny cannot be changed: "The witches have eaten up your *kra*" (BF, p.524).

Isobel having considered her family as illusionary "from behind the invisible glass wall of her disguised madness" (BF, p.22) anticipates her references to the safety of glass enclosures and bottles, especially those containing preserved foetuses. The flashback, "She and Jason had seen" Hitchcock's film *"Vertigo"* (BF, p.17), reflects the theme of mental breakdown and illusion in *Blown Figures.*

On her journey Isobel is exposed, in fact and in memory, to many grotesques of body and mind, the deformed and the compulsive, the eccentric and the uncaring, who represent a failed or imperfect humanity. Such individuals demonstrate Isobel's own imperfect vision and lack of insight. Her obsession makes her at times paranoid, as she seeks an uncertain release from "her crime against her dead child" (BF, pp.484-485). She considers herself a failure as a mother, overlooking her two living children. Mothers are not seen favourably in *Blown Figures*. Isobel's mother-in-law is a forbidding woman, perceived as a threat to unrestrained lovemaking and effectively characterized by an interest in crewel work and dried flowers:

> Jason's mother arranged dried flowers and dried grasses in huge copper urn...brought in the Hoover and the yellow dusters and...did her crewel work by the fire (BF, p.437).

Her mother-in-law performs real, but not arduous work. This is a role that keeps her happily and usefully "busy from early dawn to twilight,"[11] whereas Isobel's journey to search for the lost child makes her reject the established canon of patriarchy.

Even Isobel's eccentric mother wanted her daughters to walk on glass splinters. The legacy of Isobel's own impulse to leave and preoccupation about her mother's disappearance haunts her memory:

> Isobel's mother always put her hat on when she went out, calling over her shoulder that she was never coming back. Isobel would lie on her bed and listen to her mother's determined footsteps fade and sink into the cold grey pavement of the street (BF, p.450).

Marriage and sex, for Isobel, seem to have little common ground. Whereas Isobel associates lust with a sort of joyous, animal abandonment, she finds love, which here connotes sexual relations within marriage to be not a letting go of self but a holding back. She explains:

> With Richard she had yelled and moaned and laughed – with Jason only sometimes. In his mother's house they had learned to be quiet, hardly moving, like skin divers in enemy waters.... They were like deaf-mutes (BF, p.95).

Sex with Jason meant procreation and, in view of Isobel's fears, it is equated with blood, death and denial.

Glass barriers and containers figure in Isobel's mind. Glass signifies Isobel's wish to escape the demands of her mind and body. However, it is also associated with her wish for, and fear of intangibility: "By the time they reached the border she would be all gone. There would be nobody. No body. Personne" (BF, p.168). The idea of glass suggests how the literal and metaphorical become connected in *Blown Figures*. On board the *Pylades*, at dinner, Isobel sees through the self-absorbed and uncharitable Mrs. Hankinson "as though she were made of glass" (BF, p.66).

Visualising the eating and digestive processes she is "made fully aware for the first time of the foulness we all carry within us" (BF, p.67), and of the farcical pretence of civilization. This projection of her own unclean condition is linked to her memory of an earlier treatment for pinworms: "her knowledge of the omnipresent worms" (BF, p.210) and the remedy a real viscous liquid.

In *Blown Figures*, everything is connected with the womb. The wasteland myth used in *Mrs. Blood* appears again in

Blown Figures, but with a considerably different effect. The heroic journeyer attempts to exhaust the traditional myth in order to establish a female perspective on the story: "all the fields of millet and ground-nuts, all the lush green-ness would turn brown and cracked...She felt that whatever she had to do she must finish it before the land dried up" (BF, p.217). Evil makes the crops fail and the women abort. Vultures hover over decomposing corpses. At the last phase of her journey, Isobel comes to a groove where:

> red snakes hung down and hissed at her as she passed. Rats, gnawing at a headless corpse... a man nailed through the head to a chair and another man, about to be executed, with a small knife driven through his cheeks....The rains had stopped but everything dripped... (BF, p.513).

Here the wind blows as in T.S. Eliot's *The Waste Land.* All the trees of the forest are shaken. But in the grove, the hope for the healing of the land seems contained in the female body. The egg ceremonies that conclude Isobel's journey divert attention from male dominance to an earlier time of female dominance.

Greek Myths echo in *Blown Figures* to emphasise the potential of a woman's body. Isobel dreams of water "covered with spots of blood," an evocation of the river Charon where "On the other bank her child held out his arms to her" (BF, p.169). The spots are menstrual blood, which is a symbol of female reproduction. Like Homer's *Odyssey, Blown Figures* contains twenty-four sections. The Dutch boy sexually rejuvenates her, just as Calypso does Odysseus. Miss Miller, like Athene, functions as an omniscient ear. Rivers, the open sea and gardens proliferate in *Blown Figures.* Isobel looking into a mirror "sees a man with one eye blind and whitely translucent" (BF, p.163). References to pigs recall the Circe episode. However, seen through the Circe's eyes, the focus alters. It shifts into what the poet in Atwood's Circe poems calls "the story that counts."[12] It is the story of the land, of the future, of procreation, and of love. The souls of the dead wander in and out of the epic journey. Isobel travels not to receive her father's blessing. Her journey is a return, an odyssey back, to a lost member of the family, the dead baby. Isobel undertakes the journey to exorcise her own demons.

Isobel records a veritable gallery of heads separated from their bodies. These clearly stand for the almost continual menace she feels as well as for the reason and balance she has forsaken. George Bowering has said, "Headlessness suggests craziness, one guesses, and bears an acute relationship with the image of the abandoned womb."[13] Isobel believes her child was removed from her in pieces. Her intense recognition of "her enemy the sun" (BF, p.210) symbolizes the unsparing light of a clear and unclouded perspective. The references to water are for escape than cleansing: "But water, a boat, the idea of being carried somewhere, of once having embarked the impossibility of further choices" (BF, p.111).

Isobel tends to read significations in all things, as everything in the real world appears to accuse her of guilt: "Why did things take on such awesome significance?" (BF, p.218) Barbara Godard has written of "the true subject of the book, the creative act taking place in our minds."[14] Disconnected words and unusually structured pages reflect the material of Isobel's womb, the broken baby. They also dramatically represent the traditional isolation of the female voice: "Innocent words detached themselves from sentences, grew big as signs" (BF, p.32). Her ability to read periodically fails: "the letters jumped around the page like fleas" (BF, p.137). Isobel suffers a terrifying aphasia. She imagines her ears and lips have been cut off: "so that speech was hardly audible" (BF, p.453). She seems to be "Squashed by the words, strangled by the sentences," (BF, p.193) and worries about her compulsion to tell tales. An old man reiterates, "A tale, a tale, Let it go and let it return" (BF, p.169), and the rats ask: "Do you know only one story?" (BF, p.313)

These utterances with the idea to combat Isobel's fears document the novel.

The femininity of the text is also reflected in the colours of the story. Isobel looks at the people who are waiting for the boat to leave. She sees a red-cheeked man. "A magenta" streamer "flicked and snapped in the breeze" (BF, p.13). As the journey begins, she remembers a bright red blanket, touched up photos of virgins with reddened lips and cheeks. She imagines: "A scarlet Isobel smiled up at a scarlet Dutch Boy" (BF, p.97), dancing together and thinks about the Red Queen in *Alice in Wonderland*. She also recalls a train ride she took with Jason. The seats of the train were covered with cracked red leather. Isobel clutches a "red washcloth" (BF, p.141) when "a man in a kakhi uniform" (BF, p.140) enters the train on which she is travelling in Africa and removes her.

The driver of the taxi she gets into wears a red cloth around his arm. It is a sign that someone has died. Even the earth turns red: "The borders of the avenue to the grove were planted with red lilies.... The earth was rusty red, the color of dried blood" (BF, p.523). Other red images spread through *Blown Figures* are a corpse clothed only in red fez, flamingoes, red ants, a scarlet umbrella, a cherry-coloured coat Isobel once owned, the evocative scarlet letter, a vermillion medicine Isobel takes to rid herself of worms, Delilah's red leotard, red traffic lights, a red butterfly that alights on Isobel's arm as she moves into the forest, red snakes hissing and hanging out of the trees and the coagulated red mud that sticks to Isobel's legs as she gets closer to the grove where she ends her journey.

The references to red accentuate the centrality of blood in Isobel's delusions. *Blown Figures* concentrates on women's blood, that is, the blood of menstruation, the blood of childbirth and the loss of blood that signals miscarriage. Isobel's dreams and delusions in *Blown Figures* take the form of blood and violence: "The carnival was over, the child had been taken away in a silver basin, the great livery placenta thrust aside into a bucket. The woman who had killed the child lay quiet in a pool of her own life's blood" (BF, p.177). Isobel recalls a ghastly vision of everyone she has ever known, that is, husband, lovers, children and parents:

> Dangling upside down from great black meat hooks, their throats slashed, their mouths open in a silent collective scream. There was a thick, fishy smell of drying blood (BF, p.29).

Isobel remembers taking her two children to the university farm, where they select a pig to be killed. The sound of the slaughter echoes in her ears. She feels "the red hot blood pour from her divided throat" (BF, p.139). She also recalls the miscarriage and the doctor's voice turned into blood, liquid and arterial. Her memories of the hospital and of the nurses and doctors from her earlier life in Africa draw attention to "the long wounds in her body" (BF, p.140).

Isobel's mythic lovemaking with the "Dutch Boy" emphasises its bloody imagery:

> In her dream the Dutch Boy came to Isobel as a long-legged bird. His feathers glowed in the moonlight. "Look," he said gently, "the stars have got caught in your hair." With his beak he began to disentangle them... blood from the sharp points of the stars ran down the back of her neck. Wherever the blood flowed crimson feathers grew. It was beautiful, his white form and her red under the thin glaze of the moonlight...catching in her long red hair.... When she looked into the eyes of Dutch Boy she saw that he was blind... her breasts began to bleed... (BF, p.338).

Descriptions of perverse intercourse with the devil are marked with blood: "From between her thighs she took some blood and marked his forehead." "See how it feels," she said, "see how it feels," (He vanished)" (BF, p.68). Isobel's psychic agony takes in such archetypal dilemmas. Beneath recollections of the miscarriage, of the birth of her two living children, of her marriage to Jason, lies the ghost of an aborted foetus conceived with her ex-lover Richard. She remains a victim as the postscript suggests: "TIME! YOU MONSTROUS MOLE. WHY ARE YOU DOING THIS TO ME?" (BF, p.547)

The novel is filled with references to disease, to female ailments, to dismemberment, to decapitation, to cannibalism. The "Terminal Hotel" (BF, p.17) in London, mentioned at the beginning of the novel, creates foreboding. Isobel suffers from insomnia:

> she lay wide-eyed and alone while the rest of them slept. She had visions of witches playing football with their heads. The knives in the kitchen grinned in the moonlight like dares (BF, p.23).

The balls are, in fact, heads. The wife of the mining engineer, on the boat to Africa, is "missing something," and she has "a little sack attached to her" (BF, p.67). In Dakar, sellers offer shrunken heads. Isobel describes an episode in which two grinning men in a taxi frightened her and her friend:

> where might you have ended up.... A headless torso in one of Harry's True Detective magazines?...Your head and bright hair would have been buried elsewhere in a feed sack (BF, pp.146-147).

She remembers the nursery rhymes, which echo her obsessions:

> Here comes a candle to light your bed. / Here comes a chopper to chop off your head (BF, p.248).

A recipe for cooking a calf's head instructs the cook to "Soak the quarters about six hours in cold water to extract the blood" (BF, p.85). The recipes that appear among Isobel's fragments identify victims, heads, or young creatures sacrificed to appetite. These are connected with the French – Canadian priest's observation to Isobel: "We have a saying here. 'You eat in Africa or Africa eats you'" (BF, p.183).

Allusions to cannibalism combine anxiety and guilt: "I ALWAYS LIKE AN ARM WHEN SHARING" (BF, p.380). The information about African ants, who when starving: "eat their own excrement...continued to chew and digest their excrement" (BF, p.381) is passed on. Personified animals suddenly metamorphose into food:

> When done, transfer Master Piglet to a large hot platter; surround him with a necklace of crisp curley parsley; remove the corncob from his mouth and place instead a nice rosy apple. Serve very hot with pan gravy and apple sauce" (BF, p.382).

In a letter printed in "DEAR DOLLY" column for the lovelorn, a young man explains that his girlfriend's "parents are cannibals...might devour me...as I am fat and healthy" (BF, p.421). Isobel's memory of a mouse in her London hotel room bothered her with "the question of his reality" (BF, p.30). She is open to hallucinatory experience so that the world of reality and dark imaginings often merge their boundaries. Animal and insect life often intrudes upon her awareness. Obsessed with the memory of guilt, she is unable to accept life at an uncomplicated level:

> A tiny lizard ran across Delilah's sandalled foot; for a terrible moment Isobel thought the child had somehow slipped out from Delilah's pants – leg and was scurrying away (BF, pp.161-162).

Isobel imagines herself in a courtroom similar to the one inhabited by Alice: "Isobel placed herself in the sinner's dock and confessed she was a witch. "I ate the child in my womb," she said. "Since then I have never been happy" (BF, p.518). Images of cannibalism multiply as the novel disconnectedly ends:

I myself, Miss Miller, ate the victim's foot.... She cooked the faeces of her sister's child and set it before her husband, although he didn't eat it. I shall die, Miss Miller, and you will eat me and my children.... After we cook the flesh we sing the snakes' song... SHE EATS GRAND PEOPLE. (BF, pp.540-543).

Various objects like eggs, balloons, and footballs metaphorically represent the womb while the land sometimes offers womb like protection:

> The sun beat down mercilessly on the top of Isobel's head; she submerged herself every few minutes, jelly-fish floating, suspended, safe as a baby in a bottle (BF, p.110).

In other places, womb and tomb join and dramatize the closeness between life and death. Throughout her dreams and delusions, Isobel's fixation merges with her obsessive fantasies about dismemberment. Isobel translates memories of being scrapped clean after a miscarriage and an abortion into deconstructed bodies. By extension, those bodies reveal themselves in a chaotic text: "A few scraps left. An embryonic finger may be, or a toe. A little lost eye" (BF, p.132). The novel has a female subject, a female narrator and a female audience, Miss Miller. These interconnections Judith Gardiner writes is a notable characteristic of women's writing, "female characters in novels by women tend to dissolve and merge into each other."[15]

Isobel recalls reading about a man so fat that he had to be buried in a piano case. She also quotes an argument for burial without a coffin, "the Mohammedan way" (BF, p.53). The cabin of the boat is small, a tight enclosure. She remembers a conversation with an analyst. She was attempting to pin point her constant anxiety:

> "I'm afraid all the time... things that shut you in. Cars, Elevators, Airplanes. Especially airplanes." (BF, p.20)

Modes of transport like cabs, buses, and cars emphasize Isobel's struggle between feelings of emptiness and fullness, construction and freedom. Enclosed spaces occupy Isobel's mind and produce anxiety.

The novel's opening shows the female body as progenitor of human life:

> Cripples, one-eyed people, pregnant women: we are all the children of eggs, Miss Miller, we are all the children of eggs (BF, p.11).

Literal allusions to eggs such as the plates of eggs served on the boat connote female nurturing. Elsewhere a stern voice advices "YOU CANNOT HAVE YOUR EGG AND EAT IT" (BF, p.72). The tension between creation and destruction is given female significance because it focuses on birth, the difference between bearing a dead and a living child.

Isobel is drawn to wordplay and puns. Words which spring into Isobel's consciousness include: ""Breakdown": collapse, stoppage, failure of health or power, negro dance" (BF, p.108); "*Scrap*. Small detached piece of something, fragment, remnant (pl.) odds and ends, useless remains, alied to *scrape*" (BF, p.132); and "(Zero[żero]m. zero, naught, cipher; freezing point; starting point; love[tennis]; nonentity, nobody [fam.])" (BF, p.114). She is also responsive to remembered African words and phrases, which act as simplification of her reactions and a base chorus to her perplexities:

> ...when I go to the witch-tree the name I go by is ODI AKESE... or SHE EATS GRAND PEOPLE (BF, p.543). EATS GRAND PEOPLE (BF, p.543).

Puns cruelly point toward Isobel's condition: "MUMMY." MUM. MOM. Persian, wax used in embalming" (BF, p.75) follows a vivid reminder of the miscarriage. The play of: "Nous allons/ Noose alone/ Nurse along/ Isobel, Beware the Eyes of Mars" (BF, p.173) is a cryptic reference to Isobel's suicidal journey, in conflict with herself, omen-ridden, and unaware of her unchangeable fate. Moreover, each term of "Diseased/Dis-eased/De-ceased" (BF, p.197) has an acute relevance to the uneasy Isobel. The bitter wordplay of "TUMMY/TUMULUS/TOMB" (BF, p.397) reinforces her masochistic association of life and death, while "Marriage/ Mirage" (BF, p.446) summarizes her interest in the family left behind, her casual adultery on the *Pylades*, and the fading of all normal connections before the strength of her obsession.

Each chapter of the novel, except for Chapter IV, concludes with an artful melange, a sequence of individual items each of which is allowed a full page of the novel. As John Moss has remarked: "The whiteness becomes overwhelming. The reader reads the emptiness.... Not since *Tristram Shandy* has the physical page between so effectively incorporated into narrative reality."[16]

The majority of literary allusions are to Lewis Carroll's Alice books and to Beatrix Potter's *The Tailor of Gloucester*. Allusion to this classic tale, including part of its preface, is addressed not to Freda but to Isobel. The fragments of Chapter XIII are rich, as the narrator confesses, "Ah, Miss Miller, I was never so good at stitching buttonholes" (BF, p.245). Isobel herself becomes the "cherry-coloured coat" (BF, p.269).

"NO MORE TWIST/TMISS MILLER/ NO MORE TWIST" (BF, p.545) is another illusion to *The Tailor of Gloucester*. It is what the little mice say to the tailor of Gloucester when they run out of buttonhole twists while making the mayor's coat. "They leave him a note saying 'No more twists.'"[17] Similarly Isobel says to "Miss Miller, 'No more twist.' She's either fed up or she's so out of control herself by this point that she knows it's no good going on."[18] The novel ends with the words "DAMIRIFA/ DAMIRIFA /DAMIRIFA" (BF, p.545) which means pity. This points to the open-endedness of the text with the disappearance of Isobel into the African landscape. Potter's citations remind of Isobel's function as maker, like a carpenter, and the anxious threat of incompletion.

Alice in Wonderland and *Through the Looking Glass* participate in *Blown Figures* structure and imagery, sometimes by direct reference, sometimes by indirect reference and sometimes by allusion. The twenty four-chapter format reverberates with meaning. References to rabbits and cats recall Carroll's work. The Mock Turtle's emotionally appropriate sentence: "He taught Laughing and Grief" (BF, p.141), and the grim Duchess recommending beheading point to decapitation.

From *Through the Looking Glass* there are illusions drawn to the arbitrary and imperative roles of queens, exaggerated models of control, while references to the black and white kittens emphasize the schizophrenia of Isobel's condition. "Looking Glass Milk Isn't Good to Drink" (BF, p.442) picks up a pun on Mali Lait. Isobel reflects on her relationship with Delilah as "being a parody or looking-glass reversal of her own distress five years before" (BF, p.479). Alice's encounters with surrealistic, mythically self-contained, grotesque and threatening fantasy situations are close to the nature of Isobel's experience. George Bowering has written that *Blown Figures* is "a fiction that puts the reader in Alice's position."[19] An advertisement "BE TALLER" (BF, p.87) is succeeded by "I MUST BE GROWING SMALL AGAIN" (BF, p.88), signifying Isobel's fluctuations between self-control and its opposite.

The Red Queen becomes one of the narrative's characters. Madness pervades the universe of the novel. Quotations from Carroll's work appear throughout in *Blown Figures*:

> "Oh, don't go on like that!" cried the poor Queen, wringing her hands in despair. "Consider what a great girl you are. Consider what a long way you've come today. Consider what o'clock it is. Consider Anything, only don't cry!" (BF, p.125).

Sometimes Isobel imagines herself, like Alice, on the other side of the mirror, where she hears the voices of the "White Queen" and the playing card soldiers. "We are all the White Queen's Pawn" (BF, p.126). She questions her own reality. In distorted forms eggs, serpents, lions, frogs, flowers and insects duplicate Alice's dream universe. At the end of the novel, the sound of drums and the sudden materialization of a court repeat Alice's fantasies and reflect Isobel's chaotic anxieties: "Isobel laughed all the time her head was being shaved. She was saved saved saved" (BF, p.532).

A quotation from Charles Kingsley's *The Water Babies* about the very existence of these creatures is apt: "...if there were water-babies, somebody would have caught one at least..." (BF, p.171). Babies and water are re-emphasised: "There's a lot of references to the Water Babies who are drowned children, to Alice, to Beatrix Potter."[20] There are also associations, in the novel, of Tom, the chimney sweeper's transformation and eventual redemption and his obsession:

> Tom (alone on the heath) "Why, what a big place the world is!" Tom (alone in his delirium) "I must be clean. I must be clean" (BF, pp.334-335),

which operates strongly in Isobel's context. The motif is continued. A sequence of nursery rhyme selections in Chapter XIII manages to stress a forbidding world of childhood with threats and disasters only rarely relieved by any comfort:

> There was a mad man,/And he had a mad wife,/And/ they all lived in a mad lane!/They had three children all at a birth,/And they too were mad every one./The father was mad,/The mother was mad,/ The children all mad beside;/ And upon a mad horse they all of them got,/ And madly away did ride (BF, p.264).

Thomas has dedicated *Blown Figures* to her daughters and her women friends and also "To all the Alices, whatever you mothers called you" (BF, p.5). This is a dedication to the character of Alice created by Lewis Carroll. Isobel is obsessed with fairy tales and identifying with their characters admits her predicament to the fact that she has never been assertive as a person, but has modelled herself on the passive princess of a fairy tale, waiting for someone else to rescue her.

Isobel removes her "dirty, fear-soaked dress and a piece of white calico" (BF, p.522) wrapped around her in which she "began to glow, to tingle, to become electric as she felt the power of the god pass through the drum..." (BF, p.523). She feels the power of god also pass into the body of the priest. Isobel is revitalized by the ritual of atonement she undergoes. Isobel feels the need to shed her fear stained dress, which symbolizes her legacy from her family, her culture, and to search for the child which also means a search for her own self. She discards her gown in order to "shatter the established paradigms of dominance and submission associated with the hierarchy of gender and restore the primordial chaos of transvestism or genderlessness."[21] The last sight of her is visible as she plunges into the forest on the far side of the village healed in heart and mind.

> *Blown Figures* shows the ways in which as Michael Sprinker explains: every text is... a weaving together of what has already been produced elsewhere in discontinuous form; every subject, every author, every self is the articulation of an intersubjectivity structured within and around the discourses available to it at any moment in time.[22]

There are many allusions to Conrad's *Heart of Darkness*. Jason, like Kurtz, waits at home while Isobel penetrates deeper and deeper into the heart of Africa's darkness. Like Marlow, the narrator records the journey. She fears contamination: "That is the trouble now. How to rescue Isobel without touching her, without becoming oneself an Isobel" (BF, p.201). The physical symptoms of Isobel's suffering recall the oppressive physical intensity of *Heart of Darkness*, the sultry jungle with its central human body: "Sometimes she felt very small inside her body, a prisoner. Ran up and down the red-hung corridors, beat at the ivory gates, peered helplessly through the round windows" (BF, p.32). Marlow's phrase: "We live as we dream– alone"[23] dominates his narrative, emphasizing, human isolation and indetermination. This is also applicable in *Blown Figures*. Isobel exists in a dream state. She is alone and horror awaits her.

Blown Figures is a narrative of psychological stripping, a trip down a river toward some buried repression. The opening epigraph: "We have all Africa and her prodigies / Within us," (BF, p.9) is a quotation from Sir Thomas Browne's *Religio Medici* (1642). This quotation opens up a third frame of perception by implying that the metaphorical and hence literary nature of experience is the only reality language can express.

Odysseus's journey, like Marlow's and Kurtz's, is an archetypal male journey, whereas the patterns have been translated into female patterns in *Blown Figures*. This novel celebrates the female cycle, the woman's ability to reconstitute life. Pregnant women, eggs, holes, blood, etc., related to women dominate the text. Isobel's journey is not marked by destructive crises. She learns to celebrate the female cycle, the woman's ability to reconstitute life: "*Blown Figures* insists on certain cultural revisions that radically alter a phallocentric view of the universe."[24]

Blown Figures explicates Isobel's psychological condition. Her journey is laden with meaning. It presents a journey of silence and darkness. There are recurring references to abortions, miscarriages, dependency, eggs, blood, etc. Almost everything connected with woman's body documents the novel. *Blown Figures* "is an elaborate parody of birth" (BF, p.177). Here only women matter. Hidden parts of the female body, which seem to represent hidden or silenced stories, are exposed. Eggs focus attention on female generation. The red landscape not only reveals waste and loss but also suggests the life giving propensities of women's blood, "the redemption of just that blood so often castigated as unclean."[25] The various religious associations that coalesce around blood are consequently revised. Isobel's memories of the birth of her daughter, Mary, and of her embarrassment because of the blood-covered nightgown that betrayed her heavy bleeding indicate a beginning, a re-vision. Isobel learns to question her embarrassment: "Such rich red blood, so important to the beautiful child... The blood was a sign, an emblem" (BF, p.394). In the epics, in the Bible, in most of the world's literature, the shedding of blood is celebrated. In Thomas's female epic, the narrator reads blood differently: "Blood is offered, not wantonly spilled."[26]

At the outset of the novel, the narrator instructs to "Consider Isobel" (BF, p.11) a postulate or a fabrication. Moreover, the controlling arbitrary voice is apparent even in what Isobel does: "Once a child's wagon full of potted geraniums pulled by an unseen hand. (My hand, Isobel, my hand)" (BF, p.14). The narrator's random self-assurance recurs frequently in *Blown Figures*. Her control of Isobel's every move is declared fervently: "Ah Isobel, I who mould your head like a waterpot, how carefully I arranged you that hot September noon on the verandah deck of the H.M.S. *Pylades*" (BF, p.118).

The narrator's remarks are direct and participatory:

> I can do anything I want with Isobel. I can make her fat or thin, like a funhouse mirror. Give her an elegant back-she always wanted an elegant back-a lisp, a limp, a missing finger, a wart on the end of her nose, a lover, a husband, a dead child. Imagine her now... (BF, p.140).

Like Isobel, the narrator suffers a fear of madness: "Oh god, something has been put into my head to spoil it. How difficult it is becoming to concentrate on Isobel and her new friend Delilah – they have to complicate things ..." (BF, p.459).

Miss Miller's function in the novel is her role as fantasy dreamer. Miss Miller's dreams become part of Isobel's fantasies and dreams: "You're only a sort of thing in my dream, Miss Miller; you're only a sort of something in my dream" (BF, p.297). The narrator is not only the constructor of the story but also the critic of it. The narrator can analyze traditional female characterisation: "Why did you always feel as though you needed to be rescued.... All your life you have been as passive as a princess in a fairy tale" (BF, p.218). She can also criticize naive characterization: "We cannot wait for you forever, still running behind, breathless, a tiny school girl, your hand clutched to your side. Miss Miller and I have better things to do" (BF, p.159). But the novel also celebrates a female universe. The narrator serves the psychological function of a female dream censor and the rhetorical function of a female epic voice that extends Isobel's story from the idiosyncratic to the general: "Consider Isobel, leaning over the railing on the promenade" (BF, p.11), or "Now that Isobel has crossed the border, now that we have introduced her to the priests and walked by her side in the northern villages, it is not too difficult to bring her to the river" (BF, p.409).

Thomas comments about Miss Miller: "She's simply a reference point – a kind of old-fashioned confidante, someone the narrator talks to...."[27] The narrator occasionally confesses insecurity to Miss Miller: "The traveller who has returned from a journey may tell all he has seen, Miss Miller, but he can not explain all" (BF, p.94). Characteristic feelings of superiority are exercised against the unresponsive Miss Miller, who is called on to witness the chaos of consciousness: "So many memories, Miss Miller, things flow about so here" (BF, p.145), and hear the central notion of the tug of fate: "Once a man has stepped in the stream, Miss Miller, there is no more time to think of measuring its depth" (BF, p.157).

The narrator rhetorically seeks advice and also recognizes her mind at odds with itself: "Don't speak to me, Miss Miller. I am sure I shall split" (BF, p.190). Like Isobel, the narrator is concerned about her own ceremonial end and at times even sounds like her self-torturing subject: "Oh Miss Miller, no one went against me, I went against myself" (BF, p.342). She admits: "Ah Miss Miller, how can I tell? I am not of that country and was never there to see" (BF, p.322). Barbara Godard refers to Miss Miller as "a symbol of that analyzing and organizing force taking over Isobel's experience and turning it into narrative."[28] Miss Miller has no effect on the narrator. She is "merely a psychological projection."[29] The narrator's summoning of Miss Miller are direct reflections of her own madness. Miss Miller and Isobel become identified as one, a reason for much of Isobel's antagonism towards her: "I see you are a barren woman, Miss Miller. Take these leaves and perhaps you will conceive" (BF, p.538).

The burden that the character bears for the narrator is evident in "Ah. Isobel, how do you like belonging to another person's dream?" (BF, p.301) Audrey Thomas acknowledges: "The narrator is crazy."[30] This to a large extent justifies its perplexing organization, "more around images than along lines of narrative."[31]

Isobel's African memories frequently intrude upon her immediate consciousness. Thomas's definition of African novels, "the only kinds there are," is important here: "What I meant there was the sense of the other, the dark side of ourselves, the nightmare side of ourselves, where everything is too big, or too bright, or too beautiful, or too overwhelming."[32] Isobel's physical emptiness reflects the spiritual emptiness, transparency and mechanical quality of western humanity. Only Africa can revitalise and give peace to her spirit. Isobel's schizophrenia and madness align themselves with seeking African rituals of witchcraft, purification right, etc., as exorcism of past guilt and crimes related to her abortion and miscarriage. As she moves through the description of rituals, customs, burial rites, etc., Isobel becomes "completely mad at the end ...as it were, a witch."[33] The novel is a puzzle. Isobel reviews herself through African rituals. The blood that flows in *Blown Figures* creates a sort of blood bond. It evokes the real African primal cultural roots or origins of humanity that Isobel seeks.

The newspaper items scattered throughout the narrator's domain are ironic reminders to Isobel of the African world's imitation of her personal grief. These include a missing girl, a boy trapped by a wall, burial without a coffin, a child-theft, a piece on deception in male-female relationships, and a columnist's reflection on "a very thin dividing line between the inmates of our mental hospitals and those of us outside them" (BF, p.416). The narrator's selection of such tragedies as incongruities specifies Isobel's condition. The advertisements chosen from African newspapers are ironic directions to Isobel. Isobel is urged to "FEEL YOUNG AGAIN FAST" (BF, p.135). Her past is alive for her on this journey. A picture of two African boys: "They can always change clothes...but they wear their skin for a lifetime," (BF, p.186) suggests the deep rootedness of Isobel's problem. "Lorexane Head Lotion" (BF, p.235) points to the psychological source of her distress, less directly addressed by:

> De Witt's Kidney and Bladder Pills: WHEN LIFE SLOWS DOWN...Clean out your system, revitalize the blood...get back your health and strength... then enjoy life again (BF, p.419).

Isobel is also exposed to a number of advisory and reproving voices from newspapers. These include EI Mohr who interprets dreams, and Dolly who counsels on romantic and sexual matters. The letter to her: "I HAVE SEX WITH A BOY OF TEN" (BF, p.123) is a rude echo of Isobel's affair with a Dutch boy on the *Pylades*. "YOUR STAR TODAY" proffers direction for:

> LIBRA... Domestic and family problems will preoccupy most of you today SCORPIO...You may have to go on a short trip for your health's sake (BF, p.422).

Both signs are intimately of Isobel's condition. The various weather reports included by the narrator are another version of the prophetic assurance Isobel so earnestly seeks:

> YOUR WEATHER TODAY Mild harmattan conditions will prevail... except for local mist or fog patches it will remain fair... or showers are expected to break out...(BF, p.457).

Thomas has said her fiction is "very controlled... extremely structured although it might not seem to be when you pick it up and it falls all over the place."[34] *Blown Figures* has 547 pages. Only fewer than half of them are filled with lines. The rest are nearly blank pages, with some black marks on them or words and pictures. These may be single sentences uttered by Isobel Carpenter or African comic strips or African letters from the lovelorn or misremembered nursery rhymes or items of etymology. Regarding the title Thomas has said, "it just goes BOOM. That's why it's called *Blown Figures*. It just goes out."[35] Isobel is a figure blown by every wind of memory and psychosis. Her surname "Carpenter" signifies a joiner or maker. *Blown Figures* is an explicator's paradise or nightmare. Her return is "more likely to be neurotic, compulsive, fixated. Or it might be a deam."[36]

George Bowering comments on the title of *Blown Figures*:

> WHAT ARE FIGURES, and what is blown? There are fly-blown corpses, and corpses were once figures. Craftsmen blow figures in glass. If you don't have a good figure you'd better turn the light off if you want to be blown. Bad counters blow their figures. Poets who reach for effects blow their figures up fat. Some flute-players blow outlandish figures. Add your own....[37]

There are references in the novel to "Blown Figures" "dissolving... in the sunlight" (BF, p.227), and figures being "burnt to death" (BF, p.228) in bushfires, which infuses these created figures with the idea of violent disintegration and confirms their association with the grotesque, parodic and carnivalesque aspects of the text. Margaret Atwood praises Audrey Thomas that in *Blown Figures,* she "approaches the height of her powers," and "with each of her books, the reader feels that the next will not only be better but different in some unimaginable way."[38]

Blown Figures, with its blowing of figures, is a writing concerned with and aware of the inevitable shifting of identity in the slippage of the signified. Isobel's recognition of linguistic shift makes her aware of the always present "other" possibilities available on the paradigmatic chain as:

> Cild>child. My cild was killed. My child was chilled. In my womb, the cild-hama, the child curled like a shrimp or a sea horse and clung to the slippery decks (BF, p.82).

Robert Kroetsch suggests: "Violence, physical violence, proposes an ending....We must resist endings, violently. And so we turn from content to the container. It is the form itself, traditional form that forces resolution. In our most ambitious writing, we do violence to form."[39] The "ultimate violence that might be done to story is silence."[40] In *Blown Figurers,* blank pages or a single line comic strip, a newspaper clipping, a joke on the otherwise empty pages suggests this violence: "THOU HAST CLOTHED ME WITH SKIN AND FLESH AND HAST FENCED ME IN WITH BONES AND SINEWS" (BF, p.366).

Blown Figures is female text. The delusions and dreams it describes result from idiosyncratically female experiences, that is, miscarriage and an abortion. The consequent condensations and displacements are female both in imagery and in organization. Eggs, blood, womb like enclosures, bodies falling apart, people feeding on each other–all the images reflect the female body and describe a dominant female obsession. Told to a woman, by a woman, about a woman, the narrative attempts to open the hidden parts of the female body. Secrecy is transformed into confession, silence into speech, disconnected episodes into narrative. The male voice has disappeared in *Blown Figures*. The psychologically female experience is total through a woman's primeval imagination and dominated by delusions and dreams that speak the inner self. The novel is an exercise in the reading of the female body: "about the move from imagining the womb as a store, a cavity, a hump, a riddle, or a bleeding wound to imagining the womb as the transformative matrix of primordial change."[41]

ENDNOTES

1. Audrey Thomas, *Blown Figures* (Vancouver: Talonbooks, 1974), p.68. All subsequent references in parentheses belong to this edition of the text.
2. Elizabeth Komisar, "Audrey Thomas: A Review/Interview," review of *Blown Figures, Open Letter*, 3rd Series, No.3 (Late Fall, 1975), p.60.
3. Quoted by Lizbeth Goodman, Helen Small and Mary Jacobus, "Madwomen and attics: themes and issues in women's fiction," *Approaching Literature: Literature and Gender*, ed. Lizbeth Goodman, (Routledge: The Open University, 1996), p.115.
4. Phyllis Chesler, *Women and Madness* (New York: Avon, 1972), p.31.
5. Sandra Gilbert and Susan Gubar, *The Madwoman in the Attic: The Woman Writer and the Nineteenth–Century Literary Imagination* (New Haven: Yale University Press, 1979), p.73.
6. *Ibid.*, p.77.
7. Barbara Rigney, *Madness and Sexual Politics in the Feminist Novel* (Madison: University of Wisconsin Press, 1978), pp.126-127.
8. Sandra Gilbert and Susana Gubar (1979), *op. cit.*, p.16.
9. Lorna Irvine, *Sub/Version: Canadian Fictions by Women* (Toronto: ECW Press, 1986), p.62.
10. Louis K. MacKendrick, "A Peopled Labyrinth of Walls: Audrey Thomas' Blown Figures," John Moss ed., *Present Tense: A Critical Anthology, The Canadian Novel,* Vol.IV (Toronto: NC, 1985), p.174.
11. Caroline A. Soule, *The Pet of the Settlement: A Story of Prairie-Land* (Boston: A. Tompkins, 1860), p.195.
12. Margaret Atwood, *You Are Happy* (Toronto: Oxford University Press, 1974), p.68.
13. George Bowering, "The Site of Blood," review of *Blown Figures, Canadian Literature*, 65 (Summer, 1975), p.88.
14. Barbara Godard, "Dispossession," review of *Blown Figures*, 3rd Series *Open Letter*, No.5 (Summer, 1976), p.82.

15. Judith Gardiner, "On Female Identity and Writing by Women," *Critical Inquiry*, 8, No.2 (Winter, 1981), p.355.
16. John Moss, *A Reader's Guide to the Canadian Novel* (Toronto: MaClelland and Stewart, 1981), p.273.
17. Elizabeth Komisar (1975), *op. cit.*, p.61.
18. *Ibid.*, p.61.
19. George Bowering, "Snow Red: The Short Stories of Audrey Thomas," *Open Letter*, 3rd Series, No. 5(Summer, 1976), p.29.
20. Elizabeth Komisar (1975), op.cit, p.61.
21. Sandra Gilbert, "Costumes of the Mind," *Critical Inquiry* Vol.7, No.2, (Winter, 1980), p.416.
22. Michael Sprinker, "Fictions of the Self: The End of Autobiography," *Autobiography: Essays Theoretical and Critical*, ed. James Olney, (Princeton University Press, 1980), p.342.
23. Joseph Conrad, *"Heart of Darkness," Great Short Works of Joseph Conrad* (New York: Harper and Row, 1966), p.237.
24. Lorna Irvine (1986), *op. cit.*, p.65.
25. *Ibid.*, p.70.
26. *Ibid.*
27. Elizabeth Komisar (1975), *op. cit.*, 60.
28. Barbara Godard (1976), op.cit, p.82.
29. Louis K. MacKendrick (1985), *op. cit.*, p.172.
30. Elizabeth Komisar (1975), *op. cit.*, p.60.
31. George Bowering, "The Site of Blood," *Canadian Literature* (1975), *op. cit.*, p.88.
32. Pierre Coupey, Gladys Hindmarsh, Wendy Pickell, Bill Schermbrucker, "Interview/Audrey Thomas," *The Capilano Review*, No.7 (Spring, 1975), p.91.
33. Elizabeth Komisar (1975), *op. cit.*, 61.
34. *Ibid.*
35. George Bowering, "Songs and Wisdom: An Interview with Audrey Thomas," *Open Letter*, 4th Series, No.3 (Spring, 1979), p.9.
36. George Bowering, "The Site of Blood," *Canadian Literature* (1975), *op. cit.*, p.86.

37. *Ibid.*
38. Margaret Atwood, review of *Blown Figures, The New York Times Book Review*, (February 1, 1976), p.8.
39. Robert Kroetsch, "The Exploding Porcupine: Violence of Form in English –Canadian Fiction," *Open Letter*, 5th Series, 4 1983, p.57.
40. *Ibid.*, p.58.
41. Sandra Gilbert and Susan Gubar (1979), *op. cit.*, p.34.

Chapter 4

CREATOR AND ARTIST

SECTION –I

LATAKIA

"I want revenge. I'll get that bastard. I'll put him in a novel."

Audrey Thomas's heroines shift from one perspective to another, covering and recovering the same ground from varied angles, full of disparities, taking into account everything. Very often her protagonists are swinging in the deep engulfing swirls of light and darkness: "It is as though the exploration of one situation demands and calls into being the exploration of its opposite."[1] Ultimately, there is the emergence of the victorious self who may not be rebellious or militant but is capable of keeping freedom aloft and is more concerned about reflecting upon the relation between art and life: "An experience which seemed not at all memorable at that time...had been transformed into something curiously meaningful...and complete."[2]

Latakia depicts the portraits of a male artist and a female artist. The novel is in the form of letter, which Rachel, an established writer, writes to her absent lover Michael who is an unpublished writer. She describes him as the most fascinating man:

> tall, with a large eagle-like nose, a rich full beard and a mass of dark wavy hair...his eyes...oval and slightly slanted... He looked like Rasputin perhaps, or a young sheik.[3]

Rachel's letter, "the longest love letter in the world," (LAT, p.21) includes Michael's letters and dialogue along with the words of many other characters.

Rachel is a divorcee. She has three young school going daughters. She meets Michael, an upcoming novelist, at a graduate seminar conducted on the only afternoon of the week she spent away from her children. Rachel is "powerfully attracted" (LAT, p.34) towards Michael. She has already published her four novels and is working on a new one. She admits before meeting him she "lived in a house full of friends and children and was admired and doing good work," but still felt lonely: "... my body was very, very lonely" (LAT, p.20). "The attraction between Rachel and Michael is less their shared interest in literature than their sexual compatibility."[4] At this moment of isolation ""Just sex" can be a pretty big thing" (LAT, p.20). Rachel muses about their relationship, which relieves the loneliness of divorce and restores her sexual confidence: "When you touched me, my flesh smoked..." (LAT, p.24). However, this angers her children and blocks her writing. Michael, "bored and restless" (LAT, p.20) with Hester after seven years of marriage, enjoys this relationship.So this chance meeting turns out to be a good escape for both of them.

To write, Michael and Rachel travel by boat around the Mediterranean. They stop off in Latakia, the Syrian port. Here the crisis occurs when their roles as writers/lovers get confused. Rachel feels abandoned when Michael goes back to join his wife at Dar-e-Salam. Rachel suffers. *Latakia* explores "the male-female struggle."[5] Rachel writes to him of her experiences in his company for two years. She also narrates the turmoil in her mind between Rachel the woman, and Rachel the artist. Rachel's focus is on the imagined presence of Michael. She writes from her secluded rooftop in

Crete and endeavours to capture the look, feeling, sound, taste and scent of the place.

Rachel writes in the present observing herself, her past, Michael, the people who were on the boat with her and Michael ; the violence of people and systems in Latakia, her present, Heleni the village woman, the people in the square, in the stores, and on the beach. "Rachel's ultimate romance is with her *self,* her female-defined identity, and not with Michael nor with the patriarchal world that he represents."[6] Earlier divorced from her husband and now abandoned by her lover, Rachel momentarily thinks of herself as an "Invalidi...crippled (or wounded) by war and by work" (LAT, p.99), for whom seats are reserved in the trains and the buses of Rome and Naples. Rachel, at the end of the novel, joyfully waiting for the arrival of her friend Robert and her three daughters rededicates herself to writing. She decides to "enjoy this rare spaciousness and keep on observing ... keep on going and try to make "progress"" (LAT, pp.171-172). She knows a true artist/mother takes "a whole lifetime to learn how to live, and then...another one to put it all into practice" (LAT, p.172).

Michael's relation with Rachel's daughters is quite indifferent: "My daughters did not like you.... They thought you were loud and noisy and aggressive" (LAT, p.23). The daughters enjoy good relationship with their father whom they visit during vacation. Michael is "jealous and resentful" (LAT, p.118). He plays the part of sibling rival rather than supportive father to Rachel's daughters.

> And I... began to apologize. No wonder my daughters stared at me contemptuously... you certainly stirred up our quiet, essentially female life... (LAT, p.85).

The initial "intense electric glare" of their attraction is replaced by "long dark shadows," both of which serve only to "eclipse" Rachel's sensibility and blot "everything else out" (LAT, p.21) so that she can see nothing but Michael.

Rachel realizes she has become the battleground for an exhausting struggle between her children, her lover and her writing:

> I was to adjust myself to you in every way....The children felt I neglected them for *you*....I were being torn apart by all of you. I was never allowed any privacy or solitude (LAT, p.24).

The egotistical, immature, and competitive Michael has never experienced the divided attention that goes with being a parent. He therefore expects her to be "always free to sit down and have a long talk about literature or life... always free to retreat to the bedroom and make love" (LAT, p.22). Rachel is mature and realistic. She sums up the multiple and contradictory roles he needs her to perform:

> You wanted me to be your *soror mystica,* you mystical sister, who would talk art all day and make love all night and miraculously still find time to do the housework and cook your dinners (LAT, p.39).

When Rachel would give vent to her fatigue and frustration and ask for help: "Even geniuses sometimes clean bathrooms," he would storm out of the house, acting as if her demands are totally unreasonable and calling her a "fucking bitch" (LAT, p.41). He is "not interested in anything or anyone who ties him to some kind of responsibility" (LAT, p.86). She finds him "a complex person... a paradox" (LAT, p.138).

Michael appreciates the financial benefits of a partner who brings in money, but still needs the security of the old domestic arrangement: ""look up to" men, to be the "little woman"" (LAT, p.137). Michael's definition of a wife is "someone who is always there when you need her." Rachel disagrees, ""No," ... "that's the mother of a child under five"" (LAT, p.39). She longs for empathy and not the old style of merging and submission for woman. Moreover, Rachel's success as a writer (her fifth book is about to be published) threatens Michael on both professional and personal levels: "...you came to believe that anything nice which happened to me somehow lessened you in the world's eyes" (LAT, pp.108-109). His work is unknown, while Rachel criss-crosses Canada on speaking engagements. He resents that she neither takes her identity from him nor sacrifices her art for love of him. He wants her to "be defined in terms of man, as his other."[7] Rachel realizes: "I want both (love and art), but I can't give up the second for the first" (LAT, p.73).

Hester, "very small and slim, with long brown hair...friendly, but rather shy," (LAT, p.84) is an artist, who has neglected her career as a painter to give Michael her full attention. She is "the perfect wife" for Michael: "There is absolutely no doubt in her mind that you will succeed, that the fame and recognition you deserve will, of necessity, be yours" (LAT, p.73). She is happy to bask in reflected glory as "Wife of the rising young novelist" (LAT, p.40). Michael desires to be mothered, a role which Rachel rejects but to a certain extent Hester fulfils: "She is the wife as mother... all her maternal instincts can be directed towards you" (LAT, p.73). She fulfils the mother/servant function of the domestic woman, earning the debasing epithet of "dog-wife" (LAT, p.86) from Rachel:

I once heard a friend who was having a hard time with the man she loved, say to him, "I just want to follow you around like a dog" (LAT, p.109).

In *Latakia,* Rachel and Hester are chained by Michael. However, Rachel is able to free herself when she rejects Michael and transforms her defeat into victory by writing, and Hester chains Michael when he finally returns to her in Africa.

Rachel is enraged at the spectacle of Hester responding, like a mindless and obedient pet, to every whim of Michael. *Latakia* weaves "a tragedy about a man who loved two women" (LAT, p.65). Michael has to choose not merely between two women but two ways of life and two ways of relating to a woman. This is a choice he briefly avoids in their short-lived "ménage a trois" (LAT, p.18). The short-term "ménage a trois" arrangement: "Hester's his wife."... "I suppose I'm his girlfriend," (LAT, p.158) reveals Michael's desire to have "two separate bank accounts, both of which he wanted to keep open" (LAT, p.25). The "ménage a trois" puts severe strain on the two women. Rachel is aware of her embarrassment: "For I had been a Hester too and I knew what it was to be left, and to lie alone" (LAT, p.46).

The jealousy and insecurity of a writer still working on his first novel is seen in Michael's arrogant rationalization of his inability to relate professionally: "I have to be the most magnificent creature around. Not very nice... but there it is. I can't be with you, Rachel, because you're too fucking great." adding in parenthesis, "(That's your cross, Rachel)" (LAT, p.40). It is finally Michael's attitude towards art and life that causes Rachel the greatest disillusion, as she says:

> Michael, you cannot stand to look at pain, sickness, death, decay or failure. But isn't it only when we become aware of our mortality that we begin to create anything good (LAT, p.118).

She understands that the artist's role is to look at this chaos and organize it. However, Michael cannot afford to recognize mortality. He wants himself immortalized instead in snapshots that reinforce mythic equations of "you and me and Calypso and Odysseus" (LAT, p.46).

Rachel deconstructs the selfishness, egocentricity, individualism and combative competitiveness of the male artist. She rejects that relationship as "the PROBLEM," which led to an "awful eclipse" of her artistic sensibility: "I can't afford that kind of involvement" (LAT, p.21). She writes to her fellow writer and former lover Michael: "The "point" was to be personal growth, the expansion of the soul of the artist. You were a great fan of Stephan Daedalus. You loved me for my "life experience"" (LAT, p.66). Yet she admits, "it was precisely the result of that life experience that you hated so much: my children, my books (the fact of their publication)" (LAT, p.152). Rachel after masquerading "into a dress that was both too small and not my style" is back again in "my own comfortable clothes" (LAT, p.21) on the rooftop of her apartment in Crete. Her daughters visit their father after spending a tumultuous year of "tears and slammed doors" (LAT, p.23) with Michael and Rachel.

Rachel breaks out of her stasis after Michael leaves her alone in Crete. She begins to experience and observe life not just through her mind, but through her body, which makes her "buzz... with impressions" that she absorbs: "All of my senses are peeled – not just my eyes" (LAT, pp.25-26). The narrator is herself a writer in *Latakia* so the story draws attention to the ways a woman can write about herself and her feelings.

She enjoys her solitude in a Cretan village: "I have all the time in the world..." However, she looks back on the past to "wonder how I ever got into this mess" (LAT, p.17). She writes, "The book I am working on now is about you and me (of course)—or it started out that way" (LAT, p.30). The story of Rachel and Michael's relationship is also the story about "writing novels or trying to write them."[8]

In the process of writing this letter or "imaginary monologue" (LAT, pp.120-121), Rachel remembers the story of their personal and professional relationship from a feminist perspective. Her letter is prompted by an aerogramme she receives from Michael, after a lapse of four months, which says "GREETINGS," and has below it "a picture of a snarling leopard." Submerged in the beauty of the Grecian landscape and her memories, together with a "basket full" (LAT, p.16) of Michael's early letters from Greece and Africa, Rachel prepares "to re-read them just once more and then rid of them" (LAT, p.58).

Rachel gets up early to take "notes about the way the morning spreads down over the hill across the way, coats the hill with honey- coloured light, finally hits the houses" (LAT, p.38). Rachel struggles to capture the sounds, sights and smells of the Cretan village "with tools as worn as words" (LAT, p.60). She wants "to capture the sound of Heleni's loom" (LAT, p.30); the sight of the black clad widows "against their white stone wall" (LAT, p.60); the "Magic Boat" disappearing "through that gap in the horizon"(LAT, p.30); the smell of "the exotic fruit; the fishmonger with his white knitted cumberbund and a scarlet hibiscus flower behind his ear" (LAT, p.61); the "amazing… nameless blue" (LAT, p.99) of the sea, sky and above all "the light, the light, the light. It is like living in a diamond" (LAT, p.61). Rachel proceeds through poetic prose that comes closest to painting in words her perception of the landscape.

Rachel having "always longed to be a painter" (LAT, p.60) desires to record directly the "sensuous intoxication" (LAT, p.26) of impressions. However, she feels writing maintains a great distance between the outside world, particularly her social context, and her representation of it:

> I want a palette, not a pen. I have to say that such and such is "like" something else- I have to take the long way around when what I *really* want to do is dip my brush directly into the ocean, the sky, the sun, the eye of Heleni's donkey, the dark beard of the priest, and transfer it all to canvas.... It is like, it is like – *what* precisely is it like? I pace my study in frustration (LAT, p.61).

Rachel, feels "like one of those Impressionist painters who cheerfully sacrificed the subject, as subject, to a study of the changing effects of light," but soon realizes that the impressionist technique she verbally simulates does not decrease the distance between art and life:

> "Lovers in a landscape perhaps, but the lovers are just part of the landscape – they are shape, tone, movement (or lack of it), not STORY. The trees and rocks are just as important" (LAT, p.30).

Rachel's awakening artistic consciousness intuits the importance of people as well as environment:

> It is not just the beauty of the landscape, but the living, breathing people there, the animation of the sounds, smells, and sights that she wants to transpose into her writing, where mere verbal/visual mimetic capabilities can never suffice. [9]

Rachel observes the Cretan ladies sense of community expand outward to include her as a "mother." She is invited and does participate in their gossip and spinning. She writes:

> All the houses are joined to one another, just as all the lives appear to be joined. There are no secrets. Each woman's joy and sorrow belongs to all the rest.

Rachel understands that the "collective consciousness" (LAT, p.55) of the village will inevitably be changed by the advent of modernization and urbanization.

Rachel "passing through lives of the people on this street" in Crete, and seeing herself as a "faded snapshot" accepts change/ death. She is content to be "In their great tapestry... just one small stitch" (LAT, p.68), as she weaves them into her writing: "seeking to dislodge absences by presence through memory, and the "heteroglossia" of voices."[10]

Rachel's "vision recognizes the inevitability of change, names it through juxtaposing past/present, mortality/ immortality, youth/age, birth/death."[11] Rachel seeing "a curious shape the plastic baby baths" in the market, "like coffins," tries to remember where else she had seen them and recollects they were shaped "exactly the same shape as the ancient sarcophagi in the Herakleion Museum." Her insightful "connection between the stone coffins and the plastic baths is fantastic" (LAT, p.68).

Rachel tells Michael: "But it is not for you I must write. It is for those who *haven't* been." For them she has tried to be "artist as transporter... artist as magic carpet..." (LAT, p.61). She through her art organizes the chaos of the contradictions of human relationships, its joys and pains. She knows art is "all done with mirrors, it's all illusion." While aware of the importance of craft, she distances herself from Michael's abstract, impersonal "arrangements," and strong "critical awareness" as well as his imposing form on "material" (LAT, p.124). Her art is spontaneous:

> A reconstructive vision that seeks connections, affiliations, expanding outward, returning each time to the self before re-newing its spiralling path.[12]

Through her perspective, she attempts to make Michael "believe in the Emperor's New Clothes (LAT, p.124). She is successful in renaming herself as artist with the confidence of her own perception.

Rachel reminds Michael of a "curious conversation" they had earlier "about the difference between male and female novelists... men tended to set their stories clearly in an historical framework of fairly large proportions, whereas women did not" (LAT, p.133). Thomas explores some of the perceived differences between men's and women's writing through Rachel. Rachel suggests that for Michael, "writing is an intellectual exercise," while she writes with her "whole body" (LAT, p.124).

Rachel is an isolated woman "not only by gender, but also by occupation."[13] She replicates Thomas's view that a writer is "a diver in one of those old-fashioned diving bells, both in and apart from everything in the universe around me."[14] She as a writer cannot join the ladies because of the different perspectives she and the local woman have on the spaces they occupy. Rachel observes:

> The artist almost always lives in a Double Now. Therefore, it is not difficult for me to be up here on the roof, thinking of you, and still very much aware of the sound of Heleni's loom two doors down, and the noise of a motorbike coming down that last spiral before the village proper, and the moon slowly, surfacing behind the hill (LAT, p.58).

As Rachel watches Heleni's art, which is "obviously her great joy," as also a "great escape" from domesticity, she reads the secret of "peace and contentment" that seemed to transform Heleni in her total involvement in her work: "One uses one's whole body at these large looms" (LAT, p.55). Rachel recognizes that a true artist has to strive to have an "intuitive" approach to art, and like a "tightrope walker" do his "thinking" with "his feet, his body" (LAT, p.124).

Joining Heleni in hanging laundry and looking at the photographs she writes, "Reluctantly, I returned to my writing for a while and then went down and sat in the street with all the ladies." This leap from domestic space to artistic space and back to domestic space is followed in the novel by her explicit comparison of social activity and writing: "there's Crete and this village and this street and all that seems much more interesting than the story of how I fell in love with you" (LAT, p.30).

The scenes in *Latakia* take place in domestic locales or public areas. Discussing the Cretan village where she lives, Rachel notes that she has "never been to a watering spot before" (LAT, p.15). She, however, does mention going alone to the local bars to sip ouzo early in the morning. The fact that she enjoys a privileged position in society further alienates her from the ladies group. The two urges in Rachel one for independence and the other for attachment are in conflict. In the end, writing fiction changes from revision to revenge. It is the triumph of her independence over attachment to Michael. Rachel is head and shoulders above these illiterate village women who are performing such domestic tasks as washing children, "spinning or embroidering or winding enormous skeins of wool around their hands" (LAT, p.55). Domestic images and events associated with the female such as weaving, food preparation, and pregnancy are highlighted in *Latakia*:

> The blonde woman comes out of her house and puts my hand on her enormous belly, so that I can feel the baby kick (LAT, p.30).

Rachel's hidden desire to be pregnant for the fourth time: "I would have had your son, Michael-even a son named Minos or a daughter named Ariadne," (LAT, p.105) shows the creative urge in her. In Greek mythology, Minos was the king of Crete. He ordered Daedalus to build the labyrinth. Ariadne was the daughter of Minos and Passiphae. She gave Theseus the thread by which he escaped from labyrinth. Both these names are associated with labyrinth. Rachel believes the birth of a child might take her out of the labyrinth created around her by Michael. As a writer she gets immense satisfaction on finishing a book. Novels are her mental children. She tries to strike a balance between her creative urge as a writer and her creative urge as a woman. Here Thomas again hits back at the idea expressed by radical feminists that motherhood deprives a woman of her creative powers.

Michael wants a traditional wife at home: "loyal and helpful to whom you can dedicate your books," or "to whom you could look back on in old age" (LAT, p.42), and a beloved outside to cater to his psychological necessity of adultery:

> A hopeless, doomed, star-crossed, passionate AFFAIR.... "This way, we can love each other forever." Ah yes, from a distance!

He escapes all kinds of responsibilities of family, that is, earning a livelihood, or even washing dishes when his turn comes: "Affairs have nothing to do with washing up or toilets or making beds" (LAT, p.87). However, he does return well in time to eat, drink and sleep. *Latakia* gives an "'authentic exposure' of man from the feministic angle."[15]

Rachel quarrels with Michael about his negative attitude. Hester is a traditional woman, who willingly subordinates her creative urge to her role as Michael's wife during the seven years of their marriage. Rachel is a more cautious woman who visualizes: "No threat as a writer" (LAT, p.147) from Michael. Michael continues to enjoy life with both the women: "he's so openly exploiting us and enjoying..."(LAT, p.159). Yet both the women cannot sign him off! They reach a mutual understanding through a peculiar feminine perception:

> There would be no "losers." Hester and I both loved you; we *could* learn to love one another (LAT, p.139).

Though convinced that Michael is an emotional as well as economical parasite on their nerves, Rachel and Hester cling to him as a prize possession, but condemn the Greek expression for woman as the "stupid bird" (LAT, p.88). Hester accepts:

> It's always better in a marriage for the husband to be smarter than the wife (LAT, p.91).

Michael is unable to decide which relationship to discontinue, whether to swing between the two or to continue with both in a kind of "menage a trois." The tragic aspect of the affair is that in all the three situations he is crying. When he sleeps with his wife, he imagines her to be Rachel. When he is with Rachel he pines for Hester. ""I love you, mind *and* body," you said once, "but Hester was a better companion"" (LAT, p.24). He wants one to behave as the other and when he has both of them together in the same bedroom, his egotism refuses to permit him to sleep on the floor while the two women have their beds:

> "...I don't know about this business of being down here on the floor with you two ladies on beds up above me" (LAT, p.139).

For Michael, the woman is "the other," a land of his unfulfilled desires. She is a territory to be explored according to the impulse and fancy of man. Audrey Thomas gives a dramatic representation of the situation by making comparison between the North American Indian and man the explorer. Rachel tells:

> "The trick is to get outside one's own environment. The North American Indians, many of them, knew this. See the young braves riding ponies out into the desert—they can't go home again until they've had a vision." Well, my dear, you really rode your pony out into "the Other," - me, as well as Greece and Africa. It seems to me that you found it all too scary, too demanding, but I may be doing you an injustice. You do not clearly explain what your particular "vision" has been, but I do agree about getting out of one's own environment from time to time, whether the environment in question is emotional or "real." One doesn't *have* to leave home, of course (LAT, p.80).

Rachel understands that her relationship with Michael is more of a pact, a convenience than an understanding:

> It's like the bird who lives on the back of the hippopotamus or the one that cleans the crocodile's teeth. Such intimacies are allowed because they are mutually beneficial... these birds know that they could be crushed or swallowed at any time (LAT, p.137).

Her "self is continually breaking with him, asserting independence," but "her body remains in subjection to him."[16] The fights between Rachel and Michael melt in a forge of passion, which holds Rachel in thrall: "You gave me back my confidence in myself as a sexual being..." (LAT, p.62).

Rachel is forced to carry out the duties assigned to woman in a male dominated society. She revolts, but her revolt is not total in the beginning. She knows Michael's hatred for cooking. She divides the cooking days amongst her daughters, herself and Michael to lessen his burden: "Your cooking day was Saturday because you had never really cooked before and your workload was easier on that day" (LAT, p.51). She has to bear his insults. On the ship, he wants her to move out of the room so that he can read

Hester's letter in privacy: "You suggested that I... go out to the lounge... you'd prefer to be alone for a little while" (LAT, pp.148-149). Rachel finds Michael "surly, quarrelsome" (LAT, p.63). She informs Michael that she is no longer content "Like the moon, our symbol... to bask in reflected light" (LAT, p.47).

Michael is an egotist. He takes woman to be a territory to be explored according to the impulse of man: "Prince Charming probably chose Cinderella because she was the only one who could do housework" (LAT, p.87). He does not want Hester to bear children. He wants to seek pleasure without sharing responsibility. In the absence of children, he desires Hester's all maternal love to be directed towards him. Michael like a free lovebird wants to have fun with both the women. Rachel highlights the supremacy of the male over the female:

> I really understood the politics of male chauvinism, the conscious (or often unconscious) use of power bestowed by genitals and the System (LAT, p.24).

In *Latakia,* "the subject of the novel is... the story of Rachel's struggle to *write* that story."[17] Rachel understands the difference in priorities between a man and a woman:

> A man's first love is never his woman, but his work. That is what he has been taught; that is how he defines himself (LAT, p.85).

Michael's gift to Rachel, in exchange for her services as female muse, lover, mother, is his valuable "presence," his "*definition....* The old cock and bull story" (LAT, p.39). Rachel calls herself a "Large Bleeding Martyr" (LAT, p.86), and acknowledges she "probably deserved everything (LAT, p.70). Rachel alone in Athens after Michael leaves her is "harassed, frightened, lonely." Her "octopus-need" still hankers for his "octopus-love" (LAT, p.103).

Michael "carries before him an exaggerated version of the nature and value of his manhood."[18] Rachel punctures his exaggerated sense of phallic power through her laughter and puns. She tells him:

> Go look at the snake goddess....Go think about the Pythoness or Athena – all the great female powers. In the beginning Europe had no gods, only goddesses... (LAT, p.48).

Rachel admits although "archaic and classical sculpture" have glorified "the male figure, there are quite a few stone ladies or goddesses around as well" (LAT, p.45). Rachel decentres male history by bringing alive the ordinary women in Crete, who rewrite the "history of the street..." which "is being spun, embroidered, wound by these same women." Her activity is like the weaving work of Cretan women who use their whole bodies at their large looms. They go on "talking talking talking" (LAT, p.55) while they work. Just as these women spin yarns, Rachel writes texts. Audrey Thomas through her protagonist makes an attempt to restore the goddess to her glorious position. *Latakia* "tries to "depedestalize" the man from his eminence and the "god" is replaced by "goddess" as a sweet revenge to turn the clock back."[19]

There are ample references to women in *Latakia*. In Rome, the tensions between ancient and new views of women are evident. Stamps from Vatican show a group of women sitting at the feet of Jesus, out of keeping with the celebrations for "International Women's Year.... 'Hail Mary, Blessed Art Thou Amongst Women'" (LAT, p.95). It is on the island of Crete that Rachel writes her book under the protection of "Woman as Guardian of Culture" (LAT, p.55).

Rachel cannot hide the woman in her. Her first lovemaking session with Michael remains fresh in her memory. Sometimes she wants to turn him out of her house but can't do so. Something from within stops her. During her visit to Athens, she misses Michael. While in Rome she has a feeling of resentment against him:

> You were always wanting me to take your picture in front of something historic or picturesque. Rarely did you offer to take mine (LAT, p.92).

This act of his makes her unhappy. It gives her the feeling that she does not occupy the centre place in his mind. She is on the margin-invisible, inarticulate and ineffective in his life. She is "Victimised intellectually, emotionally and physically" [20] by him.

Rachel feels jealous when Michael breaks the news of his going to Hester on her birthday. Rachel divorced her husband after fourteen years of marriage: "a part of me doesn't want a full-time husband at all... I had contracted my focus – a husband was no longer part of it. Then I fell in love with you..." (LAT, p.131). She shares with Michael not an emotional or spiritual relationship, but a purely physical one.

Hester understands the idea of living in a male dominated society. She accepts Michael's extramarital relations with Rachel. However, she does not want to lose him to her. She makes it clear that Rachel shall not bear Michael's child. She fears the birth of a child may strengthen the bond of love between them. Rachel pities Hester for her lack of understanding the nature of Michael:

> Except you. And you came back to him, good faithful dog-wife, as soon as he whistled. All kicks forgotten. All those cold nights outside (LAT, p.86).

Rachel's strength and her subordination is revealed when she admits she is the:

> "real villain (ess) of this piece. I pretended to be someone I was not... I could *never* have given you what you wanted, and every time you recognized this and were ready to leave, I would cry, "No, no, I'll be good. I'll try harder. I *can* make you happy." And it wasn't true. I wasn't good. I never tried harder. I didn't budge one inch.... I was not willing to be your Traditional Wife anymore than you were willing to be my Traditional Husband. All your final talk of responsibilities towards and commitments to Hester was nonsense: you missed her and would not live without her commitment and responsibility towards *you*....You talked

> a lot about "taking risks."... I think you take calculated risks; I think you make sure you cover your bets. So how did I get from me as villainess to you as villain? I'm not sure - you always did tease me about my logic. And it's so comfortable sitting here alone, drinking retsina and scolding (LAT, pp.131-32).

She, however, ends up proving Michael is the villain. Moreover, she refuses to be subordinated by him.

Rachel is not blind to the dangers marking her way. She announces to Michael, "I have a terrible time balancing all the demands made on me" (LAT, p.34) as mother, writer, teacher, and lover. She sees negation in the roles of nurturer of others and creator of works of art. An artist must "develop the selfishness necessary to pursue one's art, whatever happens" (LAT, p.47), whereas "real mothers weren't supposed to have obsessions like writing or separate identities" (LAT, p.51). Just as she did not cease to be a mother when she became a novelist, so she couldn't cease to be a mother and writer when she got divorced or when she became Michael's beloved. Rachel's stay with "Michael the egotist, the liar, the hypocrite, the coward," (LAT, p.35) makes her "really very strong" to "love someone and hate him at the same time" (LAT, p.44). She rejects Michael: "it's over, it's over" (LAT, p.98) to pursue her profession as a novelist and to spend more time with her daughters to establish a relaxed and conjugal atmosphere at home.

Latakia is a renowned port for exporting the narcotic and sedative substance, tobacco. Rachel and Michael stay in Latakia before they separate. The episodes of the past and the full story of the relationship with her now departed lover are unfolded with the help of the "collage"[21] technique. Although frustrated Rachel is not torn apart. She transforms her split into creative response to experience, which is explained in terms of dress making. The "blouse" may seem beautiful to a layman, whereas the tailor would:

> turn it inside out... how badly it had been put together....A good seamstress... understands fabrics and darts and interfacing, can put together a blouse that is not only beautiful, but also well –made (LAT, pp.123-124).

Rachel emerges as a self-conscious writer and craftswoman. She finds her identity and purpose even at the cost of losing the two men she loves. Her relations with her ex-husband do not find much scope in the context of the novel: "I loved him; I bore his children. I depended on him for support. He got bored and walked away..." (LAT, p.132).

Rachel's choice of the letter format echoes Thomas's view: "You can write your book any damn way you want to as long as it works." [22] The letter is written to an absent lover and within the letter is space created for Michael's letters and dialogues. There is also Hester's voice, and also the voices of Cretan villagers. Michael's peevish assessment of Rachel's art "Your books are absolutely self-centered" (LAT, p.118) reflects Barbara Godard's review of Thomas's work: "The book is kept self-centred."[23] Her letter is a "Labyrinth: a maze, a place full of lanes and alleys" (LAT, p.160) in which it is possible to lose but also to find one's self. *Latakia* is made up of Rachel's letter to Michael, and Michael also writes to her, and receives letters from both Rachel and Hester. All this transcends through language:

> In the poste Restante, there is a pile of love letters for a guy called Karl Reicker. Practically every day another letter comes in. They are decorated with red heart-seals and little kisses. Obviously Karl is not where he is supposed to be.., (LAT, p.89).

Language functions not as a medium through which selves and intentions are channelled but as a "signifying system which exceeds all bounds of individual 'presence' and speech."[24]

Latakia is "filled with paradox, quips, and puns."[25] "All Cretans are liars" (LAT, p.29) called "the paradox of

Epimenides"[26] is used by Rachel in its strong form: ""Michael, I love you." It was a lie when I said it and yet as soon as I said it, it was true" (LAT, p.45). The protagonist is an artist within artist. Thomas tries to bring forth Rachel's hidden feminist qualities with the help of the Cretan paradox. Rachel defines the contradictions of her "bloody complicated" relationship with Michael by writing down the "irresolvable problem":

> I HATE YOU
> I LOVE YOU
> _ _ _ _ _ _ _ _ _ _ _ _ _ _ _
> EVERYTHING ABOVE THIS LINE IS TRUE (LAT, p.29).

The epigraph at the beginning of *Latakia*:

> When two vowels go walking.
> The first one does the talking (LAT, p.11)

shows the nonsense stemming from dichotomy of the statements. "The doubleness of language, both its inadequacy to net the complications of life and its necessity for human communication, runs like an obsession"[27] through *Latakia*. The metaphor of the labyrinth describes the structure of *Latakia*. Rachel is lost and found in the labyrinth of words and letters which is *Latakia*:

> sometimes the voices are simply illustrative; sometimes they are indications that some other mazewalker recently, or years ago, arrived by other paths at the same juncture. Sometimes the voices concur; often they dispute with us about the path to take. There are always echoes in the maze.[28]

Many voices speak in the labyrinth of *Latakia*. There are the echoes from other pieces of Thomas's writing – the "Horizontal Woman" from *Mrs. Blood* (LAT, p.32), and bits of the Africa of *Blown Figures*. There are the echoes of Michael's words to Rachel, Rachel's words to Michael, Michael's words to Hester, and Hester's words to Michael and Rachel.

Latakia becomes a type of epic letter. It is a long narrative based on myths and cultures. The voyage by sea connects with similar voyages in other epics like *Odyssey* and romances like *The Tempest* and *A Winter's Tale*. Like *The Tempest* and *A Winter's Tale, Latakia* involves travel to a land where the distinction between reality and unreality becomes vague. Michael is the grand patriarchal hero Poseidon, the ancient Greek god of the sea, with the power to cause earthquakes. Rachel turns Michael's grandiose heroics and catalogued Olympian mythology into farce: "The guardians of the underworld have become an old man and an old woman sitting in a public lavatory beneath the city" (LAT, pp.112-13). Rachel through her long letter attempts to dislodge the god from his majestic Olympia dwelling.

One night on shipboard, Rachel reminds Michael of the classical myth:

> Odysseus rejected immortality with Calypso in order to return home. Was he not saying what you have said? "I have to be the centre of attention." I've often wondered, considering I was trying to hang onto you, why I chose to tell you that particular tale. I guess I was all along telling you to go back to Ithaca and chaste Penelope (LAT, p.148)

Odysseus, the adventurous hero of *Odyssey*, took ten long years to return home to Ithaca after the Trojan war. Calypso, a sea nymph, detained him on the island of Ogygia for seven years. His wife Penelope remained faithful to him during his long absence and prayed for his safe return. Rachel compares herself to Calypso, Hester to Penelope, and Michael to Odysseus. She takes Michael's return to Hester in the right perspective: "Your success-or failure- is not going to affect my life either way" (LAT, p.147). Her desire to tell the story is "a gesture of longing to recover the past in such a way that one experiences both a sense of reunion and a sense of release."[29]

While thinking about Michael and the trip to Greece and Latakia, Rachel slightly misquotes a line from Spenser's

The Faerie Queene: ""Let Grill be Grill." .... "And keep his swinish ways"" (LAT, p.101), and exposes an interesting problem. She is a contemporary female novelist, but all she can think of is an excerpt from a sixteenth century male work in which all the female characters are either weak, nonexistent, and beautiful like Una, or strong and independent, but given demonical souls and mutated bodies.

Rachel moves beyond the:

> male linguistic and literary frame work to create a linguistics and structure that, if not female-oriented, is at least conscious of her position as a woman and does not convolute feminine mythology.[30]

She rejects male belief and definition of women poetically enshrined in Byron's "Love to a man, `tis but a thing apart. `Tis woman's whole existence" (LAT, p.73).

The last line of Rachel's letter is an altered version of a Spanish proverb about living with failed romance: "The best revenge is living well."[31] In an interview, Thomas has spoken about her being impressed by Pablo Casalas's artistic vision:

> to the effect that it's important to be an artist, but the quality of the man or woman is important, too, the quality of their lives... you can't just create. You have to live.[32]

Art and life, living well and writing well, come together in Rachel's artistic perspective, tinged with the desire for connection, community, nurture, and reconstruction.

The canvas of the novel is very vast. Rachel travels from North America to the Mediterranean as far as Latakia in Syria, back westward to Crete, then to Athens where the lovers separate. She breaks the barriers of confining her novel to one country. *Latakia* is an international novel with the heroine travelling through different countries. This makes explicit that Thomas's most common metaphors for the problematic nature of languages is "travelling in foreign countries, adrift on the cross-cultural confusions and the multiple meanings of words."[33]

Rachel's fascination with words – her own words, Michael's words, the foreign words she hears in Syria, Greece and Crete show Thomas's love for language. Rachel realizes the futility of words while living in a foreign country as she cannot understand their language. Her crisis of despair over failures in communication occurs at Latakia where she is confused with indecipherable Arabic:

> "Oh, the whole question of language, of communication, its impossible. Why didn't we just stick to gestures and grunts." "I'm surprised at you, of all people." "Trying to make things clear. We invent alphabets and language systems in order to make things *clear*. ...Once you get beyond letters, into words, into emotions and ideas, it doesn't help at all." "That's nonsense." "Is it?" Nothing ever changes...And people who speak the same language don't even speak the same language. You. Me. All of us (LAT, p.171).

Rachel remembers her confusion on being confronted with the Arabic script written "in one direction." The early Greek scribes too determined the directions of their writing to suit spatial considerations. She saw the way the writing was going in "both directions." She equates it with her own situation:

> "Hello, Michael
> UOY ERA WOH" (LAT, p.170).

Her alienation and feeling of being lost is significantly equated to infants:

> A baby must feel like that when it first realizes sounds are being made...which he does not understand. I keep trying to remember what it was like.... I came close in Latakia (LAT, p.169).

The Syrian epiphany reveals to her the infant state out of which she is determined to grow.

Latakia signifies a "country of failure,"[34] a "successful telling of a failure in communication." [35] It is a place where Rachel's "crisis of despair over failures in communication"[36] occurs. Rachel seeks divorce after failure in communication with her husband. Another failure of communication pertains to Rachel and Michael's relationship. This failure helps Rachel to succeed in gaining her artistic vision, which manifests itself in her later writing.

Latakia, the place of revelation becomes a metaphor:

> Months later, all we had to do was say, "Latakia" and we'd both start to laugh hysterically....It became a private metaphor for any situation in which, for whatever reasons, you were in over your head. In the end, it became a metaphor for you and me (LAT, p.167).

It stands for the chaos and contradictions they experience in a foreign land, signifying not only their turbulent relationship but for Rachel also the chaos and contradictions of language and meaning through which they define and are defined.

In the end, Rachel writes: "The war is over between us and I wish you well" (LAT, p.147). The time of concluding her letter, corresponding with their situation, is "sun down. Moon up" (LAT, p.171). Rachel emerges from her Cretan experience alone and in full possession of her creative powers. Looking down from her rooftop, Rachel sees the sea beckoning "smooth and grey as a skating rink." Echoing Stephan Dedalus at the end of Joyce's *Portrait of the Artist as a Young man*, she writes:

> "Life calls. Goodbye, Michael, I love you, my dear. I'm going skating. And remember, the best revenge is writing well" (LAT, p.172).

Joyce had depicted his hero's ecstatic "Welcome, O Life"[37] just at the moment he runs away from everything he has ever known, Thomas looks forward to acceptance of her protagonist's words. The novel ends in metaphor with Rachel understanding that skating is not the same as swimming, just as writing is not the same as talking and making love.

She leaves her rooftop/tower to go down again into life. She has made a clear choice and there are no regrets:

> But the thing that interests *me,* the reason I'm sitting up here on this roof and writing ... is that, although I love you in some very real way, I do not miss you (LAT, p.21).

Latakia is the story of resistance and rebellion offered by a female against sexual power politics. Rachel attains emotional balance, endurance and maturity. She realizes that her own voice was drowned under the imposition of Michael's speech. But the revelation that writing is the best revenge registers a growth in the changing perception of Rachel "confirmed in her female-defined identity, in love with herself."[38]

ENDNOTES

1. G.R. Helbbard, *The Making of Shakespeare's Dramatic Poetry* (Toronto: University of Toronto Press, 1981), p.20.
2. Alice Munro, *Dance of the Happy Shades* (Toronto: Mc Graw-Hill Ryerson, 1968), pp.201-202.
3. Audrey Thomas, *Latakia* 1979; rpt. (Vancouver: Talonbooks, 1989), p.122. All subsequent references in parentheses belong to this edition of the text.
4. Wendy Keitner, "Real Mothers Don't Write Books: A Study of the Penelope – Calypso Motif in the Fiction of Audrey Thomas and Marian Engel," *Present Tense: A Critical Anthology*, ed. John Moss, *The Canadian Novel,* No. IV, (Toronto: NC Press Limited, 1985), p.197.
5. Ellen Quigley, "Characters and Strategies in Audrey Thomas's Feminist Fiction," *Essays on Canadian Writing,* No. 47 (Fall, 1992), p.46.
6. Ellen Quigley, "Redefining Unity and Dissolution in Latakia," *Essays on Canadian Writing,* No. 20 (Winter, 1980-81), p.202.
7. Jonathan Culler, *On Decontruction: Theory and Criticism after Structuralism* (Ithaca: Cornell University Press, 1982), p.166.
8. Coral Ann Howells, *Private and Fictional Words: Canadian Women Novelists of the 1970s and 1980s* (London: Methuen, 1987), p.145.
9. Krishna Sarbadhikary, *Dis-membering / Re-membering: Fictions of Audrey Thomas* (New Delhi: Books Plus, 1999), p.129.

10. *Ibid.*, p.133.
11. *Ibid.*
12. *Ibid.*, p.134.
13. Dennis Denisoff, "The Rare Space of the Female Artist: Impressionism in Audrey Thomas's 'Latakia,'" *Mosaic* 26, 4 (Fall, 1992), p.82.
14. Audrey Thomas, "Basmati Rice: An Essay About Words," *Canadian Literature* 100 (Spring, 1984), p.315.
15. Shyam Asnani, "Audrey Thomas' Latakia: Depedestalising Man," *Canadian Literature and Indian Literature: New Perspectives*, ed. A.G.Khan, (New Delhi: Creative Books, 1995), p.45.
16. Barbara Godard, *Audrey Thomas and Her Works* (Toronto: ECW Press, Year not given), p.61.
17. Pauline Butling, "The Cretan Paradox, or Where the Truth lies in Latakia," *Room of One's Own*, Vol.10, Nos.3 and 4 (March, 1986), p.108.
18. Suzanne Kehde, "Voices from the Margin: Bag ladies and Others," *Feminism, Bakhtin And the Dialogic*, eds. Bauer and McKinstry, (Albany, New York: State University of New York, 1991), p.31.
19. Shyam Asnani (1995), *op. cit.*, p.45.
20. Toril Moi, "Feminist, Female, Feminine," *The Feminist Reader: Essay in Gender and the Politics of Literary Criticism*, eds. Catherine Belsey and Jane Moore, (London: Macmillan Press Ltd., 1989), p.119.
21. Robyn Gillam, "Ideals and Lost Children: An Interview with Audrey Thomas," *Paragraph: The Canadian Fiction Review*, Vol.18, No.1 (Summer, 1996), p.6.
22. Eleanor Wachtel, An Interview with Audrey Thomas," *Room of One's Own*, Vol. 10, Nos. 3 & 4 (March, 1986), p.45.
23. Barbara Godard, review of *Latakia, The Fiddlehead*, No.126 (Summer, 1980), p.122.
24. Christopher Norris, *Deconstruction: Theory and Practice* (New York: Methuen, 1982), p.27
25. Ellen Quigley (1992), *op. cit.*, p.208.
26. Barbara Godard, *Audrey Thomas and Her Works*, *op. cit.*, p.59.
27. Coral Ann Howells (1987), *op. cit.*, p.145.
28. Shirley Neuman and Robert Wilson, *Labyrinths of Voice: Conversations with Robert Kroetsch* (Edmonton: NeWest, 1982), p.xi.

29. Bell Hooks, "Writing Autobiography," *FEMINISMS: An Anthology of Literary Theory and Criticism*, eds., Robyn R. Warhol and Diane Price Harndl, (USA: N.J. Rutgers University Press, 1996), p.1038.
30. Ellen Quigley, "Redefining Unity and Dissolution in Latakia" (1980-1981), *op. cit.*, p.217.
31. Ellen Snowdon, "Body/Language: Three Feminist Positions in Novels by Audrey Thomas," M.A.Thesis (University of Manitoba, 1994), p.77.
32. George Bowering, "Songs and Wisdom: An Interview with Audrey Thomas," *Open Letters* 4th Series, No.3 (Spring, 1979), p.25.
33. Barbara Godard, review of *Real Mothers, The Fiddlehead*, No.135. (January, 1983), p.111.
34. Barbara Godard, review of *Latakia* (1980), *op. cit.*, p.123.
35. Pauline Butling (1986), *op. cit.*, p.110.
36. Coral Ann Howells (1987), *op. cit.*, p.146.
37. James Joyce, *Portrait of the Artist as A Young Man*; 1916 rpt., (Markham, Ontario: Penguin Books, 1982), p.253.
38. Barbara Godard, *Audrey Thomas and Her Works, op. cit.*, p.15.

SECTION-II

INTERTIDAL LIFE

"Here we are: woman.
What are our lives to be
about? Who are we?
Domesticity, personal relations,
personal intimacies, stories…."

Intertidal Life focuses on the disintegration of the "happy family" of Alice and Peter Hoyle and their "three Misses Canada… ever so happy. Everybody said so."[1] The narrative is the emotional saga of Alice's inability to accept that after three children and fourteen years of stay together, her husband Peter sees their marriage as "gangrenous, incurable," and struggles to comprehend how "he could amputate it in one day" (IL, p.45).

Intertidal Life is divided into three sections. Section I begins with Alice "standing at the bottom of the government wharf... very early in the morning" (IL, p.3). She recollects, "Years ago, when they had first come" (IL, p.4) to this island and bought a house, which "looked like a broody white hen with a red comb.... The house had no foundation; it sat low... was suffering from rot..." (IL, p.19). However, Peter fixed it up.

Impressed by the scenic beauty of the island and its serene atmosphere, Alice decides to live there permanently. She suggests Peter to sell the house in town and put the money in a savings account. She promises to contribute to the family income from her writing. Peter doesn't agree to Rachel's suggestion and there grows an enormous distance between them: "Their relationship wasn't intense. There was neither intense love nor intense hate" (IL, p.36). They decide to stay separately after Peter admits before the children "Your mother and I can't relate to one another any more" (IL, p.28).

Anne-Marie, the common friend of Alice and Peter, is an "extremely beautiful, a real Grecian goddess" (IL, p.26). Peter falls for her. However, he keeps changing his female friends: "found another friend and then, eventually, Stella" (IL, p.42). Alice and Peter meet Stella a "small and olive–skinned" girl during their first visit to the island. Her brother Glenn was "a tall, very beautiful young man" with "a smooth, almost sexless face, "like an angel with grannie glasses"" (IL, p.54). Stella was visiting her father on the island after the death of her lover Robert in California. Stella introduces Alice to h[illegible] friend Trudl:

> She and Stella had been friends since high school a[illegible] Trudl had left her husband and was looking for a [illegible] the island (IL, p.60).

Trudl and Glenn fall in love. Stella introduces Harold to Alice who finds him "great....all energy and life," (IL, p.59) despite his deafness. Alice feels quite comfortable in the presence of Trudl and "wished that Peter didn't have to come out here. It would be nice to have some friends who were exclusively her own" (IL, p.61).

Peter comes across Raven and Selene on the wharf and brings them home. Selene and Raven are hippies encamped at Coon Bay. Raven the "bearded man with soft brown eyes... and... very few teeth... was only about twenty -five" (IL, p.33). They become very close to Alice and her daughters: "With Raven there the kids wouldn't worry if she were away for a considerable length of time" (IL, p.109). Raven has a daughter "about the same age as Flora" (IL, p.111). Alice missing Peter cannot resist Raven making love to her. Section I concludes with Alice, her daughters and her friends—Glenn, Harold, and Stella making preparations for the Christmas eve:

> They made a large anatomically correct snow man ...drunk on mulled wine, took turns pulling Flora and Christobel up and down the snowy ridge road..."(IL, p.127).

Section II begins with Alice alone in the house. The girls were in town to meet father, "Raven was back on Vancouver Island, Selene was in New York.... Stella and Harold had gone to Victoria. Trudl and Christobel and Glenn would probably not come out tonight, it was raining" (IL, p.133). Alice missing Peter wraps his "dressing grown around her shoulders" (IL, p.134). She laments Peter "was courting Penny" (IL, p.153). The time spent with her friends haunts Alice's memory. In their company, she found less [illegible]ne for writing. However, she "held on tightly to their [illegible]dship" to be *"all right"* (IL, p.164).

[illegible] the absence of Peter, Alice and the daughters come [illegible] On weekdays Anne got up early every morning, lit [illegible]n stove and made Alice a cup of coffee..." (IL, p.147). Section II ends with Alice remembering "all the good times" (IL, p.242) spent with Peter, children and friends: "...in spite of the ache, in spite of everything" (IL, p.102).

In section III, Anne and Hannah go to town for studies. Alice is left alone with her youngest daughter Flora. Both of them read fairy tales:

> "You're very nice," Flora said. "You're a bit fat, but you're funny and kind and an awfully good cook." "I have nice hair and nice skin," Alice said. "Don't forget that." "And a beautiful young daughter" (IL, p.261).

Alice and Flora "brought crab from the girl who sold fish and they made real mayonnaise" (IL, p.252). Alice while writing the novel and fulfilling her duties as a mother looks forward to the "fun" to be had in the coming winter when she and Flora plan to " write a spoof" (IL, p.272). "On the last morning," Alice put "Flora on the ferry ...stood waving, watching the ferry, until it disappeared" (IL, p.279). The novel ends with Alice being given anaesthesia:

> "Just relax," the anesthetist said, "take a deep breath."....The needle went in. "Now will you just count for me, backwards and from ten?" Alice in a last burst of naughtiness ...began signing "10" "9" "8" Her hand fell back on the trolley... "She's under now. Let's go" (IL, p.281).

Peter in the row boat with Flora tried to comfort her: ""Flora, would you care to row?" She nodded silently and, bracing their fishpoles beneath the seats, they carefully changed places" (IL, p.282).

Alice recollects her past experience, takes another critical look at marriage, the identities of wife and mother and explores the possibilities of friendship among women, which include her daughters. All this is reconstructed and remembered by Alice who is also a writer obsessed with language and its social, ideological, and individual contexts. Alice's sense of having failed to "live up to the ideal housewife or ideal mother or ideal lover" (IL, p.209) image required of a woman critique the unrealistic standards set for women by the patriarchal society. Nancy Wigston categorizes *Intertidal Life* as a "breakthrough"[2] in Audrey Thomas's literary career.

Her daughters are a great source of strength to Alice after her separation from Peter. Alice's relationship with her daughters is "the most positive relationship in the novel."[3] Flora becomes Alice's companion on the island after Hannah and Ann become less frequent visitors, because of the painful memories of their parents break up seven years ago. *Intertidal Life* becomes a metaphor for female life caught between the tides of attraction to the male. Alice and Flora spend the summer studying "seaweeds and intertidal creatures," (IL, p.12) looking at stars and the moon by night, sunbathing on the rocks by day, sometimes reading aloud Harlequin romances and laughing over the fairy tales of *"Nurse Prue in Ceylon"* (IL, p.11). They also end up studying through memory, the female creatures of that island. After her separation from Peter, Alice realizes she has failed to learn the necessary intertidal lesson of the limpet, who knows how to hang on "for dear life or limpet life" (IL, p.60).

Audrey Thomas's friend and publisher Bob Amussen's comment on *Intertidal Life* is interesting:

> what the book is, is a turned around Harlequin romance, inverted. It begins in a sense when all the happiness is over in the relationship between Peter and Alice.[4]

Flora's reading of the Harlequin romance confirms this: "They always end at the beginning of the 'real' marriage anyway, even if they've been married for ages. They always end when they both admit to one another that they're madly in love" (IL, p.261). Alice's romance begins as her marriage ends with Peter's acceptance of no love for her. Alice asks, ""Peter, do you love me?".... He sighed. "In your terms, I don't know. I just don't know anymore"" (IL, p.34).

In *Intertidal Life,* Thomas exposes the patriarchal myth of possession and installs in its place the true plot of the maternal romance, that is, the mother-daughter plot of bonding with each other. Alice and her daughter Flora note that the initially indifferent heroes, with their inevitable "Aquiline" or "hawlike" features get transformed by the tender nature and care of the heroines. Flora's Harlequin romance tale has a blind hero and Alice assures her: "He won't stay blind, you wait and see" (IL, p.13). Alice's uneasiness at her daughter getting addicted to "such nonsense" is abated by Flora's also reading "*Madame Bovary*." Alice feels it "is a good antidote" (IL, p.14), depicting as it does the sad end of a protagonist who mistakes the illusory romance for the real. Alice consoles herself with the fact that "*Madame Bovary*" (IL, p.11) is the tale of a woman whose reading of such romances brings about her death. Alice's own anti-romance becomes the place to put together the pieces of "jigsaw puzzles" of her broken romance as well as the "1,000 Interlocking Pieces" (IL, p.158) of her own self.

Sandra Gilbert and Susan Gubar point out that the plurality of stories which reflect the massive social transformations resulting from women's entry into the public sphere with "the stability of the biological fact of (female) maternity,"[5] come up against two interesting literary phenomena. One is the increasing impulse of women writers to "historicize and analyse"[6] the maternal experience and the institutionalization of motherhood. The second is the emergence of the "mother-writer in the mid twentieth century."[7]

In *The Madwoman in the Attic,* these writers dramatized the dilemma of the nineteenth century women writers through a discussion of the tale of Snow White. They argued that any kind of self-assertive action on the part of a maternal figure results in metamorphosis from good queen to wicked stepmother: "it is as if a good mother had died and been replaced by a wicked stepmother,"[8] so that the tale highlighted the "contradiction between socially prescribed characteristics of femininity... and the rebellious woman artist's desire for power and freedom...."[9]

This also points symbolically to the contradiction between biological maternity and aesthetic creativity. However, for contemporary twentieth century women the Snow White story has "an entirely different premise... women are no longer inexorably silenced and privatized by their culture."[10] There need not to be a murderous conflict between Snow White and her mother, and also "given that there are new ways for women to negotiate between procreativity and creativity,"[11] there need not necessarily be a split between the two functions.

Alice reads in the "book of rules," that at first, "the Queen is the Piece placed nearest the King" (IL, p.135). In the beginning, she is encouraged by Peter to write but later feels his jealousy and rejection. He accuses her of being too involved in her "bloody book" (IL, p.21). She finds new ways to negotiate between motherhood and writing without a necessary split between mother and artist, but with an unfortunate split between marriage and a career.

Alice looks back at the seven year period of separation from Peter in which she found "... no peace. Everything's in pieces" (IL, p.66). Alice wrote ""Lover".... Then drew a line across the L" (IL, p.137) to show that all was over between her and Peter. She heard "the "end" in "friend,"" and saw "the "rust" in "trust"" (IL, p.30). Alice asks, "Who can see the "other" in mother?" (IL, p.136) Her ambiguity towards her mother identity is brought out in her joined entry of etymological roots for *"Mother."* She explores its various origins from "a female parent" to a "hysterical passion" to the dual meaning of *"Mummy"* (IL. p.136). "Her verbal play underlines the erasure of women's specificity and complexity in limiting definition."[12] She is ""...Hannah's mummy." "This is Anne's mummy"- to make identification easier for the teacher. All wrapped up in her family" (IL, p.136).

Intertidal Life presents a portrait of the woman artist as mother and creator. For biological and social reasons women have had a different relationship to creation and to being an artist than men have. Alice wonders: "Can you imagine a man thinking, well, once I get married I can think about being a composer or a painter or whatever! Once I find the right woman" (IL, p.179). Women relate to the moon which determines their bodily rhythms as surely as it does the rhythms of the tides:

> Men are related to the sun. The sun never changes his shape. Sisters of the moon we are, shape shifters but oh so predictable in our shifting. We hold the waters of the world in our nets (IL, p.206).

Motherhood can also be an extension into creativity, as Alice illustrates through her writing: "Integration, connection, reaching out, a defence against drift... a way to relate, a way to write-this too is motherhood as seen by mothers."[13] Alice likens her interrupted writing to "trying to interrupt a pregnancy and then take it up again....I'm always scared the little creature will have died" (IL, p.107).

She nurtures her book as well as her daughters, "writing, writing, writing by candlelight so it won't disturb the children" (IL, p.31). Her response to her friends' query "Would you rather be with a man than writing your novel?" is an incurably romantic one, "I want the whole works! I want to be with a man...*and* be writing my novel." She wants enough time to write and to play with her children. She fantasizes "supper miraculously appear and the children instantly fall asleep," and a nanny who encourages her to stay out, "and then my man and I go off down the road in the moonlight to make love in the woods" (IL, p.179).

Alice sees no contradiction between heterosexual love and her maternal vision, which is inclusive of Peter and her children. She attributes the delimiting of her maternal identity to the father's laws. Alice talks of "Musical chairs" being played at the children's birthday celebrations in which "someone must always be left out," (IL, p.51) and usually it is the mother.

When Alice alludes to the "Immaculate Conception" being followed by "the maculate delivery" (IL, p.52), she seems to echo Kristeva's provocative question cited by Susan Rubin Suleiman: "After the Virgin (Mary), what do we know about the inner discourse of a mother?"[14] Kristeva too sees no contradiction of motherhood and creativity. She states that motherhood can by itself, or under favourable circumstances favour a certain feminine creation:

> To the extent that it lifts the fixations, makes passion circulate between life and death, self and other, culture and nature....[15]

Summarizing Kristeva's ideas, Suleiman says, "If to love (her child) is for a woman, the same thing as to write, we have in that conjunction a modern secular equivalent of the word made of 'flesh.'"[16]

Alice admits: "I think ... the minute I became a mother he was unable to love me any more. Romantically, I mean" (IL, p.154). Women as artists have a double role to perform. Here Alice is a mother as well as writer. She cannot sacrifice the female functions like pregnancy, giving birth, and mothering on the altar of writing. She admits Peter left her because her mother and writer roles took up most of her energies:

> Artists are never 'always there' and mothers generally put children before husbands (IL, p.161).

Alice does not have to write the book and deny the child "or love the child and postpone/ renounce the book."[17] She does both, while also transforming herself. For Alice, motherhood not only brings with it pain and responsibility but also yields power and gives strength: "Having children has made me strong-or strong enough" (IL, p.243).

Alice continues to develop and change, challenging Freud's dictum:

> There are no paths open to further development for a woman over thirty, who is physically fixed and drained in the effort of becoming a woman.[18]

Adulthood does not necessarily signify completion. Alice distances herself now from the crustaceans, crabs and barnacles that proceed to "build the shell of the adult form around their body" (IL, p.263), but finds affinity with the "very strange creatures" ...that "Grow back" the "lopped off" (IL, p.212) part of their bodies.

Household chores like soup making, woodcutting, fire stoking, garden planting etc., bring Alice and her daughters closer. Her continuing bonding with children and her developing, changing self, confirms:

> it isn't possible to split off mother and woman, to view one without viewing the effects of the other.[19]

Alice retains and values the connection while respecting her daughters and her own differences: "There's a lot of that Capital–M Mother in me" (IL, p.181). She acknowledges, but tries to be on guard.

Contemplating on whether "women whose cycle *did* correspond to the moon's, now, were more stable, or less," Alice observes, "the tides have a point where there's no perceptible rise or fall, a kind of still moment. There must be that in women too....That might be our most stable time if we could locate it precisely" (IL, p.194). She achieves stability as she learns to retain what is important, the maternal connection and power:

> to think of the power of our mothers have over us, no matter how old they are, no matter how old we are. The mother may have been reduced, through age, through time, to a

> tiny old lady who walks with sticks. But in our hearts, our psyches, she's still the giant shadow mother ... (IL, p.180-81).

Alice turns to other forms of relations out of choice, not by rejecting the maternal vision but reclaiming and re-forming it:

> The metaphor of the intertidal zone washed by the moon, controlled by the tides and warmed by the masculine sun, is an image of unity to which after much torment, Alice finally gives consent.[20]

The night Peter breaks the news about Anne-Marie to Alice, he demands nurturance without ties: "I can't make love to you anymore...but would you hold me tonight?" (IL, p.38) Alice does, but her own desire for care and comfort, the hope that "some Great Parent would swoop down....and tuck her into bed" (IL, p.123) cannot be got from the same individual. The "sun" for her is missing and she does learn to do without his warming. However, it does not lead to a total rejection of the male or denial of the desire for a sensitive, caring, heterosexual relationship:

> Raven came in....took off his clothes and came to bed. It had been weeks since any man had touched her with affection... (IL, p.113).

Moreover, a single incident of "strange communion" (IL, p.168) with Selene is also an outcome of her loneliness for Peter.

She concedes to Trudl that "it's natural to want to be loved," but affirms: "we can't make that our whole life, our whole reason for being" (IL, p.171). Towards the end of the novel, Alice though still loving Peter is able to resist the "dark pull of the man" (IL, p.218). She is able to forgive Peter but cannot forget him:

> "'I love you'.... Knowing she must not say, 'Please, I want you back'" (IL, p.83).

Unlike her female friends, she escapes his authority, "as though he controlled the tide," and is content to be "left behind on the shore" (IL, p.218) amidst a proliferation of the creatures of the intertidal pool which she and Flora study. Alice aligns herself with the element of nature, tends her garden with loving care, and watches it: "growing and swelling, changing color" (IL, p.212), and bonds with her daughters: "Each one could feel the others' presences in the night. Sorority. In the best sense" (IL, p.147).

The suggestion that woman can be possessed and then discarded is to be found in Alice's lack of any sense of exhilaration at the momentous event of man's setting foot on the moon. She is upset at the first moon landing at the thought of "a flag and a footprint... on the virgin moon" (IL, p.16). At a later stage, still struggling to get used to her separation from Peter, Alice and her female community take a look at women's complicity in their "conquered" status:

> Women have *let* men define them, taken their *names* even, with marriage, just like a conquered or newly settled region, *British* Columbia, *British* Guiana, *New* Orleans, *New* Jersey, *New* France, *New* England, etcetera (IL, p.171).

The female characters in the novel confront the problems and contradictions of modern womanhood. The "Moon-ladies" are shown to revolve around Peter:

> the sun, the hub, around which first Alice, then Anne-Marie, then Penny, now Stella and Trudl, revolved (IL, p.239).

Alice feels Peter was cleverly: "taking her friends away from her, gathering them in under his magician's cape...with his magic box of colors, his warm sympathetic voice... his strength..." (IL, p.218). However, it is women and the friendship of women which offer ways for Alice to deal with the crisis and to survive the "great tidal wave, a hurricane, of hatred" (IL, p.75) that engulfed her when Peter left her. Through her daughters and her female friends on the island, Alice learns about herself and about women in general.

From the initial state of dependence and weakness Alice learns slowly to move on, putting aside passion.

The island is an idyllic Eden, which has not only Adam (Peter) and Eve (Alice), but also three children (Hannah, Anne and Flora). Much of the narrative is devoted to Alice's relationships, especially with other people on the island. Alice, her daughters and a group of women friends move towards a new direction in interpersonal relations. Here the focus is on "women's relationships with other women" as well as their "relationships with men."[21] Alice sees them as:

> All Eve's sisters bobbing for apples. All connected like some vast archipelago. Herself. Selene. Stella. Trudl. The girl children. Connected by femaleness and by blood and by the moon. Yet can't do without Adam (IL, p.92).

She recalls the move to the island seven years ago as "a new beginning" to their marriage. This was a new beginning for Peter, but not with Alice "I guess what I saw as a sunrise, you saw as a sunset" (IL, p.20).

Alice's friends Anne-Marie, Selene, Raven and Trudl are each a foil for Alice's self-discovery. However, each of them is also "represented as a complex individual endowed with personal and social problems.[22] There is Stella, whose promiscuity does nothing to assuage her emptiness. For a while, Stella and Peter are lovers. There is Raven. Alice and Raven are occasional lovers. She does not want to establish a permanent relation with him. She is quite fond of Raven's friend Selene and Raven also loves Selene.

"Writing, in this, as in many women's novels, is overtly connected with pregnancy and birth."[23] Alice finds herself connected to her cat, Tabby. Both are associated with their offspring:

> Alice picked up her sleeping youngest whose cheeks were flushed from the fire...and padded off to bed mother – catlike, in her soft green dressing gown (IL, p.119).

She felt her condition was no better than Tabby. Like Tabby, she had her children alone:

> The night Hannah was born.... Alice wanted to talk to Peter but he didn't come. He had left at the ending of visiting hours even though she was already in labor. He had been holding her hand but as soon as the head sister rang the little bell out in the hall he dropped her little hand...kissed her forehead and went away (IL, pp.250-51).

Tabby and Alice are linked in *Intertidal Life* by sexual play on the word "pussy." "What a marvelous pussy you are/ you are/ What a beautiful pussy you are" (IL, p.32).

Alice recalls at a moment of personal crisis the words of the "Cheshire Cat-"we're all mad, or we wouldn't be here"" (IL, p.123). Alice is named after the heroine of *Alice in Wonderland* who faces trouble making sense of the new maleless world into which she has fallen. In this novel, Alice, mirror doubles herself between journal entries in the first person and a novella in the third person where Alice represents herself as she writes a story of abandonment.

Images of domesticity and Alice's maternal figure are present in the novel through her involvement in baking, cooking, as well as her writing from the kitchen table. *Intertidal Life* develops what Nina Baym refers as "closed and structured social space," frequently the home, which often contracts into even smaller spaces, "the room of her own that is the heroine's particular territory, identified with her self."[24] After three summers, Alice desires to "live there all the time, forever and ever" (IL, p.19). A shrewd Peter convinces Alice:

> "You have this fantasy about the simple life,".... "but complex people don't lead simple lives....Let's have a trial run. At the end of a year, if everybody's happy, we'll make it permanent."

He decides to "come over on Friday nights and go back Sundays" (IL, p.20). "Having installed the wife/mother in her domestic space, the father is free to walk away."[25]

Marriage is believed to be the destiny of a woman within a patriarchal culture. She is placed at a disadvantage when she signs the marriage contract which is "a mutual bet for gaining ascendancy in power, personal autonomy, and self-realization."[26] *Intertidal Life* is a novel about friendship and also about marriage-its rituals, its expectations and its disappointments. Alice and Peter look at life from different perspectives. Alice transcends the narrow confines of her individual self and desires to be an autonomous and independent writer. The attitude of a woman towards the institution of marriage is:

> to be explained and defined with reference to marriage whether she is frustrated, rebellious, or even indifferent in regard to that institution."[27]

It is through the projection of the marital problems of Alice and Peter that Thomas reprehends the actions of married people. For Alice, love means affection, respect and space whereas Peter led by passion hankers after glamour and a free lifestyle.

Alice leaves Flora to learn through her own experiences, hoping only for a happier future for her daughter:

How to prepare Flora? Not possible ....She may be hurt, but there is no way to stop that. Just try and make her strong. There are no rules. Each time it will be different... (IL, p.276).

The subtle hint of her "passing on the matrilineage"[28] occurs when during the sorting out and discarding of books and clothes, preparatory to Alice's departure, Flora asks for the taffeta evening dress that belonged to sixteen years old Alice: "Let me have it. I can use it for fancy dress even if styles don't change." "It's yours" (IL, p.278). Alice after putting Flora on the ferry sits alone, surrounded by her garden and her pets, affirming women's real and symbolic links with nature. She indulges in self-analysis:

> "I am a good woman".... "I let myself be persuaded that I wasn't that I was, in my personal relations anyway, a failure..." (IL, p.279).

The novel is divided into three sections, each preceded by an epigraph from *A Spanish Voyage To Vancouver,* which Alice has been reading since her stay in her island home. The selections all point to the early explorers preparations for their journey. The explorers' quest parallel's Alice's preparations for exploration of her failed romance of human relationships, and of her own creative abilities. Maritime imagery and language are used as she struggles to set in order her floating memories, "currents hot and cold, lagoons and clashing rocks" (IL, p.134), in her attempts to chart her journey of recovery from being "love amps" wandering around with her heart "permanently missing" (IL, p.242).

The exploration theme is also linked to that of creation, for Alice feels that the early ages of maritime discovery, which inspired the language of John Donne-that of maps, new lands, compasses, etc., are now finding their modern equivalent in her own writing about human relations: "what's happening to men and women today is just as exciting and terrifying as the discovery that the earth was round, not flat" (IL, p.171).

The background setting of the novel is the entire period of the 1960s and 1970s Hippy Culture which is subjected to a scathing attack by Thomas through Alice, for its passive, irresponsible lifestyle and its code of dope and sex. Alice finds she has little patience for Kahlil Gibran: "Give your hearts, but not into each other's keeping" (IL, p.274). Alice observes that Raven and Selene the "takers... did not care to change the world or make it better.... It was as though they had had the moral equivalent of a stroke" (IL, p.97). Their flabby or casual attitude offends her. Puns, verbal play or personal word associations are made part of the normal fabric of Alice's language. Peter is metamorphosed from

"Peter the Rock" to "Peter Pan" (IL, p.225). He is "One of the "lost boys"" (IL, p.92), with increasingly drug induced sexual appetite for younger women.

Alice's idea of "quest together" was "hand in hand," like Milton's Adam and Eve" (IL, p.141). Her rebellious thought that it was the "turn of women, now, to go out exploring" (IL, p.69) is followed by the practical difficulties and doubts involved: "One didn't bring along three kids, a lame dog and a spiteful cat" on a "true quest" (IL, p.141). Alice steps out of the male defined ideal wife/mother role, and as a writer subverts the romance through irony and intertextuality. Alice accepts her different fate. The epigraph to Section III of the novel:

> "We put out our oars, endeavouring with them to counteract the current, but alas the efforts of the sailors were in vain" (IL, p.245),

suggests a victory of the female moon and the power of her waters, the "intertidal life" force.

In bed, missing and desiring her absent husband, Alice offers: "*Pudendum*, n. (usu. in pl. *–da*)/ Privy parts –. (L. *pudere*, to be ashamed.)" (IL, p.80). What is remarkable is Alice "plays on words, the non-sense of sense, laughter."[29] Alice as writer is a modern female Adam. She is a namer "I could change my name to Alice Apple or Alice Blackberry..." (IL, p.39). Names are of obvious significance in *Intertidal Life*, both in their symbolic echoing and in their relation to things. Alice composes a list of "Household Words" made up of the names of people who had given their names to things:

> Lord Cardigan /Quisling /The Earl of Sandwich /L.Von Sacher Masoch/ The Marquis de Sade/ M.Guillotin /Mr. Condom (nationality unknown)/ Mr. Hoyle (IL, pp.146-147).

Alice is also interested in the etymology and variant meanings of words. "L. *volupt*-as, pleasure.-L. *volop*, adv. agreeably.-L.*vol*.-o, I wish" (IL, p.32). After marrying Peter she became "Mrs. Hoyle…A couple, a unit. I loved all that stuff" (IL, p.172), but her husband: "Peter Peter Pumpkin eater. Had a wife and couldn't keep her" (IL, p.70).

On being asked by Flora to give her the book, Alice asks, "Which one? *Madame Bovary* or *Nurse Prue in Ceylon*?" There is a pun on the word Prue when she says, "They'll have to change that one to *Nurse Sue in Sri Lanka*. (IL, p.11) because the name of Ceylon has been changed to Sri Lanka.

Edward Said expresses the opinion: "writing today is no longer seen as a single and unique inscribing. That image of writing gives way now to one of parallel script."[30] In *Intertidal Life,* the most extended source of intertextual reference is Margaret Atwood's *Life before Man.* Atwood's heroine Elizabeth, a mother of daughters plays on the word: ""*Mummy.*" A dried corpse in a gilded case. *Mum,* silent. *Mama,* short for mammary gland."[31] This is very close to Alice's extended play on the meanings and forms of mother and mummy:

> *Mummy* c.1. Body of human being or animal embalmed for burial; dried up body. 2. Pulpy substance or mass, esp. *beat* (thing) *to a–* .3. Rich brown pigment….Mummy^2, n. Mother (nursery form of MAMMA) (IL, p.136).

In *Life Before Man,* Elizabeth reads a child's riddle book that contains a saying which she relates to her sister's death by drowning and to her own possible demise. Alice too cites a riddle in her daughter's book: "Q. What does a Baby Ghost call his parents?" The reply is "Dead and Mummy" (IL, p.240). Thomas seems to have borrowed ideas about marriage, disintegration of human relations, how men cope with solitude and parental responsibility from Margaret Atwood's novel *Life Before Man.*

Intertidal Life can be described as metafictional novel. Alice Hoyle is a writer and the fabric of the text is made from the texts of the past. George Bowering's *Burning Water,* a novel with its metafictive concern for writing and exploring is always present in the background of *Intertidal Life*. The trunk label, "NOT WANTED ON VOYAGE" (IL, p.277) refers to Timothy Findley's novel of the same name. Another reference is to the biblical book of Daniel 'MENE, MENE TEKEL, UPHARSIN (IL, p.118). Alice gets disturbed on reading the divorce document: ""Peter Hoyle, teacher" and underneath, "Alice Hoyle, housewife."" She replaces "that housewife business: with "Writer,"" and writes a letter to the lawyer that "she had no intention of signing until the document had been officially changed." The incident makes her recall the Duke and Dutchess of Windsor. Duke of Windsor always put:

> "nothing" under "occupation" on his passport after he stepped down from the throne. ... Mrs. Simpson put. "Companion to ex-King?" Perhaps she should have crossed out "housewife" and put "castaway" or "reject" or even "lunatic, part-time" (IL, p.157).

These references suggest a connection with Findley's *Famous Last Words*, another novel about the novelist as witness.

There are many more references in *Intertidal Life* to other works of literature. Audrey Thomas has the habit of "borrowing from other artists/writers."[32] Nora, Joyce's wife, has an even more symbolic function, in the intertidal life of women: "N.Barnacle, God's holy name for us all" (IL, p.263). Alice's visit to the lighthouse with her daughter Flora reflects back on Mrs. Ramsay's and James plan to visit the lighthouse in Virginia Woolf's novel *To The Light House. Intertidal Life* abounds with death references and Virginia Woolf's novels are very much in the background. *The Waves* and *To The Light house* keep haunting Alice's mind. There is a mention of suicide of the light housekeeper's wife: "...killed herself some years ago. She had been Danish or Norwegian and had committed suicide while home on holiday" (IL, p.6). After her separation from Peter, Alice sees the death of her marriage. She also fears her possible death in surgery. When the Indian cloth is spread on the rug and everyone sits down on floor for dinner, Alice sitting at one end of the rug finds affinity with Virginia Woolf's Mrs.Ramsay. Like Mrs. Ramsay, staring down at the diner table, she asks herself, "But what have I done with my life?"(IL, p.125)

Peter, like Mr. Ramsay, is lost in his own world. Although separated Alice cannot escape remembering him at every turn of her life. She on the verge of mental collapse is reminded of Virginia Woolf's suicide. Woolf left "a note saying she's been so happy." Her husband Leonard Woolf confessed that "she wasn't strong enough to have children" (IL, p.243). Alice thinks she would have done the same. However, having children, the mother within her prevented her from taking such a drastic step. Motherhood gives woman the strength to overcome negativity, sorrows, and frustrations in life. Peter having left her, Alice continues to live and work for her daughters.

There are also other literary echoes of death in *Intertidal Life*. Alice calls the west 'the land of the dead' (IL. p.230). She makes a reference to Joyce's story "The Dead" (IL, p.119). While contemplating the notion of being buried in her beloved garden and thus nourishing it, Alice cites T.S.Eliot: "that corpse you buried in your garden / has it begun to sprout' (IL, p.258). Her garden has flourished after years of care, and her daughters too (the youngest is called Flora) flourish well.

When Peter and Alice discuss how to get the things settled before they part Alice makes an abrupt remark "Something Doctor Aziz said in *A Passage to India*. About the English" (IL, p.31). Alice remembers the first present Peter "brought her was Rilke's *Letters to a Young Poet*" (IL, p.51).Looking at the painting of Stella and Trudl, Alice is reminded of Thoreau's quote "marching to a different drummer." She associates the hippies, now, the Coon Bay people "as the lotus-eaters in Tennyson's poem: "on the hills like gods together / careless of mankind (IL, p.67). She recalls Emily Dickinson, "One need not be a chamber to be haunted." She hears "the drums on Kuyper Island, the dancers practicing." She wants to go to them and say," Help me to dance away my grief," (IL, p.125). The reference to Emily Dickinson is a reminder, to Alice of the frightening peculiarities and personal limitations of the female writer.

There are other repeated references to books about women: "a line from *Justine*: "We have gone different ways. We have all of us taken different paths now"" (IL, p.242), throws light on the disintegration of the family life of Alice, and how Peter, Anna, Hannah, Christobel and Alice move towards different directions. Alice always writes from the kitchen table, she never gets the desired room to write. ""When can I have a room to write in, "she would say to Peter, "when?"" (IL, p.238) The desire for a room of her own refers to Virginia Woolf's work *A Room of One's Own*. Alice looks forward to self-actualization while balancing her roles as a mother and writer. In Irigary's scenario women writing makes an attempt to reclaim "the characteristics associated with the mother and the speaking of the feminine language."[33]

In *Intertidal Life*, as in Susan Swan's *The Biggest Modern Woman of the World,* women are constantly associated with water, with the sea, but also with tears, cups of tea, menstrual blood and the waters that break at birth. In Alice's particular geographical locality, water has also been that which men have used as a means of exploring, of getting somewhere, of finding a land to conquer. However, these two different associations with water are not unrelated. In imagery reminiscent of that of Atwood's moving poem "Death of a Young Son by Drowning" in *The Journals of Susanna Moodie,* Alice sees that "Babies drop out of us from our most secret places, through channels the fathers have charted and laid claim to. Rivers of pain and blood" (IL, p.205).

As in T.S. Eliot's *The Waste Land,* water is an ambivalent image here. It is both the female source of life and the cause of death. Alice sees herself at the end of the novel as a version of Ophelia being wheeled into the operation room, a "Horizontal Woman" (IL, p.280). Alice does not feel her life is in order as she faces surgery. Flora and Peter in the row boat suggest Virginia Woolf's James and Mr. Ramsay. Lily Briscoe's words "I have had my vision,"[34] at the end of *To The Light House* echo in Alice's speech at the end of the novel *Intertidal Life:* "I forgive," she said, "but I don't forget. And that's hard" (IL, p.279).

Women's language "produces in writing circularity diffusion, spontaneity, indefiniteness and playfulness."[35] It is both as a novelist and mother that Alice knows the pains and pleasures of birth. There is a short fragment that suggests an abortion "fear and pain and all those vast quantities of blood, and the little, dead thing in the basin." This caused a "sea change of a most terrible sort'" (IL, pp.189-190) in Alice. This fragment is followed by her explanation why she had to kill Tabby's kittens:

> I had to kill a litter of Tabby's kittens...put them in a sack ....Nobody said they were willing to take them when they were old enough. I thrust in stones and sand. Then I tied the neck tight and walked nearly to the end of the island, where I knew the current would be terrible and swift, and I threw it out into the water (IL, p.190).

Alice in *Intertidal Life* is torn between the past and the future, between the mother's frustrations and her extravagant hopes for the daughters: "The uncertainty of women poised between past and future, between mothers and daughters, frustration and hope."[36] The book of Ashanti proverbs Alice finds in a second hand bookshop gives her wisdom:

"The story comes, the story goes. Off with the rat's head." One story was over; she must let it go, let Peter go...for her daughters' sakes as well as her own...she must nevertheless get on with the business of living (IL, p.225).

This is a novel about language and consciousness and the inseparability of the two. It is about the impositions of language and behaviour, and response, the conditioning effect of language, the extent to which women's experience, especially is determined by the linguistic realities we live within. The novel shifts "coherently and cleverly"[37] between journal entries in the first person of the explorer of the female psyche through proverbs, songs, quotations, etc., and the third person commentary of the observant writer. After being left alone by her husband, Alice living on the island writes a story of abandonment and exploration. She recollects her past and present, her marriage and divorce, mothering and writing.

ENDNOTES

1. Audrey Thomas, *Intertidal Life* (Toronto: Stoddart Publishing, 1984), p.26. All subsequent references in parentheses belong to this edition of the text.
2. Nancy Wigston, "A Novel of Riches," review of *Intertidal Life, The Globe and Mail* (December 22, 1984), p.E20.
3. Joan Coldwell, "Natural Herstory and Intertidal Life," *Room of One's Own*, Vol. 10, Nos. 3-4 (March, 1986), p.145.
4. Eleanor Wachtel, "An Interview with Audrey Thomas," *Room of One's Own*, Vol. 10, Nos. 3 and 4 (March, 1986), p.29.
5. Sandra Gilbert and Susan Gubar, *No Man's Land: The Place of the Woman Writer in the Twentieth Century*, Vol. 3, *Letters From the Front* (New Haven, Yale University Press, 1994), p.378.
6. *Ibid.*
7. *Ibid.*
8. *Ibid.*, p.360.
9. *Ibid.*
10. *Ibid.*, p.389.

11. *Ibid.*
12. Krishna Sarbadhikary, *Dis-Membering/Re-Membering: Fictions of Audrey Thomas* (New Delhi: Books Plus, 1999), p.71.
13. Susan Rubin Suleiman, "Writing and Motherhood," *The (M) other Tongue: Essays in Feminist Psycho-analytic Interpretations*, eds. Shirley Nelson Garner, Claire Kahane, Madelon Sprengnether, (Ithaca: Cornell University Press, 1985), p.358.
14. *Ibid.*, p.368.
15. *Ibid.*, p.366.
16. *Ibid.*, p.367.
17. *Ibid.*, p.360.
18. Marianne Hirsch, *The Mother/Daughter Plot: Narrative, Psychoanalysis, Feminism* (Bloomington: Indiana University Press, 1989), p.166.
19. Vivien E. Nice, *Mothers and Daughters* (New York: St. Martin's Press, 1992), p.232.
20. Joan Coldwell (1986), *op. cit.*, p.148.
21. Eleanor Wachtel, "The Guts of Mrs. Blood," *Books in Canada*, (November, 1979), p.50.
22. Judith Fitzgerald, "Audrey Thomas: Her Time Has Come," review of *Intertidal Life, The Whig – Standard Magazine*, (Kingston), (November 17, 1984), p.19.
23. Linda Hutcheon, '"Shape shifters': Canadian women novelists and the challenge to tradition," *Amazing Space: Writing Canadian Women Writing* eds. Shirley Neuman and Smaro Kamboureli, (Alberta: Longspoon Press, 1986), p.223.
24. Nina Baym, *Woman's Fiction: A Guide to Novels by and about Women in America - 1820-1870* (Ithaca: Cornell University Press, 1978), p.188.
25. Krishna Sarbadhikary (1999), *op. cit*, p.68.
26. Dair L. Gillespie, "Who has the Power? The Marital Struggle," *Women: A Feminist Perspective*, ed. Jo Freeman, (California: Mayfield Publishing Co., 1975), p.70.
27. Simone de Beauvoir, *The Second Sex*, trans. And ed. H.M.Parshley (London: Penguin Books, 1997), p.445.
28. Krishna Sarbadhikary (1999), *op. cit.*, p.78.

29. Julia Kristeva, *Polylogue* (Paris: Seuil, 1971), p.14, trans. Naomi Schor, '"Female Paranoia'. The Case For Psychoanalytic Feminist Criticism," *Yale French Studies*, 62 (1981), p.212.
30. Quoted by Linda Hutcheon (1986), *op. cit.*, p.225.
31. Margaret Atwood, *Life Before Man*, (Toronto: McClelland and Stewart, 1979), p.250.
32. Martin Kuester, *Framing Truths: Parodic Structures in Contemporary English-Canadian Historical Novels* (Toronto: University of Toronto Press, 1992), p.126.
33. Donna Bennett, "Naming the home," *Amazing Space: Writing Canadian Women Writing* (1986), *op. cit.*, p.239.
34. Virginia Woolf, *To The Lighthouse* (London: Penguin Books, 1945), p.237.
35. Donna Bennett (1986), *op. cit.*, p.240.
36. Nancy A. Walker, *Feminist Alternatives: Irony and Fantasy in the Contemporary Novel by Women* (London: University Press of Mississippi 1990), pp.14-15.
37. David Staines, "Feminist Matter Fashioned into Fine Novel Mapping the New War between the Sexes," review of *Intertidal Life, The Gazette* (Montreal), (January 12, 1985), p.H 12

SECTION-III

GRAVEN IMAGES

"So it is that I am sitting here,
many years later,
still grappling with these visitations
from the past...it is to be a therapeutic experience,
An old fashioned catharsis, an enema."

In *Graven Images,* Audrey Thomas gives us at last the story the mother and the daughter tell together. Here Charlotte writes about her mother Frances, her friend Lydia, and herself. She declares: "I don't believe in biological determinism; if I did I might slit my throat"[1] to convince herself that she has not inherited her mother's emotional problems and character traits. *Graven Images,* written more that two decades after *Songs My Mother Taught Me,* has the middle-aged Isobel/Charlotte still trying to work out her ambiguous relationship with her ninety-year-old mother. She calls her "the Aged Pea" (GI, p.5) with grudging affection.

Graven Images opens on "October 16, 1987." Charlotte twisted her "ankle the night of Captain's Farewell Party." She and Lydia visit the infirmary where a "large woman in white" (GI, p.1), who could speak only Polish applies iodine on her foot. Charlotte is a "journalist" and "writer." She is a "Canadian" from "Vancouver." She is in London and confesses that she travels a lot. Her old mother "lives in a senior citizens' home in Massachusetts" (GI, p.4). She has been "in the senior citizens' home "for eighteen years, having decided at the age of seventy-two that she couldn't cope on her own..." (GI, p.261). Charlotte lives "in another country and thousands of miles away." She admits that she likes to "keep distance and a border between my mother and myself." She is no longer:

> afraid of her; my heart no longer pounds when I hear high, rather nasal voice on the telephone, nor do I feel anxious and afraid when one of her letters arrives in the mail (GI, p.5).

Charlotte denies maternal love and connection: "I think I am *nothing like* my mother," only to add "that is the biggest lie of all" (GI, p.227). Her mother in old age "looks soft, like a decaying angel, with her pink, wrinkled skin and her white white hair" (GI, p.6).

Charlotte is:

> in England for three reasons: One (the one that pays for two and three), to write up an account of the last transatlantic sailing of the Polish ocean liner the *Stefan Batory,* for the Toronto *Globe and Mail* and for *Departures* magazine....Two,

> to try and find the missing link between the Robert Corbett (Corbit, Corbet, Corbin) who showed up in Massachusetts around 1660 and the Corbet/Corbetts back in England.... Three is my secret project, a novel.... The novel will be about my mother (GI, pp.20-22).

Her mother does not want to be buried at Corbettsville: "I've left my body to Harvard Medical School and I've told them, when they've taken all the spare parts they can use, they can chuck the rest of it out. Just chuck it out in the garbage" (GI, p.17). However, later on she changes her mind ".... bad enough to have fresh medical students poking around one's muscles and bones so I decided to pay now for cremation..." (GI, p.116).

Frances sits alone in the home for the aged, "chewing on stale grievances" (GI, p.78). Charlotte worries about her mother's loneliness, bitterness and passivity. She seeks answers to Frances's aversion for the Corbetts and her adamant refusal to be buried in the family cemetery in Corbettsville. Charlotte is aware of the association between the Corbett name and the word "raven" (GI, p.184). However, she is still unaware of its link with Frances. She struggles to complete the puzzle before her mother "croaks (her words)" (GI, p.21), and tries to understand her mother's metamorphosis "from beauty into beast" (GI, p.165).

Charlotte in her relationship with Frances acts "like a psychiatrist or social worker, distanced, professional, uninvolved" (GI, p.18). She experiences an "emotional fatigue" (GI, p.19) after every visit to her mother. However, she "don't want to think about her death" (GI, p.18). Charlotte traces the history of Corbetts starting from her "mother's grandfather, Marshall Corbett" (GI, p.16). She requests her mother: "Tell me everything you can remember about the Corbetts" to complete the "family tree" (GI, p.21).

Charlotte is unable to tear apart the sickening memories of her childhood:

> The words my parents shouted at one another were stones, sticks, knives, shards of glass... the words bounced off the walls of the dining room downstairs, flew up the hot-air ducts and into my room where I lay still as a statue underneath the bedclothes (GI, p.62).

The unpleasant memories of her parents' fights still chase the middle-aged Charlotte.

Charlotte in her young age was desperate to join "as a stewardess on a freighter or passenger liner" (GI, pp.50-51) to get rid of her tormented and anguished childhood. She met Michael "on holiday in St. Ives.... He was a potter... studying with Bernard Leach." He was "gentle and loving" (GI, p.226), and wrote to her regularly. They married and "After our first child was born we emigrated to Canada" (GI, p.227) where Charlotte gave birth to two more daughters. In the beginning, Michael encouraged her to write, "when I wasn't chopping wood or hauling water. When I wasn't playing with the babies...it was more fun baking bread or feeling in the nests for eggs, more fun playing with the babies." However, Charlotte "One summer... managed to finish two stories." She "won a contest" and built "a writing shed" (GI, p.228) for herself. Michael never forgave her for this.

Charlotte remembers meeting Lydia Sorenson:

> when we were seven years old and she was little Heather Fulford, a child evacuee who had been brought over from England to America by one of the richest families in our town (GI, p.8).

They studied together in Kindergarten. Afterwards Hester went away to a different summer camp, and then to a boarding school. Charlotte lost touch with her. She met Lydia again "In our fourth year at college" (GI, p.46) and she rarely called her Charlotte: "It was Harlot or Harlotta or Lotte Lena or Vacant Lottie" (GI, p.47). Larry, Lydia's first husband was a poet. He could not understand and respect her sentiments. She divorced him. She spent some time in a convalescent home and then served as "a waitress at Schraffts" (GI, p.64).

Lydia's second husband Stephen was "a journalist who specialized in travel - writing." He was ten years older than her and looked "very dashing with his bush jacket and his camera slung around his neck" (GI, p.107). He disappeared after eight years of marriage during their visit to the Ivory Coast. One day when Lydia and Stephen were sitting in the bar two chunky looking men walked in, and Stephen left with them. "Nobody ever saw him again."

Charlotte, on a holiday with her two eldest daughters, met Lydia after seventeen years by chance "on the steps of the Victoria and Albert" (GI, p.109). After meeting they began an exchange of letters. Lydia unable to work on Stephen's old job wrote to Charlotte to take on as the "pay was good," (GI, p.114) and she would get an opportunity to travel a lot. Lydia's foster parents did a lot for her and left her a huge amount of money but the question "who am I?" (GI, p.122) disturbed her. She went to England to search for her parents. One day Charlotte received a letter from Lydia. She sent her a photograph of "Heather, my half-sister, known to the world as my cousin Heather" (GI, p.304). Heather's mother and Lydia's mother were real sisters. Her aunt told Lydia that she was "her husband's child.... My mother never told; it was my uncle, just before he died, last year, who told Heather" (GI, p.307). Charlotte accompanied Lydia to Ontario "for a few days" (GI, p.310) as Lydia needed to talk to her, and Soren "Lydia's third husband" (GI, p.12) went back to Stockholm.

Moreover, the Corbett family skeleton locked away for forty years is finally unlocked at the end of the novel by Frances, who emerges from the shadows to tell how she had been awakened one night by strange noises. Coming out on to the landing, she had stood looking down, ""and my father looking up, from the bottom of the stairs...and his hands were covered in blood".... And he saw me"" (GI, p.317). In the end, the "graven image" of the god-like Lawrence is broken, releasing Frances and Charlotte to come together in a new relationship of closeness and affiliation.

Ambivalence, a central concept in writing about mothers and daughters, itself becomes a problematic element when it is not considered normal. The Freudian view of motherhood denies that mothers too can have ambivalent feelings towards their offspring; it is only the child's ambivalence that needs to be turned into hate and anger for normal development. According to Freud, "It is the special nature of the mother child relationship that leads with equal inevitability to the destruction of the child's love."[2] In Freudian theory, construction of the subject is thus founded on the repression of the mother. A continuing allegiance to the mother is seen as regressive even by Julia Kristeva, and this in a way reinforces the Freudian Electra complex, emphasizing the daughter's alignment with the father, and her need to "murder" the mother.

Maternity has always been the repressed term in the family plot. Associated with blood and flesh, "mater-iality," the mother's threatening immanence necessitated that literary and cultural authority transcend or repudiate her being. Therefore, "She had to be executed, or exorcized, most often by her sons but also at times with the connivance of daughters."[3]

In *Graven Images*, there are references to Charlotte's childhood spent at grandfather's house "Journey's End," (GI, p.223) with signs "NO TRESPASSING.... TRESPASSERS WILL BE PROSECUTED" (GI, p.214), and at the mental hospital during her adolescent years:

> It was here... that I spent my summers, moving from ward to ward as I was needed —shock ward, ambulatory wards, the O.R.,... but ending up, more and more, on female geriatric, Ward 88, "The Shit Ward" (G I, p.164).

These are linked experientially with Isobel of the earlier trilogy to suggest that Charlotte is none other than Isobel. For her, "telling the story of my growing up years was intimately connected with the longing to kill the self I was without really having to die...to kill that self in writing."[4]

In *Graven Images,* Charlotte writes her story which includes, in italics, her biographical novel which is a translation of her mother's letter writing and oral family history as well as the terrible secret of what her mother saw of a criminal abortion implicating Frances's father. She also writes about Lydia. She keeps her mother supplied with envelopes and stamps for the endless outpourings of family gossip."Mothers don't write, they are written."[5] She allows herself to be lured by the "new tidbit" (GI, p.115) of a mad spider's words, pertaining to the history of female suicides, madness, and children's deaths, as well as a history of family quarrels and sibling estrangements. Through her "autobiographical act"[6] of choosing a matrilineage of forms, including gossip, letters, clippings, photos and local histories, Charlotte challenges those "generic contracts that reproduce patrilineage."[7]

Charlotte's creating space in her autobiographical text for her mother's words is a process of making contact and connection with her. The sequential movement of the maternal discourse begins with Frances's partial revelation; ""I saw something".... "When I was small. Eight, maybe nine years old"" (GI, p.22). She writes to Charlotte about "those experiences that were deeply imprinted"[8] in her consciousness. Charlotte gets ready with pens and notebooks, knowing "she would tell me eventually" (GI, p.23). She does not have to wait long. The "few sentences" that set her off to write her biographical novel on her mother are inscribed in Frances's letter:

> "I saw a baby in a bucket outside the hired girl's room. The tops of the carrots we had for dinner were floating all around

it, like seaweed or ferns. And my father, just closing the door" (GI, p.86).

The floating body of the child brings forth the moments of "birth and death."[9] Charlotte understands the powerlessness of the women and children of the Corbett family and their cruel and insensitive victimization. The revelation is immediately followed by the italicized biography, a dramatized account of the Corbett children's interest in water-babies, which anticipates the sisters' later trauma:

> *They were always searching for the water- babies, ever since Mama read them the book.... Betty said, "If we find a water-baby where will we keep him?" "In the bath," Frances said, but wasn't sure. She'd have to think about it. "We could give him to Mama," Betty said, "to make up for Baby Grace"* (GI, pp.86-87).

It is only at the end of the novel that generic borders and borders of subjectivity are effaced in the merging of the first and third persons in Charlotte's biographical novel. Frances's biography begins "*August 1904. Ready or not, here I come*" (GI, p.313), the rest of the passage continues to relate events in the third person, until the final disclosure nails Lawrence Corbett to the crime. The autobiographical "I" finally merges with "my mother," who is named and can emerge from the shadows to describe the horror. The slippage of the "I" occurring at this only instance erases the "atomized privacy"[10] of the unitary selves of Charlotte and Frances, allowing the continuity of dialogue, with Frances's oral account positioned on the last page between bits of the daughter's italicized novel:

> "What I saw," says my mother, pulling at her fingers, "what I saw was a baby in a bucket, and my father... He had just come out of the hired girl's room and his hands were covered in blood."..."And he saw me" (GI, p.317).

As a writer and journalist, Charlotte knows "There are lies one tells to engage and entertain and there are the facts one uses to instruct" (GI, p.88). Her attempted collaborative family history is not going to be "just a boring enumeration but something livelier" (GI, p.21). In pursuit of that goal, knowing that facts "could keep one from the larger view" (88), Charlotte prepares to delve into boring facts and lively fiction. Charlotte lands in England armed with a box full of Frances's letters, two stones from the Susquehanna river her mother swam in, a button from mother's sewing box to inspire her, books on the Norman Conquest, and an envelope full of old photographs referred to as "Book of Begats" (GI, p.25). She is greeted by "signs twisted" (GI, p.1) everywhere announcing "DANGER KEEP CLEAR" of "lopped off" and "uprooted" (GI, p.79) trees. However, the greater danger comes not from all the "ancient stuff" (GI, p.21) of the family tree, or the reasons for the first Corbett to emigrate from Britain to America, but from a mystery close to home.

Graven Images takes the form of a "jigsaw puzzle" (GI, p.219). Charlotte is trying to reach the "Minotaur at the centre" of the "original maze" (GI, p.19) of her mother's mind. Charlotte's "mother has an enormous number of the pieces tucked away in drawers and in her head." However, every time Charlotte comes upon "Another piece of the jigsaw puzzle," she is reminded that "there is no box with a picture on the cover to show me what the finished product will look like" (GI, p.219). She has to "struggle to put together the missing pieces, whether in the archival records in England, or in the recesses of her mother's memory."[11] Certain things were becoming "numinous" (GI, p.172) for Charlotte. She came upon a copy of *"The Water- Babies"* (GI, p.122) concealed in the bottom drawer of Frances's cupboard and tried to fit the piece into the "jigsaw" of the family history.

Charlotte in search of more missing pieces of the puzzle finds many surprises stored away in her mother's secret drawer. One such piece is a beautiful oval picture frame which Frances offers Charlotte. Curious about the missing picture she is told it had been of Grace Corbett, Frances's mother, but "I tore it up" (GI, p.238). The words reverberate with the continuing cycle of maternal ambivalence. Charlotte's inherited blank photo frame, and its elusive silence, "become symbolic of the silencing of the Mother," but they hint as well at "a subversive potential, in as much as Charlotte will refuse to be framed the same way as the others."[12] In trying to read meaning into that blank space, she has to see beyond the maternal figure as an "ancient spider... storing up venom, thrumming" (GI, p.13), or to recognize herself as "my mother's daughter. Or, as she would say, a chip off the old block" (GI, p.227). In the process of writing with, as well as about, her mother, she finally breaks "the cultural icon" of the "angry abandoning or abandoned mother."[13]

Graven Images is also a crossword puzzle which has to be defined and its missing meanings claimed. The "linguistic "plot" is to be found in a sequence of definitions"[14] for "hag," which moves from an "evil spirit, daemon, or infernal being, in female form" to " holy, saintly, as in hagiarchy, the rule, or order, of saints" (GI, p.234-35). Charlotte acknowledges that "No one suggests a possible relationship between saints and witches, visions and nightmares" (GI, p.235). Her true plot is an endeavour to transform her mother from a "hag" into something more "saintly," as a friend of her intuits, "Is this trip, all these trips... an attempt to forgive your mother?" (GI, p.214)

The contradiction between Frances's active youth and passive old age confronts Charlotte. Looking at a picture taken of her eight-year-old mother and aunt Betty in a canoe, Charlotte finds her mother "Regular outdoor girl" GI, p.220). She is puzzled over the forty-year silence maintained by Frances. A 1906 photograph of the Corbetts "This is a *family* picture," (GI, p.149) stresses Charlotte. It shows a nine-year–old Frances, staring straight at the camera, a slightly smiling grandmother Grace, "great - grand mother, Alice Corbett," and "great-great-grandmother, Juliet Corbett...children," and Charlotte's "Great-grandfather Marshall J." (GI, p.148), the only male in the group. The photographer might have been Lawrence Corbett "like an old-fashioned detective looking for clues." Charlotte studies the faces of Frances and Grace through a magnifying glass and wonders, "Was this before or after?...the hired girl is not in the picture proves nothing" (GI, p.149). The stereotypical family photograph discloses few hints to Charlotte of the tensions and unhappiness behind the scene.

Frances's views Hell as "an empty place where there is only herself in a long white nightgown, at the top of the stairs, and her father, below, looking up" (GI, p.234). Charlotte is forced to acknowledge that "the god of my childhood" (GI, p.223) was a man who fornicated with the governess without qualms and removed the traces of the crime, while his wife lay ill.

A strange hallucinatory experience makes Charlotte sense the "Not transparent but substantial" presence of all her dead ancestors, including her grandfather who "did not look at me," because "He knows I know" (GI, p.275). In this way Charlotte finally lays to rest her ancestral ghosts, including the original Robert Corbett who emigrated to America. She pays a last visit to Coram's Field Museum before departure from England and confirms for herself that "Fate - in the form of hurricanes or dolls or whatever – was going to bring me right back to where I started" (GI, p.173).

The wives and daughters of the Corbett family were considered irrational or mad. Frances's "gossips" about mental breakdowns in the family becomes for her a catharsis of pain and guilt. Frances writes to Charlotte: "It's fairly easy to commit a helpless person by just getting any two doctors' signatures" (GI, p.132). The asylum in which Charlotte worked during the summer was the same where Marshall sent his daughter who was "becoming a burden financially" (GI, p.131), and where Lawrence sent his other daughter Elizabeth. Grace Corbett also went to the same hospital *"for a rest"* after Baby Grace's death, and "A *week later Frances went as well"* for another sort of problem. Later on Frances tells Charlotte: ""They cut me down there" ..."because I was too high strung" (GI, p.167). She now understands the significance import of the "twisty smile" (GI, p.240) that accompanied Frances's objection of the Corbetts, and of Betty's breakdown:

> "she was the pretty one.... But she tried to do too much and look where it got her. Breakdown after breakdown, poor Betty" (GI, p.256).

Charlotte ponders, "Why did she smile? Was it that so long as Betty was "the crazy one" then Frances could be sane?" (GI, p.257) At the end of the search for family roots, and the maternal past, Charlotte can place Grace and Frances's "mothering" in the context of their particular time and place. "Charlotte names "the mother's "motherless" feeling in families ruled by men, where women's first duty was the service of their men, and where daughters, as well as their maternal links, were of low priority."[15]

After the establishment of the fact of Lawrence's crime, the epigraph to *Graven Images*:

> In 1892, five years before my mother was born, Julian Huxley sent a letter to his grandfather, Thomas Henry Huxley, asking about water-babies. There was a picture in Kingsley's book of T.H.H. and Professor Owen examining a water-baby. DEAR GRANDPATER HAVE YOU SEEN A WATER-BABY? DID YOU PUT IT IN A BOTTLE? DID IT WONDER IF IT COULD GET OUT?
> CAN I SEE IT SOME DAY?
> YOUR LOVING
> JULIAN (GI),

provides yet another context for Frances's revelation. Julian Huxley's letter to grandfather asking about water-babies also implicit Charlotte's own silent query to Lawrence Corbett.

Charlotte looking for gifts on Portobello Road in London comes upon her namesake, a strange-looking, porcelain doll, a fine specimen of a "Frozen Charlotte," (GI, p.76) who could be a metonym for herself, born as she nearly had been in a snowdrift. Charlotte remembers her mother telling her, "I was too high-strung and so was your Aunt Betty" (GI, p.46). Orphans, dolls and babies all require care and need to be "restrung and repaired" (GI, p.44). Her mother gave her a doll which she had carried around with her for over eighty year. "It was a doll, a young-Lady doll with a beautiful face. She had come unstrung"... (GI, p.170). In a gesture to retie the knot of bonding with her mother Charlotte restrung the doll and named it "Frances after my mother," and it "sits in my daughter's bedroom" (GI, p.171).

Frances dislikes the family name "Corbett" with its etymological links with the French for raven. However, Frances herself "resembles the raven in Ovid's *Metamorphoses*."[16] In that version of the raven's origins, "His ruin was his tongue" (GI, p.40). The bird revealed to Apollo his beloved's faithlessness, leading to that lady's death, but also to the initially white raven's metamorphosis into "black as night". The raven had not heeded the crow's warning about his own punishment for revealing to the goddess another daughter's transgressive act, and his own secret related to another irregular birth. Like Ovid's story of the raven, Frances's story also ends in sorrow for her act of transgression, of her being a "Tell-TaleTit" (GI, p.264) and revealing to her brother Lawrence the dark family secret, which led to souring of her relations with her father:

> ...who called me up and said the letter was now in his safety deposit box and it would stay there until he died. I should've kept my mouth shut (GI, p.263).

He excluded her from her inheritance: "It don't do to talk too much" (GI, p.264).

The various associations of the name, in literary and biblical discourse, somehow had a bearing on the individuals who carried it. Raven was related to "carrion" (GI, p.184), biblical prohibitions against it declared it "UNCLEAN" (GI, p.185), and old French roots proclaimed its meaning as "to take...by force, to rush, to ravage" (GI, p.186). This certainly confirmed for Charlotte the process of "Destructive Distillation," which had helped the Corbetts "built an empire of acid," that "appealed to the Corbett soul." "When they finished with one forest"... "they just moved on and built another town"" (GI, p.221) and became rich.

"Romance is, at bottom, the quest for life after separation," a kind of "halfway house" on the road to autonomy, an "enticement to leave the family."[17] The outline of this familiar romance plot entraps the young Charlotte: "I was nineteen years old, a virgin and ready to meet Mr. Right or Mr. Wrong, whoever showed up first" (GI, p.52). In search of love/romance/Mr. Right, Charlotte meets Michael. The marriage ends after fifteen years and three children. Writing led to her being "driven out of Paradise" (GI, p.251) with her children. Michael never forgave her for having "money and a room of her own... to write...."[18] Charlotte writes a "heartbreak Haiku after Michael left: I pricked my finger/I fell down/ But no prince came" (GI, p.242). The middle-aged and lonely Charlotte realizes that she is "too old for the Prince, or even King Charming or his cousin the Archduke charming." She jokingly toys with the idea of sending an advertisement: "Over fifty and still nifty" to cap a similar one she saw in a paper, "DWM, a fit 52, wishes to meet slim attractive women 19-35." However, she immediately exposes the hidden code of male self-interest: "Fifty-One, still loads of fun, Fifty-two and loves to screw." (GI, p.213).

The code of romance is revealed as a code of exploitation. Charlotte recalls Lydia's marriage to Larry who saw Lydia as "material plus material goods," and "somebody to wash his socks" (GI, p.48). He won a National Book Award for Poems in which he described Lydia's "body and her physical actions and reactions ...Every mole, every smell or excretion" (GI, p.49). "Women are used as extensions of men, mirrors of men, devices for showing men off, devices for helping men get what they want."[19]

Charlotte recognizes from family history that grandmother Grace's marriage to grandfather Lawrence also had been a fairy tale romance in the beginning. After young Lawrence Corbett had seen Grace, he marched up to his mother and announced his intention to marry Grace in six year time. The attitude of Frances's towards her father, who was Charlotte's beloved "Uncle Larry" (GI, p.149) puzzled her. She recollects he took both the sisters to Ritz Tea Rooms, flirted with waitresses, all of which she then saw as harmless flirtation to boost his ego. However, Frances considered it scandalous, his "making eyes at that house keeper" (GI, p.262). She did not appreciate his installation of his "girlfriend," "the cardboard" cut out of a woman, "In *Mother's chair*....In my mother's *chair*" (GI, p.160).

The maternal link foregrounds when ready to write a travelogue, Charlotte aboard ship, experiences the feeling of being "immersed in a warm bath of benevolence. Does a child feel like this in the womb?" (GI, p.67) Moreover, Charlotte has a "secret project" (GI, p.21), a novel which will be about her mother. On all the levels, her writing connects her with the "Womb" (GI, p.67) of personal and matrilineal history.

Charlotte, muses that the Bayeux Tapestry at Normandy, depicting the battle of Hastings and Corbetts ancestors, valorizes the heroism of conquest However, what is lost to history is the real story behind the conditions of its production: "Women had embroidered the tapestry, gossiping, telling stories" (GI, p.230). These stories are merely private/female, while what they weave is public/male. Here the tapestry marks a boundary between history and autobiography, heroic and domestic spheres. Past and present mingle as Lydia and Charlotte emulate those invisible women. Their subversive "laugher and crude remarks" (GI, p.231) introduce the private domain of gossip into the public stories of heroism.

As in the Bayeux Tapestry, wherever Charlotte looks in- public discourses, historical records, journals, or museums, she sees the image of the male Corbetts foregrounded. Charlotte herself has made a "graven image" of her grandfather, breaking the second commandment: "Thou shalt not make any graven images."[20] She has to struggle to preserve her icon from the attempts to dislodge it by her iconoclastic mother:

> The grandfather I knew there must remain separate from this other man. He was the god of my childhood and I can't let him go, not just yet (GI, p.223).

However, Charlotte has learnt to refrain from worshipping fake gods, and in their place to put absent grandmothers, absent mothers, absent babies thrust out of sight by the male Corbetts.

Charlotte locates the import of all the messages she has been receiving in the form of dolls, babies, orphans. It was really "one message in bits, like a treasure hunt" (GI, p.172). She recalls as an eight-year-old child she had asked her mother the meaning of "gelding." Frances's evasive reply had elicited a rude guffaw from grandfather Larry. Charlotte's exploration of the etymological roots of "geld (1)" lead from "a crown tax" to "geld (2) to castrate, gelding castrate related to castle, a place cut off. "With L. *Castrum* (let) a cutting off, (hence) a place cut off, hence an entrenchment....hence a fortified camp"" (GI, p.242).

Like all male children, the male Corbetts had been socialised to construct the autonomous self as a "fortified camp" against connection and relation, both of which were seen as emotional weaknesses.

Graven Images depicts Grace, Frances, Charlotte, all orphans of love, all needing nurturing. The uneven responsibility placed on the mother for the outcome of mothering leads to a recurrent tendency towards "blame and idealization," giving rise to myths and misconceptions embodied in "the fantasy of the perfect mother."[21] Charlotte recognizes that mothers also have a "little girl" within them, and that they project that presence onto their daughters who bring it to the surface in a "cyclical situation."[22] In seeking out the mother, and desiring connection, nurturance, and relational identification, Charlotte defies the social message: "As a woman you cannot have both care for yourself and adult status."[23] Although it "might be a bit like learning a new language," Charlotte and Frances, as a result of their communicative alliance and sharing of pain through gossip, learn to articulate the word "love" (GI, p.248). Charlotte learns that the "crosses" that signify "kisses" and the "noughts" that signify "hugs" (GI, p.262) need not bear the negative significance with which she has endowed them. She begins to recognize that she did not have "a monopoly on pain" (GI, p.45), and prepares to be a nurturing mother to "the ancient child" Frances (GI, p.251).

Graven Images does not end in an unrealistic upsurge of maternal love. Charlotte knows and accepts that there would be times when "the ancient, unpurged anger of the child,"[24] would surface in her and in Frances. However, her transformation lies in her acceptance that maternal anger and love can co-exist. She identifies with the pain and suffering of Frances's maternal experiences, sees the battle scarred survivor, and desires to give her a "Viking funeral," on the event of her death (GI, p.286), a thought which troubles Charlotte.

Frances kept all her precious things in the chest drawer, for safe keeping, Charlotte's memories are a similar treasure. She wanted to place them somewhere for safekeeping. "An autobiographical narrative seemed an appropriate place."[25] Charlotte's story concludes not with the murder of the mother, but with dislodging the "graven images" of the fathers. Haunted by the ghost of the repressed maternal story, Frances and Charlotte lay to rest all the ancestral and paternal ghosts, dislodge all forbidden idols, including Freud's icon, and in the process forge and strengthen the mother-daughter bond of nurture, continuity, connection. Charlotte's writing her mother's biography and her autobiography is a "way to find again that aspect of self and experience," which "is a living memory shaping and informing the present."[26] In writing about her mother, Charlotte reclaimed the past for herself which she had long ago rejected, left uncared for, as she had often felt alone and uncared for as a child.

ENDNOTES

1. Audrey Thomas, *Graven Images* (Toronto: Viking, 1993), p.54. All subsequent references in parentheses belong to this edition of the text.
2. Marianne Hirsch, *The Mother/Daughter Plot: Narrative, Psychoanalysis, Feminism* (Bloomington: Indiana University Press, 1989), p.168.
3. Sandra Gilbert and Susan Gubar, *No Man's Land: The Place of the Woman Writer in the Twentieth Century* Vol. 3 *Letters from The Front* (New Haven: Yale University Press, 1994), p.379.
4. Bell Hooks, "Writing Autobiography" *FEMINISMS: An Anthology of Literary Theory and Criticism*, eds. Robyn R. Warhol and Diane Price Harndl, (New Brunswick: N.J. Rutgers University Press, 1996), p.1036.
5. Susan Rubin Suleiman, "Writing and Motherhood," *The (M) other Tongue: Essays in Feminist Psycho-analytic Interpretations*, eds. Shirley Nelson Garner, Claire Kahane, Madelon Sprengnether, (Ithaca: Cornell University Press, 1985), p.356.
6. Sidonie Smith, *A Poetics of Women's Autobiography: Marginality and the Fictions of Self-Representation* (Bloomington: Indiana University Press, 1987), p.46.
7. *Ibid.*, p.44.
8. Bell Hooks, "Writing Autobiography" (1996), *op. cit.*, p.1039.

9. Emily M. Ahern, "The Power and Pollution of Chinese Women," *Women in Chinese Society*, ed. Margery Wolf and Roxane Witke, (Stanford: Stanford University Press, 1975), p.198.
10. Sidonie Smith (1987), *op. cit.*, p.48.
11. Krishna Sarbadhikary, *Dis-Membering/Re-Membering: Fictions of Audrey Thomas* (New Delhi: Books Plus, 1999), p.83.
12. *Ibid.*, p.86.
13. Marianne Hirsch (1987), *op. cit.*, p.170.
14. Krishna Sarbadhikary (1999), *op. cit.*, p.83.
15. *Ibid.*, p.94.
16. *Ibid.*, p.84.
17. Sharon Thompson, "Search for Tomorrow: On Feminism and the Reconstruction of the Romance," *Pleasure and Danger*, ed. Carole S. Vance, (Boston: Routledge and Kegan Paul, 1984), pp.354-355.
18. Virginia Woolf, *A Room of One's own* (London: Penguin Books, 1945), p.6.
19. Jane Tompkins, "Me and My Shadows," *FEMINISMS*: (1996), *op. cit.*, p.1091.
20. Exodus XX, p.4, quoted by Krishna Sarabdhikary (1999), *op. cit.*, p.85.
21. Nancy Chodorow and Susan Contratto, "The Fantasy of the Perfect Mother," *Rethinking the Family*, eds. Barie Thorne and Marilyn Yalom, (New York: Longman, 1982,), rpt. *Feminism and Psychoanalytic Theory* (New Haven: Yale University Press, 1989), p.96.
22. Vivien E. Nice, *Mothers and Daughters* (New York: St. Martin's Press, 1992), p.8.
23. *Ibid.*, pp.117-118.
24. Adrienne Rich, *Of Woman Born: Motherhood as Experience and Institution* (New York: Norton, 1976), p.224.
25. Bell Hooks, "Writing Autobiography" (1996), *op. cit.*, p.1039.
26. *Ibid.*, p.1038.

Chapter 5
CONCLUSION

> **"God, in his wisdom has so linked the whole human family together that any violence done at on end of the chain is felt throughout its length, and here too, is the law of restoration, as in woman all have fallen, so in her elevation shall the race be redeemed."**

Writing by women strives to redefine and valorize a woman's sphere which often appears in male writing as unproblematic, as something merely given. Since these re-definitions are explored from a woman centred perspective, the feminine text generates female centred experiences which are not merely the obverse of the male tradition or simply an imitation or revision of the writing of her male predecessors but a multi-dimensional discourse embedded in both female and male traditions. Writing by woman is difficult to define or codify, it is a "dark continent" which has never been represented or voiced in the long silence of history.

The feminine text is like a volcanic eruption that brings to the surface violently, what has been hidden in the subterranean levels of the earth. When a woman writes she puts herself into the text, into history, into the world. The woman writer "unthinks" what history has said and then writes herself anew.

Audrey Thomas's narratives stress gender issues. They celebrate a maternal domain that presents an alternative structuring to that of patriarchal systems. Each of her novel is a new voice, a new experience which is a record of the protagonist's personal her story to converge, fracture, deconstruct and rewrite male centred discourse. Her female characters are involved in the quest for self-definition or re-definition in the turbulent socio-political context of women's and men's rapidly changing roles and expectations. In a statement made to the Conference of Inter-American Women Writers at the University of Ottawa, Audrey Thomas remarked:

> There are female images and female ways of looking at the world, interior or exterior. For if there is one thing that unites all the women at the conference, that needs no translator, it is our biology. For about thirty years of our lives we prepare each month for an event which does not take place. We ovulate, we bleed. Before this event, ages one to twelve, say, and after, in our fifties and beyond, this fact is still part of our 'Becoming' or our 'Been.' I do think it is only fairly recently that women writers have dealt overtly with this kind of experience. Where Philip Sydney's muse told him to look in his heart and write, our muse has been telling us to look a little farther down. Our visceral imagination is now coming to the fore.[1]

The trilogy of Isobel is the history of the discovery of woman's voice. Audrey Thomas in the trilogy uses the past effectively to show how women, so often silenced, learn to speak and make themselves heard. Thomas in *Songs My Mother Taught Me* envisions a life in which Isobel's sexuality is a positive force rather than the means to emotional enslavement to men. Her diverse experiences in the family, her education, her sexual and creative contentment give her the confidence to retreat into a new world of adventure.

Audrey Thomas jumps ahead a decade and half in Isobel's life to link the anguished, unnamed central woman of *Mrs. Blood* to the energized Isobel of *Songs My Mother Taught Me.* In *Mrs. Blood,* the heroine is thrust into a position of "otherness" as a white woman in an African hospital, adding to her sense of alienation. The narrator in *Mrs. Blood* "lacks a clearly defined "self" that can be named."[2] She therefore constructs her narrative through Mrs. Blood and Mrs. Thing.

Concluding in stillbirth, the brutal memory of an earlier abortion and silence, the novel's final gaps and negations suggest the loss of both the woman's language making power and her potential for life. The ebb and flow of blood emphasizes the ebb and flow of woman's discourse. *Mrs. Blood* is an unusual novel. The prose style conveys the controlled hysteria of the narrator, balanced against her need for an almost ruthless exposure of her self. Audrey Thomas writes of a woman's body with revolutionary candour and without sentimentality of bravedo.

In *Blown Figures,* Audrey Thomas has displayed a perspective from which the dominating male voice has disappeared. She has constructed a psychologically female experience. It is told through women's visceral imagination and is dominated by delusions and dreams that speak the inner self. This novel is a psychological thriller, where the protagonist searches for or comes in conflict with her fragmented self. Isobel moves on a journey of self-discovery, starting from North America to the continent of Africa, and further into the country, heading towards a border, then a river, and finally arriving at a small village. Her final destination is an African sanctuary where the priest presides over a ritual for seeking salvation.

Blown Figures centers on the female body, the womb. From this space the narrative emerges and elucidates female creativity. The memory of the baby she has aborted at the behest of her ex-lover Richard, and the miscarriage suffered in Africa remain hidden in her own subconscious depths. It is this guilt / secret which has actually driven her into the north, as into the dark recesses of the past and of her unconscious. As a result of her insanity she is released from her compulsive search of the unborn child and from her quest for an order that will make her past comprehensible.

George Bowering comments on *Blown Figures*, "The first chapter gathers up Thomas' previous books, so that readers of *Mrs. Blood, Songs My Mother Taught Me*, etc., feel themselves sinking into the womb of the delivering voice."[3] The trilogy is linked through the experiences of Isobel, and traces her shift from childhood and adolescence to adulthood and marriage. Her self-division and alienation linked to a traumatic past increases from *Songs My Mother Taught Me* to *Mrs. Blood*, to climax in total disintegration in *Blown Figures*. Audrey Thomas admits:

> "I see *Songs* and *Mrs. Blood* and
> *Blown Figures* as a continuity."[4]

These three novels tell the story of one woman's attempt to harmonize her dreams and the fascination romance has for her with her actual reality, that is, her life as it has to be lived. In the character of Isobel, we study a woman character who embodies the romance of adventure but in a context of emotions more familiarly associated with horror than romance. Isobel in *Songs My Mother Taught Me* abjects/rejects mother. However, she survives the relentless experience of maternal loss/separation by abjecting "Other," the mad self and putting it on the borders of her narrating self in *Blown Figures*. In the narrative process, the trilogy whittles away at contemporary values in the form of family, love, and sexuality to reveal an emotional and rational vacuum in their love. The values, the thinking, the behaviour of the central character Isobel, a woman whose years span the pre-second world war, war time, and post-war years continuing into the present are the focal centre of the fictional world in the trilogy.

Audrey Thomas's heroines challenge the masochistic view of women and men through standards invented for the female body by masculine order of things. For Audrey Thomas the feminine body and its language is an echo of what Luce Irigaray say: "Woman's desire would not be expected to speak the same language as man's."[5]

In *Mrs. Blood* and in *Blown Figures,* Isobel and the narrator undertake to revise the language of the myths that have for generations privileged male metaphors. To put in simple words, the womb replaces the penis. These novels reflect the change by drawing attention to broken connections, with excessive use of dashes, by disrupted chronology, and by peculiar pagination.

Mrs. Blood and *Blown Figures* discover reposed voices, the physical presence of women's bodies, and the female character as representative rather than peripheral. Her novels are matrilineal. Her female characters see the world differently and what they see becomes their narratives. The female characters successfully complete both physical and spiritual journeys that afford them greatly increased personal knowledge. Her heroines are not silent sufferers but achieve a distinct and varied voice. Thus the trilogy documents female creativity, the stories emerge from women's experience.

Audrey Thomas's novels *Latakia, Intertidal Life* and *Graven Images* are about marriage, disintegration, human relations, and how women cope with solitude and parental responsibility. Her protagonists both as mother and writer, creator and artist, are vibrant images of female heroism, while male characters function only in supporting roles. Her protagonists are independent, vibrant, and are also keen to take risks in their lives to assert their individuality. They refute the awful truth that "women required husbands for social and economic security."[6] However, her heroines need warmth, company and human attachment despite having an established sensibility and a feeling of self-assuredness.

A woman is naturally creative, and thus if she has a room of her own, she can very well write not only fiction but can also defend her selfhood and narrate the story of her life. Her literary creativity cannot be a rival to her biological creativity. The real question of power resides in language. Language has split the fictions of men and women. It is language that Rachel in *Latakia* uses as the ultimate weapon on her male lover. It also exploits the ritual of "writing" with the narrator becoming text of the narration.

The novel is a voyage across oceans of emotions, sharks of tensions, and icebergs/rocks of estrangements. Rachel struggles to become a mature artist. She rejects Michael/ male artistic vision. Her more prominent feminist, independent stance privileges art and not the male artist / lover. Thomas also unravels the competition among women for a man. The romantic triangle with female pitied against female is exposed in *Latakia*.

In *Intertidal Life,* Alice remaps her life in her island encircled house with her three daughters. Peter refuses to shoulder the responsibilities of the family. He leaves Alice and has short spell affairs with Anne-Marie, Stella, and Penny only to discard them. Alice accepts both creativity and responsibility. Alice transcends her condition as victim.

Using autobiography to create identity, Charlotte in *Graven Images* breaks down the hegemony of formal "autobiography," and breaks out of the silence that has bound her culturally to discover a resonant voice of her own. Charlotte affectionately traces her genealogy as woman and writer to and through her mother in a sincere gesture of filiality, acknowledging that her autobiography cannot be inscribed outside the biography of her mother, just as the biography of her mother cannot be inscribed outside her own interpretations. Charlotte is her mother's daughter, however, much she may distance herself geographically and psychologically from her. Carrying on the matrilineal trace, she gives "birth to herself as the daughter who has passed through the body and the world of the mother."[7] Mother and daughter are allied in the end.

Her mother's biography and her autobiography signal the mother's genuine identification with the daughter. *Graven Images* speaks both of the horrifying vulnerability of women and of their fierce and commanding power. It also tells of the power of art to sustain the continuity of life and the power of interpretations to turn adversity and victimization to triumph.

Audrey Thomas's female narrators attempt to dislodge male defined female identify and engage in a continuing process of re-naming and re-remembering the self. Her female characters are often caught up in complex and conflicting emotions. However, they struggle to break free and to stop being a victim. Isobel, Rachel, Alice, and Charlotte emerge courageous and strong. They do not cling to a dying relationship. They learn to live as independent women while retaining and strengthening maternal links as both mothers and daughters.

Audrey Thomas's works examine the realities of women's lives as they struggle for a sense of selfhood (*Songs My Mother Taught Me*), or search for self (*Mrs. Blood, Blown Figures*), or struggle with the conflicting demands of children and husband/lovers (*Graven Images, Latakia, Intertidal Life*). This struggle of the contemporary women to redefine conventions is at its sharpest, because convention here coincides with our deepest emotional bonds. Isobel is the girl and woman who struggles to be defined in terms other than someone's grand daughter, daughter, mistress, wife, or mother. Rachel, Alice and Charlotte are the self-conscious writers. They are able to insist on their own identity and purpose even at the cost of losing their husbands/lovers.

Audrey Thomas's attraction to the etymology of word and her play with puns, nursery rhymes, literary refrains and intertextual allusions in these novels highlights her postmodern stance to broaden her concept of feminism. She experiments with narrative method and use of language to depict women's sense of emotional alienation, struggling with the dark side of the self, or hovering on the verge of disintegration. "Thomas the novelist," says Ken Adachi, "luxuriates in language, releasing... a torrent of crystalline words."[8]

Mrs. Blood and *Blown Figures* have African settings. In both these novels, Africa is a locale the heroine experiences as an exaggeration in terms of the physical environment, the heat and the colours, as well as the behaviour of the people living there. It is against this back ground that she creates relationships and emotions.

Audrey Thomas's novels have tremendous significance for the readers of the third world countries, especially India for the realization that "within the reality of our universal inadequacy, uncertainty and blindness is a limitless capacity to reach out to one another, to hold one another, a limitless energy, a limitless empowerment which is available and accessible directly in our finite limited condition."[9] Thomas attempts to instill pride, confidence and dignity in women through her novels. She pleads for the need to create a conducive atmosphere for the development of the personality of a woman corresponding to her tastes, interests and sensibility.

Audrey Thomas, a feminist writer makes ample use of writing in the feminine and postmodernist techniques – the refrain, wordplay, inclusion of nursery rhyme, intertextuality, self-reflexivity, etc., in her works and this places her on the fore front of the postmodern feminist writers in Canadian literature. Her novels emphasize gender and articulate from the perspective of female characters and their sense of physical dispossession. Her novels address the issue of female creativity, that is, its authenticity, its authority, its stance.

She creates narrative patterns that echo the voices of women. They direct attention to the problem through central characters who are themselves writers and who are able to simultaneously demonstrate and analyze women's writing.

ENDNOTES

1. Audrey Thomas, "My Craft and Sullen Art: The Writers Speak," *Atlantis,* 4, No. 1 (Autumn 1978), p.153.
2. Nancy A. Walker, *Feminist Alternatives: Irony and Fantasy in the Contemporary Novel by Women* (Jackson and London: University Press of Mississippi, 1990), p.79.
3. George Bowering, "The Site of Blood," review of *Blown Figures, Canadian Literature,* No.65 (Summer 1975), p.87.
4. Pierre Coupey, *et al.* "Interview/Audrey Thomas," *The Capilano Review,* No.7 (Spring 1975), p.101.
5. Luce Irigaray, "The Sex which Is Not One," *FEMINISMS: an anthology of literary theory and criticism,* eds. Robyn R. Warhol and Diane Price Herndl, (USA: N.J. Rutgers University Press, 1996), p.351.
6. Nancy A. Walker, (1990), *op. cit.,* p.8.
7. Sidonie Smith, "Maxine Hong Kingston's Woman Warrior: filiality and woman's autobiographical storytelling," *FEMINISMS* (1996), *op. cit.,* p.1077.
8. Ken Adachi, *Two in the Bush and Other Stories* (MeClelland and Stewart, 1981)-Cover page.
9. Joy Kogawa, "Is There A Just Cause?" *Canadian Forum,* 63, (March, 1984), p.211.

BIBLIOGRAPHY

Primary Sources:

Thomas, Audrey, "Henry James in the Palace of Art: A Survey and Evaluation of James' Aesthetic Criteria as Shown in His Criticism of Nineteenth Century Painting." M.A. Thesis British Columbia, 1963.

—, *Ten Green Bottles*, 1967; rpt. Ottawa: Oberon, 1977.

—, *Munchmeyer and Prospero on the Island*. New York: Bobbs-Merrill, 1971.

—, *Songs My Mother Taught Me*, 1973; rpt. Vancouver: Talonbooks, 1988.

—, *Blown Figures*. Vancouver: Talonbooks, 1974.

—, *Mrs. Blood*, 1975; rpt. Vancouver: Talonbooks, 1988.

—, *Latakia*. Vancouver: Talonbooks, 1979; rpt. 1989.

—, *Real Mothers*. Vancouver: Talonbooks, 1981.

—, *Intertidal Life*. Toronto: Stoddart Publishing, 1984.

—, *Goodbye Harold, Good Luck*. Toronto: Viking, 1986.

—, *Graven Images*. Toronto: Viking Books, 1993.

—, "A Winter's Tale," *Ten Green Bottles*. 1967; rpt. Ottawa: Oberon, 1977.

—, "Still Life With Flowers," *Ten Green Bottles*. 1967; rpt. Ottawa: Oberon, 1977.

—, "Omo," *Ten Green Bottles*. 1967; rpt. Ottawa: Oberon, 1977.

—, "My Craft and Sullen Art: The Writers Speak," *Atlantis*, 4:1 (Autumn 1978).

—, "Two in the Bush and Other Stories," *New Canadian Library*, No. 163. Toronto: McClelland and Stewart, 1981.

—, "Mademoiselle Blood," review of *Heloise*, Anne Hebert, *Books in Canada*, February, 1983.

—, "Basmati Rice: An Essay About Words," *Canadian Literature*, 100 (Spring, 1984).

—, *The Path of Totality: New and Selected Stories*. Toronto: Penguin, 2001.

Secondary Sources:

Abel, Elizabeth, "Introduction." *Writing and Sexual Difference*. Chicago: University of Chicago Press, 1982.

Adachi, Ken, *Cover of Two in the Bush and Other Stories*. Me Clelland and Stewart, 1981.

Ahern, Emily M., "The Power and Pollution of Chinese Women." *Women in Chinese Society*. Eds. Margery Wolf and Roxane Witke. Stanford: Stanford University Press, 1975.

Appelbe, Alison, "Female Loners...and the Broken Marriage Syndrome," *Leisure* [The *Vancouver Sun*], (August 31, 1973).

Archer, Anne, "*Real* Mummies." *Studies in Canadian Literature*, 9, 1984.

Asnani, Shyam "The Female Identity." *The Sunday Tribune*, (December 13, 1992).

Atwood, Margaret, *The Journal of Susanna Moodie*. Toronto: Oxford University Press, 1970.

—, *Survival: A Thematic Guide to Canadian Literature*. Toronto: Anansi, 1972.

—, *You Are Happy*. Toronto: Oxford University Press, 1974.

—, Review of *Blown Figures*. *The New York Times Book Review*, (February 1, 1976).

—, *Life Before Man*. 1979; rpt. London: Virago Press, 1983.

—, *Bodily Harm*. 1981; rpt. London: Virago Press, 1983.

Auerbach, Nina, *Communities of Women*. Cambridge: Harvard University Press, 1978.

Austen, Jane, *Persuasion*. London: Oxford University Press, 1964.

Balachandran, K. Ed, *Essays on Canadian Literature*. Bareilly: Prakash Book Depot, 2001.

Barthes, Roland, "The Death of the Author." *The Rustle of Language*, Trans. Richard Howard. Berkeley: University of California Press, 1989.

Baym, Nina, *Woman's Fiction: A Guide to Novels by and about Women in America, 1820-1870*. Ithaca: Cornell University Press, 1978.

Belsey, Catherine and Bennett, Donna, "Naming the home," *Amazing Space: Writing Canadian Women Writing*. Eds. Shirley Neuman and Smaro Kamboureli, Alberta: Longspoon Press, 1986.

Bowering, George, *Fiction of Contemporary Canada*. 1974; rpt. Erin, Ontario: Press Porcepic, 1975.

—, "The Site of Blood." Review of *Blown Figures*. *Canadian Literature*, No.65 (Summer, 1975).

—, "Snow Red: The Short Stories of Audrey Thomas," *Open Letter*, 3rd Series, No. 5 (Summer, 1976).

—, "Songs and Wisdom: An Interview with Audrey Thomas," *Open Letter*, 4th Series, No. 3 (Spring, 1979).

—, "Munchmeyer and the Marys." *Room of One's Own*. Vol. 10, Nos. 3 and 4 (March, 1986).

Boxill, Anthony, "Portraits of the Artists: Three Novels by Audrey Thomas." *The Fiddlehead*, 95 (Fall, 1972).

Bradbury, Malcolm. Ed, *The Novel Today: Contemporary Writers on Modern Fiction*. New Jersey: Rowman & Littlefield, 1977.

Brownmiller, Susan, *Feminity*. New York: Fawcett Columbine, 1984.

Burt, Sandra, "The Second Wave of Canadian Women's Movement." *Canadian Politics: An Introduction to the Discipline*. Eds. Alain G. Gagnon and James P. Bickerton, Ontario: Broadview Press, 1990.

Butler, Judith, *Gender Trouble: Feminism and the Subversion of Identity*. New York: Routledge, 1990.

Butling, Pauline, "Thomas and Her Rag-Bag." *Canadian Literature*, No.102 (Autumn, 1984).

—, "The Cretan Paradox, or Where the Truth Lies in Latakia." *Room of One's Own*. Vol. 10, Nos. 3 and 4 (March, 1986).

Carroll, Lewis, *Alice's Adventures in Wonderland*. Toronto: McClelland and Stewart, 1975.

Chesler, Phyllis, *Women and Madness*. New York: Avon, 1972.

Chodorow, Nancy, *The Reproduction of Mothering: Psychoanalysis and the Sociology of Gender*. Berkeley: University of California Press, 1978.

—, *Feminism and Psychoanalytic Theory*. New Haven: Yale University Press, 1989.

Christ, Carol P., *Diving Deep and Surfacing: Women Writers on Spiritual Quest*. Boston: Beacon Press, 1980.

Cixous, Helene, "The Laugh of the Medusa." *FEMINISMS: an anthology of literary theory and criticism*. Ed. Robyn R. Warhol and Diane Price Herndl.New Brunswick: Rutgers University Press, 1996.

Coldwell, Joan, "Memory Organized: The Novels of Audrey Thomas." *Canadian Literature*. 92 (Spring, 1982).

—, "Natural Herstory and Intertidal Life," *Room of One's Own*, Vol.10, Nos. 3-4 (March, 1986).

Conrad, Joseph, "Heart of Darkness." *Great Short Works of Joseph Conrad*. New York: Harper and Row, 1966.

Coupey, Pierre *et al*, "Interview/Audrey Thomas," *The Capilano Review*, No.7 (Spring, 1975).

Culler, Jonathan, *On Destruction: Theory and Criticism after Structuralism*. Ithaca: Cornell University Press, 1982.

Das, Bijay Kumar, *Twentieth Century Criticism*. New Delhi: Atlantic Publishers and Distributors, 2002.

Davey, Frank, *From There to Here: A Guide to English-Canadian Literature Since 1960*. Erin: Porcepic, 1974.

—, "Alternate Stories: The Short Fiction of Audrey Thomas and Margaret Atwood." *Canadian Literature*, No 109 (Summer, 1986).

David, Lyon, *Postmodernity*. Second Edition, New Delhi: Viva Books Pvt. Ltd., 2002.

Davidson, Arnold E., "Reading Between the Texts in Audrey Thomas Munchmeyer and Prospero on the Island." *The American Review of Canadian Studies*. Vol. 15, No. 4 (Winter, 1985).

Daxell, Joanna, "Body/Mind Split: The Social Logic of Schizophrenia and the Dissolution of Self in Mrs.Blood." *Intercultural Journeys/ Parcours Interculturels*. Eds. Joanna Daxell and Natasha Dagenais. Baldwin Mills: Topeda Hill, 2003.

Daymond, Douglas and Monkman, Leslie, *Canadian Novelists and the Novel*. Ottawa: Borealis Press, 1981.

De Beauvoir, Simone, *The Second Sex*. Trans & Ed. H.M.Parshley. England: Penguin Books, 1972.

Delmar, Rosalind, "What is Feminism?" in *What is Feminism?* Eds. Juliet Mitchell and Ann Oakley. New York: Pantheon Books, 1986.

De Santana, Hubert, "Wonder Women." *Today Magazine. The Toronto Star*, (December 13, 1980).

Deborah, Scharbach, "Audrey Thomas." Review of *Ten Green Bottles and Ladies and Escorts. Brick: A Journal of Reviews*, No. 4 (Fall, 1978).

Denisoff, Dennis, "The Rare Space of the Female Artist: Impressionism in Audrey Thomas's 'Latakia.'" *Mosaic*, 26.4 (Fall, 1992).

Dhawan, R.K. Ed, *Canadian Literature Today*. New Delhi: Prestige Books, 1995.

Dobbs, Kidare, "A Novelist Explores the Circles of Hell." Review of *Munchmeyer and Prospero on the Island. The Toronto Star* (April1, 1972).

Docherty, Thomas, Ed, *Postmodernism: A Reader*. New York: Columbia University Press, 1993.

Dorscht, Susan Rudy, "On Blowing Figures...and Bleeding: Post structuralist Feminism and the 'Writing' of Audrey Thomas." *Canadian Fiction Magazine*, No.57, 1986, [*Tessera*, No.3].

—, "Blown Figures and Blood: Toward a Feminist/Post-Structuralist Reading of Audrey Thomas's writing." *Future Indicative: Literary Theory and Canadian Literature*. Ed. John Moss. Ottawa: University of Ottawa Press, 1987.

Ecker, Gisela. Ed, *Feminist Aesthetics*. London: The Women's Press, 1985.

Eco, Umberto, "Reply." *Interpretation and Overinterpretation*. Ed. Collini. Cambridge: Cambridge University Press, 1992.

Ehrmann, Jacques, "Homo Ludens Revisited." *Game, Play, Literature*. Ed. Jacques Ehrmann, 1968; rpt. Boston: Beacon Press, 1971.

Ellmann, Mary, *Thinking About Women*. New York: Harcourt, 1968.

Federman, Raymond. Ed, *Surfiction: Fiction Now and Tomorrow*. Chicago: Swallow, 1975.

Felman, Shoshana, "Women and Madness: the Critical phallacy," *FEMINISMS: an anthology of literary theory and criticism*. Eds. Robyn R. Warhol and Diane Price Herndl. New Brunswick: Rutgers University Press, 1996.

Fitzgerald, Judith, "Audrey Thomas: Her Time Has Come." Review of *Intertidal Life. The Whig–Standard Magazine* (Kingston), (November 17, 1984).

Flax, Jane, "Postmodernism and Gender Relations in Feminist Theory." *Feminism and Postmodernism*. Ed. Linda J.Nichoslon, New York: Routledge, 1990.

Fleenor, Juliann. E, *The Female Gothic*. Montreal: Eden Press, 1983.

Foucault, Michael, *The History of Sexuality: An Introduction*. Vol.1. Trans. Robert Hurley, New York: Vintage Books, 1980.

Freedman, Jane, *Feminism*. New Delhi: Viva Books Pvt.Ltd. 2002.

Freeman, Jo. Ed, *Women: A Feminist Perspective*. California: Mayfield Publishing Co., 1975.

Friedan, Betty, *The Feminine Mystique*. 1963; rpt. Middlesex: Penguin Books, 1983.

Friedman, Susan Stanford, "Creativity and the Childbirth Metaphor: Gender Difference in Literary Discourse." *FEMINISMS: an anthology of literary theory and criticism*. Eds. Robyn R. Warhol and Diane Price Herndl. New Brunswick: Rutgers University Press, 1996.

Fromm, Erich, *The Sane Society*, 1955; rpt. New York: Fawcett Publications, 1966.

Gardiner, Judith, "On Female Identity and Writing by Women," *Critical Inquiry*, 8, No.2 (Winter, 1981).

Gilbert Sandra and Susan Gubar, *The Madwoman in the Attic: The Woman Writer and the Nineteenth –Century Literary Imagination*. New Haven: Yale University Press, 1979.

—, "Costumes of the Mind." *Critical Inquiry* 7, 2, (Winter, 1980).

—, *No Man's Land: The Place of the Woman Writer in the Twentieth Century*. Vol. 1. *The War of the Words*. New Haven: Yale University Press, 1994.

—, *No Man's Land: The Place of the Woman Writer in the Twentieth Century*, Vol. 3, *Letters From The Front*. New Haven: Yale University Press, 1994.

Gillam, Robyn, "Ideals and Lost Children: An Interview with Audrey Thomas." *Paragraph: The Canadian Fiction Review*. Vol. 1, No. 1 (Summer, 1996).

Gillespie, Diar L., "Who has the Power? The Marital Struggle." *Women: A Feminist Perspective*. Ed. Jo Freeman, California: Mayfield Publishing Co., 1975.

Godard, Barbara, "Dispossession." Review of *Blown Figures. Open Letter.* 3rd Series, No. 5 (Summer, 1976).

—, *Audrey Thomas and Her Works.* Toronto: E C W Press, year not given.

—, Review of *Latakia. The Fiddlehead.* No.126 (Summer, 1980).

Godard, Barbara Review of *Real Mothers. The Fiddlehead,* No.135 (January, 1983).

—, "Redrawing the Circle: Power, Poetics, Language." *Feminism Now: theory and practice.* Eds. Marilouise Kroker *et al.*, Montreal: New World Perspectives, 1985.

Goodman, Lizbeth *et al*, "Madwomen and Attics: Themes and Issues in Women's Fiction." *Approaching Literature: Literature and Gender.* Ed. Lizbeth Goodman. Routledge: The Open University, 1996.

Grimke, Sarah M, *Letters on the Equality of the Sexes and the Condition of Women,* 1838; rpt. New York: Source Book Press, 1970.

Gubar, Susan, "'The Blank page' and the Issues of Female Creativity." *Critical Inquiry.* Vol. 8. No. 2 (Winter, 1981).

—, "The Birth of the Artist as Heroine: (Re) production, the *Kunstlerroman* Tradition, and the Fiction of Katherine Mansfield." *The Representation of Women in Fiction.* Eds. Carolyn Heilbrun and Margaret Higonnet. Baltimore: The Johns Hopkins University Press, 1983.

Gunn, Barbara, "Writer with Dazzling Gift for Short Fiction." Review of *Goodbye Harold, Good Luck. The Vancouver Sun* (June14, 1986).

Hassan, Ihab, "Making Sense: The Trails of Postmodernism." *New Literary History,* 18.2, 1987.

Hatch, Ronald, "Stories for Now." Review of *Goodbye Harold, Good Luck. The Canadian Forum* (August-September 1986).

Hay, Linda Mackinley, "Recurring Themes in the Fiction of Audrey Thomas." M.A. Thesis, New Brunswick, 1975.

Heilbrun, Carolyn, "Women, Men, Theories and Literature." *Profession,* 81 (MLA Publication).

Hekman, Susan J., *Gender and Knowledge: Elements of a Postmodern Feminism.* Boston: Northeastern University Press, 1990.

Hirsch, Marianne, *The Mother/Daughter Plot: Narrative, Psychoanalysis. Feminism.* Bloomington: Indiana University Press, 1989.

Hofsess,John, "A Teller of Surprising Tales." The Canadian. *The Toronto Star,* (May 6, 1978).

Homer, *The Odyssey*. Trans. and Ed. Albert Cook, London: W.W.Norton and Company, 1993.

Hooks, Bell, *Feminist Theory: From Margin to Center*. Boston: South End Press, 1984.

—, "Writing Autobiography" *FEMINISMS: An Anthology of Literary Theory and Criticism*.Eds. Robyn R. Warhol and Diane Price Herndl. New Brunswick: N.J. Rutgers University Press, 1991.

Horney, Karen, *Feminine Psychology*. Ed. Harold Kelman, New York: W.W. Norton, 1967.

Howells, Coral Ann, "Margaret Lawrence: *The Diviners* and Audrey Thomas: *Latakia*." *Canadian Woman Studies*. 6, No. I (Fall, 1984).

Howells, Coral Ann, "No Sense of an Ending: *Real Mothers*." *Room of One's Own*, 10, No.3-4 (March, 1986).

—, *Private and Fictional Words: Canadian Women Novelists of the 1970's and 1980's*. New York: Methuen, 1987.

Hoy, Helen, Review of *Real Mothers*. "Letters in Canada 1981: Fiction." *University of Toronto Quarterly*, 51 (Summer, 1982).

Hutcheon, Linda, '"Shape Shifters': Canadian women novelists and the challenge to tradition." *Amazing Space: Writing Canadian Women Writing*. Eds. Shirley Neuman and Smaro Kamboureli, Alberta: Longspoon Press, 1986.

—, *The Canadian Postmodern: A Study of Contemporary English Canadian Fiction*. Toronto: Oxford University Press, 1988.

—, *A Poetics of Postmodernism: History, Theory, Fiction*. New York and London: Routledge, 1988.

—, "Incredulity Toward Metanarrative: Negotiating Postmodernism and Feminisms." *Postmodernism and Feminism: Canadian Contexts*. Ed. Shirin Kudchedkar, Delhi: Pencraft International, 1995.

Huyssen, Andreas, *After the Great Divide: Modernism, Mass Culture and Postmodernism*. London: Macmillan Press, 1988.

Irigary, Luce, "The Sex which Is Not One." *FEMINISMS: an anthology of literary theory and criticism*. Eds. Robyn R. Warhol and Diane Price Herndl New Brunswick: N.J. Rutgers University Press, 1991.

Irvine, Lorna, "A Psychological Journey: Mothers and Daughters in English-Canadian Fiction." *The Lost Tradition: Mothers and Daughters in Literature*. Eds. Cathy N. Davidson and E.M. Broner, New York: Frederick Ungar Publishing Co., 1980.

—, "Separate Space." *Canadian Literature,* 107 (Spring, 1986).

—, *Sub/Version: Canadian Fictions by Women.* Toronto: ECW Press, 1986.

Jacobus, Mary. Ed. *Women Writing and Writing About Women.* London: Croom Helm, 1979.

Jacobus, Mary, Reading Woman: Essays in Feminist Criticism. New York: Columbia University Press, 1986.

Jay, Paul, "Autobiography and the Subject of Photography." *Autobiography and Postmodernism.* Eds. Kathleen Ashley, Leigł Gilmore and Gerald Peters. Amherst: University o: Massachusetts Press, 1994.

Jardine, Alice, "Pre-Texts for the Transatlantic Feminist." *Yale Frencl Studies* 62, 1981.

Jones, Ann Rosalind, "Inscribing Feminity: French theories of the feminine." *Making a Difference.* Ed. Gayle Green and Coppeliɛ Kahn. London: Methuen, 1985.

Joyce, James, *Portrait of the Artist as A Young Man*; 1916; rpt., Markham, Ontario: Penguin Books, 1982.

Juneja, O M P and Chandra Mohan. Ed., *Ambivalence: Studies in Canadian Literature.* New Delhi: Allied Publishers, 1990.

Kareda, Urjo, "Sense and Sensibility." Review of *Intertidal Life. Saturday Night* (January, 1986).

Kay, Jane, "The Neglected Child of Literature." review of *Ten Green Bottles,* by Audrey Thomas, and Four other books, *The Patriot Ledger* [Quincy, Mass.], (September29, 1967).

Kehde, Suzanne, "Voices from the Margin: Bag Ladies and Others." *Feminism, Bakhtin and the Dialogic.* Eds. Bauer and McKinstry. Albany, New York: State University of New York, 1991.

Keitner, Wendy, "Real Mothers Don't Write Books: A Study of the Penelope-Calypso Motif in the Fiction of Audrey Thomas and Marian Engel." *Present Tense: A Critical Anthology.* Ed. John Moss. *The Canadian Novel,* No.4. Toronto: NC, 1985.

Kekman, Susan J., *Gender and Knowledge: Elements of Postmodern Feminism.* Cambridge: Polity Press, 1990.

Khan, A.G. Ed. *Canadian Literature and Indian Literature: New Perspectives.* New Delhi: Creative Books, 1995.

Kogawa, Joy, "Is There A Just Cause?" *Canadian Forum,* 63, (March, 1984).

Komisar, Elizabeth, "Audrey Thomas: A Review / Interview." Review of *Blown Figures*. *Open Letter*, 3rd Series, No. 3 (Late Fall, 1975).

Kristeva, Julia, *Desire in Language: A Semiotic Approach to Literature and Art*. Trans. Thomas Gora, Alice Jardine and Leon S. Roudiez. Ed. Leon S. Roudeiz. New York: Columbia University Press, 1980.

—, *Polylogue*. (Paris: Seuil, 1971). Trans. Naomi Schor, "Female Paranoia: The Case For Psychoanalytic Feminist Criticism." *Yale French Studies*, 62, 1981.

—, *Powers of Horror: An Essay on Abjection*. Trans. Leon S.Roudiez, New York: Columbia University Press, 1982.

—, "Women's Time." *Feminist Theory: A Critique of Ideology*. Trans. Alice Jardine, Harry Blake. Eds. Nannerl O. Keohane, Michelle Z. Rosaldo and Barbara C. Gelpi, Chicago: University of Chicago Press, 1982.

Kroetsch, Robert, "Death is a Happy Ending." 1978; rpt. *Canadian Novelist and the Novel*. Eds. D. Daymond and L. Monkman. Ottawa: Borealis, 1981.

—, "The Exploding Porcupine: Violence of Form in English-Canadian Fiction." *Violence in the Canadian Novel Since 1960* (Conference Volume). Eds. Terry Goldie and Virginia A. Harger-Grinling. St. John's: Memorial University of Newfoundland Press, 1981.

Krouse, Agate Nesalule, "Feminism Prose Criticism." *Feminist Criticism: Essays on Theory, Poetry and Prose*. Eds. Cheryl L. Brown and Karen Olson. N.J. and London: The Scarecrow Press, 1978.

Kudchedkar, Shirin. Ed., *Postmodernism and Feminism: Canadian Contexts*. Delhi: Pencraft International, 1995.

Kudchedkar, Shirin, "Feminist Literary Criticism: the Ground Work, *Journal of Literary Criticism*, 8, 1 (June, 1996).

Kuester, Martin, *FRAMING TRUTHS: Parodic Structures in Contemporary English-Canadian Historical Novels*. Toronto: University of Toronto Press, 1992.

Lafore, Laurence, "Short Turns and Encores." Review of *Ten Green Bottles*, by Audrey Thomas, *In the Courtyards of Jerusalem*, by Chaim Brandwein, *Dear Me*, Edith Morris, and *The Best American Short Stories*, 1967. Eds. Martha Foley and David Burnett. *The Book Review*, 10 (December, 1967).

Laing, R.D, *The Divided Self*. 1959; rpt. London: Penguin Books, 1975.

Lal, Malashri, "Canadian Gynocritics: Contexts of Meaning in Margaret Atwood's Surfacing." *Perspectives on Women: Canada and India*. Ed. Aparna Basu. New Delhi: Allied Publishers, 1995.

— Ed., *Feminist Spaces: Cultural Readings from India and Canada*. New Delhi: Allied Publishers Limited, 1997.

Laurence, Margaret, *A Jest of God*. 1966; rpt. Toronto: McClelland and Stewart Ltd., 1982.

Lee, Dennis, "Cadence, Country, Silence: Writing in Colonial Space." *boundary 2, 3*, No.1 (Fall, 1974).

Levin, Martin, "Review of *Mrs.Blood*." *The New York Times Book Reviеu* (January 3, 1971).

Lyotard, Jean-Francois, *The Postmodern Condition: A Report on Knowledge*. Trans. Geoffrey Bennington and Brian Massumi. Manchester: University of Manchester Press, 1984.

Prabha, M. Sneha, *Canadian Studies: New Perspectives*. New Delhi: Creative Books 1998.

Mackendrick, Louis K, "A Peopled Labyrinth of Walls: Audrey Thomas' *Blown Figures*." *Present Tense: A Critical Anthology, The Canadian Novel*. John Moss. Ed., Vol. IV. Toronto: NC, 1985.

Mallinson, Jean, "Songs Sung Blue." Review of *Songs My Mother Taught Me*. Leisure [*The Vancouver Sun*], (April 5, 1974).

Marks, Elaine, "Women and Literature in France." *Signs*, 4, No. 3 (Summer, 1978).

Marlatt, Daphne, "Musing with mother tongue." *In the Feminine: Women and Word*. Edminton: Silverspoon Press, 1985.

McAlpine, Mary, "'I Cannot Wear Your Mark Upon My Back.'" Review of *Munchmeyer and Prospero on the Island*. *Saturday Night* (July, 1972).

McCormick, Marion, "Love, Marriage and Related Disasters." Review of *Ladies and Escorts*. *Quill and Quire* (July, 1977).

McDowell, Judith H., Review of *Munchmeyer and Prospero on the Island*, Audrey Thomas, and *Daughters of the Moon*, Joan Haggerty, *World Literature Written in English*, No.12 (April, 1973).

McKenna, Isobel, "Women in Canadian Literature." *Canadian Literature*, 62 (Autumn, 1974).

Miller, Arthur, *Psychology and Arthur Miller*. Interviewer Richard Evans, New York: E.P. Dutton, 1969.

Millet, Kate, *Sexual Politics*. USA: Equinox Books, 1971.

Moi, Toril, "Feminist Literary Criticism." *Modern Literary Theory: A Comparative Introduction*. Eds. Ann Jefferson and David Rubey, London: B.T. Batsford Ltd., 1968.

—, *Sexual /Textual Politics: Feminist Literary Theory*. London: Methuen, 1985.

—, "Men Against Patriarchy." *Gender and Theory*. Ed. Linda Kauffman. Oxford: Basil Blackwell, 1990.

Moir, Nikki, "A Symphony of Birth That Is Unforgettable." Review of *Ten Green Bottles. The Province* [Vancouver],(January 12, 1968).

Monk, Patricia, "Shadow Continent: The Image of Africa in Three Canadian Writers." *Ariel*. Vol. 8, No.4 (October, 1977).

Moore, Jane. Ed., *The Feminist Reader: Essays in Gender and the Politics of Literary Criticism*. London: Macmillan Press Ltd., 1989.

Mores, Elaine, *Literary Women: The Great Writers*. New York: Doubleday, 1976.

Moss, John, *Sex and Violence in the Canadian Novel*. Toronto: McClelland and Stewart, 1977.

—, *A Reader's Guide To The Canadian Novel*. Toronto: McClelland and Stewart, 1982.

Munro, Alice, *Dance of the Happy Shades*. Toronto: Mc Graw-Hill Ryerson, 1968.

Nancy, Poland, "Margaret Drabble: 'There Must Be a Lot of People Like Me." *Midwest Quarterly*, XVI, 3 (April, 1975).

New, William H., "In Defence of Private Worlds: An Approach to Irony in Canadian Fiction." *Journal of Commonwealth Literature*.10 (December, 1970).

—, "Africanadiana: The African Setting in Canadian Literature." *Journal of Canadian Studies*. Vol. 6, No. 1 (February, 1971).

Niall, Lucy. Ed., *Postmodern Literary Theory: An Anthology*. Oxford: Blackwell Publishers Ltd., 2000.

Nice, Vivien E., *Mothers and Daughters*. New York: St. Martin's Press, 1992.

Nietzsche, Friedrich, *Beyond Good and Evil*, Trans. Helen Zimmern, *Complete Works*. Vol.12. Ed. Oscar Levy. New York: Russell and Russell, 1964.

Norris, Christopher, *Deconstruction: Theory and Practice*. New York: Methuen, 1982.

Novak, Barbara, "Lunar Distractions." Review of *Real Mothers. Books in Canada* (February, 1982).

Olsen, Tillie, *Silences*. New York: Dellacorte, 1978.

Ostriker, Alicia, *Stealing The Language*. Boston: Beacon Press, 1986.

Pearlman, Mickey, Ed., *Canadian Women: Writing Fiction*. Jackson: University Press of Mississippi, 1993.

Peterman, Michael, "Introduction" *Journal of Canadian Studies / Revue d' etudes canadiens*. 13, No.3 (Fall, 1978).

Plessis, Rachel Du, *Writing Beyond the Ending: Narrative Strategies of Twentieth- Century Women Writers*. Bloomington: Indiana University Press, 1985.

Prabhakar, M., *Feminism/Postmodernism: Margaret Atwood's Fiction*. New Delhi: Creative Books, 1999.

Pratt, Annis, "The New Feminist Criticism." *College English*, 32, No.8, 1971.

—, "Archetypal Approaches to the New Feminist Criticism." *Bucknell Review*, 21, No.1, 1973.

—, *Archetypal Patterns in Women's Fiction*. Bloomington: Indiana University Press, 1981.

Prentice, Chris, "Re-Writing Their Stories, Renaming Themselves: Post-Colonialism and Feminism in the Fictions of Keri Hulme and Audrey Thomas." *SPAN: Journal of the South Pacific Association for Commonwealth Literature and Language Studies*, 23, 1986.

Quigley, Ellen, "Redefining Unity and Dissolution in *Latakia*." *Essays on Canadian Writing*, No. 20 (Winter, 1980-81).

Quigley, Ellen, "Characters and Strategies in Audrey Thomas's Feminist Fiction." *Essays on Canadian Writing*, No. 47 (Fall 1992).

Raskia, Anita, Review of *Ten Green Bottles. News*. [Savannah, Ga.], (October 8, 1967).

Rich, Adrienne, "An Old House in America." *Poems: Selected and New* (1975) reproduced in *Adrienne Rich's Poetry. The Poet on her Work: Reviews and Criticism*. Eds. Barbara Charlesworth Gelpi and Albert Gelpi, New York: W.W. Morton and Co., 1975.

—, *Of Woman: Born Motherhood as Experience and Institution*. New York: Norton, 1976.

Richards, Janet Radcliffe, *The Sceptical Feminist: A Philosophical Enquiry*. London: Routledge and Kegan Paul 1980.

Ricous, Laurie, "Phyllis Webb, Daphne Marlatt and simultitude in Amazing Space." *Amazing Writing Canadian Women Writing*. Eds. Shirley Neuman and Smaro Kamboureli, Edmonton: Longspoon Newest 1986.

Rigney, Barbara Hill, "After the Failure of Logic: Descent and Return in Surfacing." *Madness and Sexual Politics in the Feminist Novel: Studies in Bronte, Woolf, Lessing and Atwood*. Madison: University of Wisconsin Press, 1978.

Robinson, Sally, "The Anti-Logos Weapon: Multiplicity in Women's Texts." *Contemporary Literature*. Vol.29, No.1 (Spring, 1988).

Rossi, Alice, "Women of Action: Frances Wright." *The Feminism Papers from Adams to de Beauvoir*. New York: Columbia Press, 1973.

Rudzick, O.H.T, Review of *Munchmeyer and Prospero on the Island. Letters in Canada 1972: Fiction*. University of Toronto Quarterly, 42 (Summer, 1973).

Rule, Jane, Review of *Latakia. The Globe and Mail*, 22 (December, 1979) Section Entertainment.

Sadoff, Dianne, *Monsters of Affection: Dickens, Eliot and Bronte on Fatherhood*. Baltimore: The Johns Hopkins University Press, 1982.

Said, Edward, *Beginnings: Intention and method*. New York: Basic Books, 1975.

—, *Orientalism*. London and Henley: Routledge and Kegan Paul, 1978.

Salat, M.F, *The Canadian Novel: A Search for Identity*. New Delhi: B. R. Publishing Corporation, 1993.

Sarbadhikary, Krishna, *Dis-Membering /Re-Membering: Fictions of Audrey Thomas*. New Delhi: Book Plus, 1999.

Santana, Hubert de, "Wonder Women." *Today Magazine. The Toronto Star* (December 13, 1980).

Schneiderman, Stuart, *Jacques Lacan: The Death of an Intellectual Hero*. Cambridge: Cambridge University Press, 1983.

Seller, Susan, *Language and Sexual Difference: Feminist writing in France*. London: Macmillan Education Ltd., 1991.

Shakespeare, William, *"Macbeth." The Living Shakespeare: Twenty-Two Plays and The Sonnets*. Ed. Oscar James Campbell, New York: The Macmillan Company, 1958.

Showalter, Elaine, *A Literature of Their Own*. Princeton: Princeton University Press, 1977.

—, "Feminist Criticism in the Wilderness." *The New Feminist Criticism: Essays on Women, Literature and Theory*. New York: Pantheon Books, 1985.

Shulman, Alix Kates, "Surviving Childhood." review of *Songs My Mother Taught Me*, by Audrey Thomas, and *Now Molly Knows*, by Merrill Joan Gerber, (April, 1974).

Sim, Stuart. Ed, *The Routledge Companion to Postmodernism*. London and New York: Routledge and Taylor and Francis Group, 1998.

Singh, Raghwendra Pratap, *Philosophy: Modern and Postmodern*. New Delhi: Intellectual Books Corner Pvt. Ltd., 1997.

Singh, Sushila, *Feminism: Theory, Criticism Analysis*. Delhi: Pencraft International, 2004.

Smith, Paul Julian, *The Body Hispanic*. New York: Oxford University Press, 1989.

Smith, Sidonie, *A Poetics of Women's Autobiography: Marginality and the Fictions of Self-Representation*. Bloomington: Indiana University Press, 1987.

Snowdon, Ellen, "Body/Language: Three Feminist Positions in Novels by Audrey Thomas." M.A. Thesis, University of Manitoba, 1994.

Soule, Caroline A, *The Pet of the Settlement. A Story of Prairie-Land*. Boston: A. Tompkins, 1860.

Spacks, Patricia Meyer, *The Female Imagination*. New York: Avon 1975.

Sprinker, Michael, "Fictions of the Self: The End of Autobiography." *Autobiography: Essays Theoretical and Critical*. Ed., James Olney.Princeton: University Press, 1980.

Staines, David, "Feminist Matter Fashioned into Fine Novel Mapping the New War between the Sexes." Review of *Intertidal Life*. *The Gazette* (Montreal), (January 12, 1985).

Stanley, Don, "Stories Audrey Told Me." *Leisure* [*The Vancouver Sun*], (September 9,) 1977.

Stape, John H, "Dr. Jung at the Site of Blood: A Note on Blown Figures." *Studies in Canadian Literature*. Vol. 2 (Summer, 1977).

Strauss, Levi, *The Elementary Structure of Kinship*. Trans. James Harle Bell *et al.*, Boston, Mars: Beacon Press, 1969.

Suleiman, Susan Rubin, "Writing and Motherhood." *The (M) other Tongue: Essays in Feminist Psycho-analytic Interpretations*. Eds. Shirley Nelson Garner, Claire Kahane, Madelon Sprengnether. Ithaca: Cornell University Press, 1985.

Thomas, Clara, "Happily Ever After: Canadian Women in Fiction and Fact." *Canadian Literature,* 34 (Autumn, 1967).

—, "Heroinism, Feminism and Humanism." *Atlantis*, 4, No. 1, 1978.

Thompson, Sharon, "Search for Tomorrow: On Feminism and the Reconstruction of the Romance." *Pleasure and Danger*. Ed. Carole S. Vance, Boston: Routledge and Kegan Paul, 1984.

Tomasevski, Katarina, *Women and Human Rights*. London and New Jersey: Zed Books Ltd., 1993.

Trikha, Manorama.Ed, *Canadian Literature: Recent Essays*. Delhi: Pencraft International, 1994.

Turkle, Sherry, *Psychoanalytic Politics: Jacques Lacan and Freud's French Revolution*. London: Burnett Book, 1979.

Tuttle, Lisa, *Encyclopedia of Feminism*. New York: Facts on File Publications, 1986.

Vevaina, Coomi S. and Barbara Godard, *Intersexions: Issues of Race and Gender in Canadian Women's Writing*. New Delhi: Creative Books, 1996.

Wachtel, Eleanor, "African Images: The Image of Africa in the Fiction of Audrey Thomas." *Room of One's Own*. Vol. 2, No. 4, 1977.

—, "The Guts of Mrs. Blood." *Books In Canada* (November, 1979).

—, "Contemporary Triangles." Review of *Real Mothers* and *Two in the Bush and Other Stories*. *Saturday Night* (April, 1982).

—, "An Interview with Audrey Thomas." *Room of One's Own*, Vol. 10, Nos. 3 and 4 (March, 1986).

—, "Putting up Fences in the Garden." Audrey Thomas talks to Eleanor Wachtel, *Tessera*, 5 (September, 1988).

Walker, Nancy A, *Feminist Alternatives: Irony and Fantasy in the Contemporary Novel by Women*. Jackson: University Press of Mississippi, 1990.

Walker, Susan, Review of *Songs My Mother Taught Me*. *Quill and Quire* (January, 1974).

Weedon, Chris, *Feminist Practice and Poststructuralist Theory*. London: Basil Blackwell, 1987.

Weed, E. Ed., *Coming to Terms: Feminism, Theory, Politics*. New York: Routledge, 1989.

Wigston, Nancy, "A Novel of Riches." Review of *Intertidal Life. The Globe and Mail* (December 22, 1984).

Williams, David, *Confessional Fictions: A Portrait of the Artist in the Canadian Novel*. Toronto: University of Toronto Press, 1991.

Wilson, Lionel. Ed. The Artist in Canadian Literature: Themes in Canadian Literature. Toronto: Macmillan of Canada, 1976.

Wollstonecraft, Mary, *A Vindication of the Rights of Woman*, 1792; rpt. *Penguin Classics*. London: Penguin Books, 1985.

Woodcock, George. Ed, *The Canadian Novel in the Twentieth Century*. Toronto: McClelland and Stewart, 1975.

Woolf, Virginia, *A Room of One's Own*. London: Penguin Books, 1945.

—, *To The Lighthouse*. London: Penguin Books, 1945.

—, *Three Guineas*. London: Hogarth Press, 1947.

Yanofsky, Joel, "Thinking Small." Review of *Goodbye, Harold, Good Luck. Books in Canada* (June-July 1986).

INDEX

N

P

R

S

T

W

Y